THE JAMES JOYCE – PAUL LÉON PAPERS

IN

THE NATIONAL LIBRARY
OF IRELAND

THE JAMES JOYCE – PAUL LÉON PAPERS
IN
THE NATIONAL LIBRARY
OF IRELAND

A CATALOGUE

Compiled by Catherine Fahy

NATIONAL LIBRARY OF IRELAND

First published in 1992 by The National Library of Ireland
© 1992 The National Library of Ireland
Previously unpublished material by James Joyce
© 1992 The Trustees of the James Joyce Estate
Previously unpublished material by Ezra Pound
© 1992 The Ezra Pound Literary Property Trust

ISBN 0-907328-49-0 (Paperback)
ISBN 0-907328-20-2 (Cased)

British Library Cataloguing-in-Publication Data.
A catalogue record for this book is available from the British Library.

Cover design by Bill Bolger, NCAD
Typeset by Typeform
Printed by Genprint

FOREWORD

In the autumn of 1940 the city of Paris was occupied by the German army. James Joyce, Nora Joyce, their son George and their grandson Stephen were staying in the village of Saint Gérand-le-Puy near Vichy. Paul Léon who was Joyce's confidant and friend and had acted as his agent, secretary and legal advisor during the 1930s had also come to live in St Gérand in the June of that year but returned to Paris on or about the 4th of September.

An account of his actions on his return has been left by his wife Lucie Noel in her memoir *James Joyce and Paul L.Léon: the story of a friendship* (New York, 1950). She described how Léon first of all wrote his letter of resignation as secretary of the Archives of Philosophy and then attended to the Joyces's affairs: 'Paul put all the important papers and documents in a large brown suitcase. Then he took all of his and Joyce's private correspondence over the years of their friendship and put it in a large envelope...He took the envelope personally to Count O'Kelly, then head of the Irish legation in Paris and asked him to place them in the Dublin Library.' Lucie Noel goes on to describe how her husband subsequently rescued many books and family belongings from the Joyces's apartment. These, she says, were all returned to Mrs Joyce after the war, as was the suitcase containing important papers and contracts.

The papers that Léon handed to Count O'Kelly were accompanied by a typed statement which reads as follows: 'Nineteen envelopes sealed containing private and business correspondence between James Joyce and Paul Léon in the years 1930-40 and the latter's correspondence business and otherwise, relating to Mr Joyce, his family and work. This is the property of Paul Leon, 27 rue Casimir, Paris. To be returned to him at his request. In case of death to be handed to Mr James Joyce. In case of both being dead to be deposited with the Public Library of Ireland or the British Museum to be made accessible for literary use fifty years after Mr Joyce's death; directions to be sought at present from Mr C. Curran and at any time agreement of Mr Joyce's family.'

The Joyces left St Gérand-le-Puy for Switzerland on the 14th of December 1940 and arrived in Zurich on the 17th. On the 7th of January 1941 Joyce became acutely ill and died on the 13th of January of a perforated duodenal ulcer. Léon in Paris received the news with shock. However, conscientious as always, he thought of the papers he had left with Count O'Kelly and wrote a letter dated 17th January 1941 in which he confirmed that the nineteen envelopes were 'destined to be donated to the National Library of Ireland in Dublin' and that 'As this correspondence involves thrid [sic] persons and is partly of an intimate character I must put to this donation the condition that access to it for biographers and litterary

[sic] persons should not be granted until fifty years after Mr Joyce's death and that the representatives of his family should be consulted before any publication is allowed.'

Paul Léon was subsequently arrested by the Gestapo and spent some months interned in camps at Drancy and Compiegne. In the spring of 1942 he was moved to Silesia and was killed probably on the 4th of April 1942.

Following the expiration of the fifty year period stipulated by Léon the papers were opened in the National Library of Ireland. The nineteen envelopes were found to contain correspondence and other papers in a rough chronological order. The papers fell into five main groups: the correspondence of James Joyce and Paul Léon, the correspondence of James Joyce and Paul Léon with Harriet Shaw Weaver, general correspondence with Joyce's friends, acquaintances and admirers, business correspondence with his solicitors, agents and publishers and miscellaneous personal and household accounts.

The most interesting and important group of papers are the two hundred and twenty odd letters exchanged between Joyce and Léon. Most of these letters were written when Joyce was away from Paris. When Joyce was at home Léon talked with him either in person or by telephone and received instructions daily though there were periods when Léon complained to Miss Weaver that he saw Mr Joyce seldom and that Mr Joyce refused to tell him what he wanted. The major themes running through these letters and indeed through the entire collection are the major themes of the last decade of Joyce's life: his efforts to get *Ulysses* published in England and in America and to finish and publish *Finnegans Wake*, his money worries, his concern for his daughter Lucia and his efforts to secure publication of her illuminated letters or *lettrines*, and his own ill health. Where Léon's side of the correspondence survives his letters are in the form of carbon typescripts which he kept intermittently.

Joyce's publishers, solicitors and friends were all under instructions to communicate with him through Léon at Léon's apartment on 27 rue Casimir-Périer. This included at times even Miss Weaver who came to rely on Paul Léon to keep her in touch with the Joyces. The collection includes two hundred and thirteen letters exchanged between Miss Weaver and Léon, the letters from Léon again surviving in the form of carbon typescripts, though some of the originals can be found in the collection of Harriet Shaw Weaver papers held by the Manuscripts Department of the British Library.

The files of business correspondence are extensive. Léon was fairly systematic in keeping carbons of business letters so the files read straight through and give a detailed picture of the sometimes complex and acrimonious negotiations leading to the American and English publication of both *Ulysses* and *Finnegans Wake*.

In describing the letters an attempt has been made to indicate as fully as possible their subject matter rather than to reproduce their style. This is not always easy as Léon's manner of expressing himself tended to be convoluted. Any of his letters may contain passages that were dictated or written directly by Joyce as well as paraphrases of Joyce's instructions and Léon's own opinions and interpretations. All of the letters written by Léon are carbon typescript copies unless otherwise specified and he nearly always wrote from his Paris address at 27 rue Casimir-Perier. Each item described consists of one page only unless otherwise specified.

The National Library of Ireland has released a very limited number of papers of a purely personal family nature to Stephen James Joyce, grandson of James Joyce, and, having regard to the wishes of Paul Léon, has decided not to allow access to or publication of certain of the papers prior to the 31st day of December 2050. The collection of papers deposited with the Library in accordance with Paul Léon's instructions did not include any letters from Nora Barnacle Joyce to James Joyce or from him to her.

It remains to acknowledge the work of the staff of the Manuscripts Department of the National Library who sorted and catalogued these papers, in particular Catherine Fahy who compiled this catalogue, Brian McKenna, Gerard Lyne, Kevin Brown, Tom Desmond and Pat Sweeney. We would also like to acknowledge Dr Noel Kissane who assisted with the index, Eugene Hogan, John Farrell and lastly Sarah Smyth and Ludmilla Borisovna Seregina of the Department of Russian, Trinity College, Dublin. The papers have been conserved by the Delmas Bindery and thanks are due to Muriel McCarthy and her staff for their careful work.

Patricia Donlon
Director
National Library of Ireland

TABLE OF CONTENTS

LIST OF LETTERS BY JAMES JOYCE

Includes correspondence between James Joyce and Paul Léon and other letters from James Joyce including letters in the handwriting of James Joyce but for signature by Paul Léon and annotations and draft replies by James Joyce on letters received. Letters etc from James Joyce not in the main James Joyce-Paul Léon sequence are listed in italics.

1912
19 September 1912   *to W.B. Yeats.*
16, 25 December 1912   *to W.B. Yeats*

1930
22 November 1930   *to Harriet Weaver*
[4 December 1930?]   *to Faber*

1931
20 July 1931   to **Paul Léon**
16 September 1931   to **Paul Léon**
18 December 1931   *to Benjamin H. Conner*

1932
[? January 1932]   *to Benjamin H. Conner*
[? February 1932]   *to Padraic Colum*
9 February 1932   *to Hamish Miles*
[c. 24 February 1932]   *to Padraic Colum*
[c. March 1932]   *to James B. Pinker & Sons*
8 March 1932   *to T.S. Eliot*
[April 1932]   *to Mayor of Florence*
2 April 1932   *to Bennett Cerf*
9, 10 April 1932   *to Mayor of Florence*
18, 26 April 1932   *to Monro Saw & Co*
22 April 1932   *to Clark Tourist Co*
[? May 1932]   *to Professor Y. Okakura*
2 June 1932   *to David Charles*
7 July 1932   **George Borach**   to **Paul Léon**
12 July 1932   to **Paul Léon**
14 July 1932   **Paul Léon**   to **James Joyce**
'recd July 17 1932'   to **Paul Léon**
20 July 1932   to **Paul Léon**
22 July 1932   to **Paul Léon**
31 July 1932   to **Paul Léon**
[post 8 August 1932]   to **Paul Léon**
8 August 1932   *Jean Henley*   *to James Joyce, annotated by Joyce*
                              pp Sylvia Beach

17 August 1932		to **Paul Léon**
20 August 1932		to **Paul Léon**
25 August 1932		to **Paul Léon**
28 August 1932		to **Paul Léon**
30 August 1932	**Paul Léon**	to **James Joyce**
31 August 1932	**Paul Léon**	to **James Joyce**
3 September 1932		to **Paul Léon**
8 September 1932		to **Paul Léon**
8 September 1932		to **Paul Léon**
[? September 1932]		to **Paul Léon**
9 September 1932	**Paul Léon**	to **James Joyce**
14 September 1932		to **Paul Léon**
15 September 1932	**Paul Léon**	to **James Joyce**
19 September 1932	**Paul Léon**	to **James Joyce**
20 September 1932		to **Paul Léon**
25 September 1932		to **Paul Léon**
27 September 1932	**Paul Léon**	to **James Joyce**
28 September 1932	**Paul Léon**	to **James Joyce**
2 October 1932		to **Paul Léon**
3 October 1932	**Paul Léon**	to **James Joyce**
5 October 1932	**Paul Léon**	to **James Joyce**
6 October 1932		to **Paul Léon**
7 October 1932		to **Paul Léon**
7 October 1932	**Paul Léon**	to **James Joyce**
11 October 1932		to **Paul Léon**
12 October 1932		to **Paul Léon**
after 12 October 1932		*to The Albatross Press*
15 October 1932		to **Paul Léon**
17 October 1932	**Paul Léon**	to **James Joyce**
28 November 1932		*to M.C. Wegner*
6 December 1932		*to Monro Saw & Co*
1933		
[1933]		*to W.B. Yeats*
6 February 1933		*to W.K. Magee*
16 February 1933, *postmark*		to **Paul Léon**
10 May 1933		to **Paul Léon**
[30 May 1933]		to **Paul Léon**
[c. June 1933]		*to J. Kingsley Martin*
14 June 1933	*A. Establet*	*to James Joyce, annotated by Joyce*
4 July 1933		to **Paul Léon**
4 July 1933		to **Paul Léon**
6 July 1933		to **Paul Léon**
6 July 1933	**Paul Léon**	to **James Joyce**
7 July 1933		to **Paul Léon**
9 July 1933		to **Paul Léon**

10 July 1933	*Bernard d'Avout*	*to James Joyce, annotated by Joyce*
12 July 1933		to **Paul Léon**
19 July 1933		to **Paul Léon**
23 July 1933		to **Paul Léon**
25 July 1933	**Paul Léon**	to **James Joyce**
31 July 1933		to **Paul Léon**
4 August 1933		to **Paul Léon**
7 August 193[3?]	*Basil Burton*	*to James Joyce, annotated by Joyce*
c. November 1933		to **Paul Léon**
1934		
1934		to [?]
22 January 1934		*to John Gadsby*
15 April 1934		to **Paul Léon**
24 April 1934		*to John Gadsby*
9 July 1934		to **Paul Léon**
12 July 1934	*J. Holroyd-Reece*	*to James Joyce, annotated by Joyce*
19 July 1934		to **Paul Léon**
20 July 1934		to **Paul Léon**
21 July 1934		to **Paul Léon**
22 July 1934		to **Paul Léon**
2[3] July 1934		to **Paul Léon**
23 July 1934		to **Paul Léon**
25 July 1934		to **Paul Léon**
27 July 1934		to **Paul Léon**
28 July 1934		to **Paul Léon**
30 July 1934		to **Paul Léon**
2 August 1934		to **Paul Léon**
[?2] August 1934		to **Paul Léon**
4 August 1934		to **Paul Léon**
4 August 1934		*to J. Holroyd-Reece*
5 August 1934		to **Paul Léon**
6 August 1934		to **Paul Léon**
9 August 1934		to **Paul Léon**
10 August 1934		to **Paul Léon**
14 August 1934		to **Paul Léon**
14 August 1934		to **Paul Léon**
[? August 1934]		to **Paul Léon**
[? August 1934]		to **Paul Léon**
16 August 1934		to **Paul Léon**
16 August 1934		*to J. Holroyd-Reece*
16 August 1934		*to Carolus Verhulst*
17 August 1934		to **Paul Léon**
18 August 1934		to **Paul Léon**
19 August 1934		to **Paul Léon**
19 August 1934		to **Paul Léon**

20 August 1934		to **Paul Léon**
20 August 1934		to **Paul Léon**
22 August 1934		to **Paul Léon**
[after 29 August 1934]		to **Paul Léon**
1 September 1934	*Monro Saw & Co to James Joyce, annotated by Joyce*	
7 September 1934		to **Paul Léon**
9 September 1934		to **Paul Léon**
13 September 1934		to **Paul Léon**
14 October 1934		to **Paul Léon**
[after 18 October 1934]		to **Paul Léon**
20 October 1934		to **Paul Léon**
22 October 1934,	*bill from Schiaparelli endorsed with note by James Joyce*	
23 October 1934		to **Paul Léon**
28 October 1934	**James Joyce**	
	Nora Joyce	
	Carola Giedion-	
	Welcker	to **Paul Léon**
4 November 1934		to **Paul Léon**
6 November 1934		to **Paul Léon**
9 November 1934		to **Paul Léon**
12 November 1934		to **Paul Léon**
13 November 1934	**Nora Joyce**	to **Paul Léon**
25 November 1934		to **Paul Léon**
27 November 1934		to **Paul Léon**
10 December 1934		to **Paul Léon**
[?15 December 1934]		to **Paul Léon**
20 December 1934		to **Paul Léon**, envelope
20 December 1934	*John Hinsdale*	*to James Joyce, annotated by Joyce*
	Thompson	
25 December 1934		to **Paul Léon**
'Childermas '34'		to **Paul Léon**
1935		
8 January 1935		to **Paul Léon**
[c. 10 January 1935]		to **Paul Léon**
13 January 1935		to **Paul Léon**
[1?5 January 1935]		to **Paul Léon**
16 January 1935		to **Paul Léon**
16 January 1935, 6 pm		to **Paul Léon**
31 January 1935	[] **Joyce**	to **Paul Léon**
5 March 1935	*newspaper clipping annotated by James Joyce*	
15 September 1935		to **Paul Léon**
20 September 1935		to **Paul Léon**
20 September 1935		to **Paul Léon**
25 October 1935		to **Paul Léon**

1936

25 April 1936	**James** and **Nora Joyce**	to **Paul Léon**
28 April 1936		*to F.R.D'O. Monro*
6 May 1936		*to F.R.D'O. Monro*
21 July 1936		to **Paul Léon**
8 August 1936		to **Paul Léon**
10 August 1936		to **Paul Léon**
12 August 1936		to **Paul Léon**
12 August 1936		to **Paul Léon**
13 August 1936		to **Paul Léon**
[? August 1936]		to **Paul Léon**
19 August 1936		to **Paul Léon**
21 August 1936		to **Paul Léon**
21 August 1936		to **Paul Léon**
23 August 1936		to **Paul Léon**
24 August 1936	*Edward Young*	*to Paul Léon, annotated by Joyce*
24 August 1936	*T.R.M. Creighton*	*to James Joyce, annotated by Joyce*
25 August [1936]		to **Paul Léon**
26 August 1936		to **Paul Léon**
26 August 1936	**James** and **Nora Joyce**	to **Paul Léon**
28 August 1936		to **Paul Léon**
[2? August 1936]		to **Paul Léon**
[30 August 1936]		to **Paul Léon**
2 September 1936		to **Paul Léon**
3 September 1936		to **Paul Léon**
4 September 1936		to **Paul Léon**
[?5 September 1936]		to **Paul Léon**
6 September 1936		to **Paul Léon**
8 September 1936		to **Paul Léon**
10 September 1936	**Greta Hertz** **Nora Joyce** **Wilhelm Hertz** **James Joyce**	to **Paul Léon**
[?September 1936]		to **Paul Léon**
[c. November 1936]		to [?]

1937

[c. 1937]		to **Paul Léon**
[c. 1937]		to **Madame Bertrand**
[1 April] 1937		to **Paul Léon**
[?4 April 1937]		to **Paul Léon**
6 April 1937		to **Paul Léon**
7 April 1937		to **Paul Léon**

[8] April 1937		*to F.D'O. Monro*
9 April 1937		to **Paul Léon**
11 April 1937		to **Paul Léon**
15 April 1937		to **Paul Léon**
2 May 1937		*to F.D'O. Monro*
4 May 1937	**Paul Léon**	to **James Joyce**
12 August 1937		to **Paul Léon**
14 August 1937		to **Paul Léon**
14 August 1937		to **Paul Léon**
15 August 1937		to **Paul Léon**
18 August 1937		to **Paul Léon**
19 August 1937		to **Paul Léon**
21 August 1937		to **Paul Léon**
27 August 1937		to **Paul Léon**
28 August 1937		to **Paul Léon**
5 September 1937		to **Paul Léon**
11 September 1937		to **Paul Léon**
[end December 1937 –	**Paul Léon**	to **Gerald Griffin**
beginning January 1938]		*in hand of James Joyce*

1938

23 January 1938	*Paul Léon*	*to T.S. Eliot, in hand of James Joyce*
February 1938		*'Critical appreciation [of James Joyce] by Professor Jeremiah Hogan, with brief annotation by James Joyce*
11 February 1938		to **Paul Léon**
12 February 1938		to **Paul Léon**
[1]6 February 1938		to **Paul Léon**
17 February 1938		to **Paul Léon**
19 February 1938		to **Paul Léon**
20 February 1938		to **Paul Léon**
27 February 1938		to **Paul Léon**
28 February 1938		to **Paul Léon**
9 March 1938	*J. Mullany*	*to James Joyce, annotated by Joyce*
[10 March 1938]	**[Paul Léon]**	to **[?]**,
[post 31 August 1938]		to **Paul Léon**
1 September 1938		to **Paul Léon**
1 September 1938	*Monro Saw & Co*	*to James Joyce, annotated by Joyce*
6 September 1938		to **Paul Léon**
6 September 1938		to **Paul Léon**
9 September 1938		to **Paul Léon**
11 September 1938		to **Paul Léon**
21 September 1938		to **Paul Léon**
28 September 1938		to **Paul Léon**
28 September 1938		to **Paul Léon**
30 September 1938		to **Paul Léon**

1.

CORRESPONDENCE OF JAMES JOYCE AND PAUL LÉON

220 letters with 42 assorted notes and drafts, 1931-40

James Joyce, 28B Campden Grove, Kensington, London W.8 to **Paul Léon**, *autograph letter signed*, *French*
Asks Léon to telephone Borach to find out if Professor Vogt will be in Zurich towards the end of August or beginning of September, he should also tell Borach that Joyce is still having trouble with his lawyers in London but everything will be settled soon better than expected and they will return to Paris for the 21 September and after the 8 October the anniversary of his first marriage he hopes to go to see Vogt in Zurich, will Léon also ask Borach to destroy Sullivan's record, Joyce has had them all destroyed, Léon should destroy his own also, that is the recording of *William Tell*, which is dreadful, *2p*

20 July 1931

James Joyce, 28B Campden Grove, Kensington, London W.8 to **Paul Léon**, *autograph letter signed*, *French*
Telephone Joyce's son and tell him that Joyce needs the money order immediately, encloses two letters which Léon should read and return, see Sullivan and clear things up with him, Joyce was at a première in Covent Garden and heard that Sullivan was in prison in Palermo for having boxed a manager, *2p*

16 September 1931

George Borach, Carlton Elite Hotel, Zurich on behalf of **James Joyce** to **Paul Léon**, *autograph letter signed*, *French*
Mr Joyce wants Léon to telephone Mr Colum and tell him to telephone Mlle Barney immediately, she has not sent back the proofs of the *lettrines* T and N which Mr Joyce wants to get as quickly as possible to show to a silk merchant who is one of his old friends, these *lettrines* demonstrate Miss Joyce's talent, she has already done some textile designs, a telegram yesterday gave news of her arrival at Feldkirch, Mr Joyce will see Prof Vogt after a few days rest and will then go to Lucerne, Léon should arrange to have money sent, Mr Joyce would like to have the *lettrines* by Monday morning as his meeting is on Monday afternoon, *4p*

7 July 1932

12 July 1932   **James Joyce**, Carlton Elite Hotel, Zurich to **Paul Léon**, *autograph letter signed*
Thanks for letters, Miss Barney did not return the two proofs, Joyce opened the parcel at Miss Beach's in the presence of Sullivan and Budgen and it contained only Lucia's seven *lettrines* made at L'Haye-les-Roses, Joyce got the *T* proof and the cheque which was crossed, he wants open cheques sent to him in future, he has not heard from Monro Saw & Co or about Miss Beach and the 12th edition of *Ulysses*, have Eliot or Pinker replied about the Christmas book, he will show the *lettrines* and designs for stuffs to his friend Brauchbar, the news from Feldkirch is fairly good, he and Mrs Joyce are both very tired owing to the heat, will Léon inform Goll, Gillet, Miss Beach and the Colums of the contents of Vogt's report on his eyes and send a copy of the following paragraph to Giorgio, Miss Weaver and Eliot, *5p, paragraph printed in Letters of James Joyce, Volume III, edited by Richard Ellmann, London, 1966*

14 July 1932   **Paul Léon** to **James Joyce**
Contract is signed, hopes Mr Joyce received the cheque, Léon attended to Boothroyd matter with Reece, will see Wegner about the criticisms of *Ulysses* to be printed on the inside covers, Miss Beach said that Mr Joyce had been very generous with her, *Pomes Penyeach* is marked 'out of print', Mr Joyce will receive contracts and memorandum of agreement with Miss Beach, Léon encloses memorandum for the Japanese translation, he saw Mr Holroyd Reece whose appearance he did not find attractive, Reece's proposal is for a right of first refusal, Reece told Léon that the power behind Albatross was the South-African copper magnate Sir Edmund Davis who was in a position to talk to the government and could secure their promise not to interfere with *Ulysses*, the only danger was from the Director of Public Prosecutions, they would bring *Ulysses* out first on the Continent and later in the year in England, Reece would find out from Sir Edmund whether he was willing to risk £5,000 on bringing out the only modern classic, Léon has not read *Ulysses* but he will, Wegner is the General Manager of Albatross, Léon handed Mr Joyce's kind thoughts from one guichet of the post office to another but they still threaten to cut off Léon's telephone, *3p*

James Joyce, Carlton Elite Hotel, Zurich to **Paul Léon**, *autograph letter signed*
Thanks for telephone call, encloses letters which aroused criticism, they are to be forwarded to Miss Weaver, will Léon thank Colum for his letter and ask him to get the *lettrines* back from Miss Barney, he is going to the station to see if Mrs Jolas is on the Paris train, hopes the balance of the money was sent, *2p*

'recd July 17 1932' [pencilled annotation]

James Joyce, Carlton Elite Hotel, Zurich to **Paul Léon**, *autograph letter signed*
Thanks for money, Léon should type letters to him, hopes Collinson and Miss Barney are settled, the Borach and Brauchbar letters should be sent to Miss Weaver who is to send them to Giorgio, the *Querschnitt* should be sent to Gilbert who should send it to Miss Weaver to return to Miss Beach, he has written to Faber offering to cancel contract, news from Feldkirch seems better, storms in Zurich, Lucia is very talented and should not be looked down on, will Léon thank his brother-in-law for the trouble he took about the cheques, messages for Kahane, when will Léon leave Paris, Miss Weaver wants to come to Zurich, what about *Ulysses* in Paris, will send Léon's boy a box of chocolates, *3p*

20 July 1932

James Joyce, Carlton Elite Hotel, Zurich to **Paul Léon**, *postcard*
Still awaiting Collinson's reply

22 July 1932

James Joyce, Carlton Elite Hotel, Zurich to **Paul Léon**, *typed letter signed*
Thanks for pamphlet and letter, Léon should not write funny messages, glad that case will come up in America in the Autumn, Colum is not seeing about Miss Barney and Lucia's *lettrines* as he is worried about his wife who has had an operation for a tumour, Joyce asked Dr Codet should Lucia be told about the proposed operation on his eyes or about Mrs Colum's operation, Mrs Jolas told Lucia a little about Joyce's eyes and Lucia sent Joyce a letter the tone of which he did not like, Feldkirch must be boring so his wife suggested Lucia and the nurse should go to Lucerne for August, Léon nearly lost the tenancy of the London flat by delaying estate agent's letter but Joyce is not angry, does not see why Léon should be interested in long letters about Lucia, Joyce cannot send Léon what he promised as he cannot realise his War Loan stock, his solicitor has not made arrangements for his monthly

31 July 1932

remittance, can Léon find out if there is any result from the talks Pinker is having with Lane, Miss Allgood and Eliot, Vogt is annoyed with Joyce, he will not accept money so can Léon arrange to get some publicity for him in the English press, *2p*

August - September 1932

Miscellaneous empty envelopes, 5 items

[post 8 August 1932]

James Joyce to **Paul Léon**, *typed letter signed endorsed on letter from Pinker dated 8 August 1932*
His eye is better, Lucia and his wife phone for him to come and work with Jolas, his notebooks have all disappeared, Borach and Ruggiero are away, he walks the Bahnhofstrasse till midnight and round his room till 3am, *draft reply from Léon to letter from unknown correspondent at bottom of page*

17 August 1932

James Joyce, Hotel zum Löwen, Feldkirch to **Paul Léon**, *picture postcard of Feldkirch*
Send him the brown notebook, Mrs Jolas is going to Paris and will tell Léon Joyce's news

20 August 1932

James Joyce, Hotel Krone am Rhein, Rheinfelden to **Paul Léon**, *autograph letter signed*
Financial arrangements, send him book on S. Pat from his flat, dictionary, what is Léon's address in Brittany, has sent book for Mrs Sullivan to give to Lucia as from himself, weekly *Irish Times*, Joyce is writing in haste as Léon may be leaving, could anybody forward mail, will send letters for Lucia in a separate envelope, his contract for *Ulysses* should be submitted to the solicitor of the Authors Society, *3p*

25 August 1932

James Joyce, Carlton Elite Hotel, Zurich to **Paul Léon**, *autograph letter signed*
Received cabled money, Léon should leave for his holiday, the doctor says Joyce's intestinal pain must be caused by nervous reaction to the stormy weather, his wife thinks it is due to overwork in Paris, Miss Weaver gives him belly ache, words of the *Soldier's Song*, asks for the Italian libretto of Verdi's *Don Carlos*, Monro Saw & Co should send his monthly cheque to Zurich, book he ordered from Brentano's, he is weak from lack of food and cannot work for some days, send a batch of papers to Lucia, Léon should make arrangements to get away, *3p*

JOYCE and LÉON

James Joyce, Hotel Löwen, Feldkirch to **Paul Léon**, *autograph letter signed*
Hopes Léon had a pleasant holiday, suspects the film people want to rush a pirate bowdlerised version of *Ulysses* into the United States if he does not agree to their terms so they should be intimidated, he agrees to Miss Weaver's modification and to Winkler's request, will Léon send him the *carnet* and Lucia's contract with Kahane which she wants, he is getting Section 1 of Part II ready for the October issue of *transition* in order to repay the Jolases for their kindness, Gilbert opened one of his boxes in Passy and sent 15 other *carnets*, the notice in the English press about Vogt and Joyce's eyes is wrong, wants an account from Sylvia Beach of sales of *Ulysses*, *3p*

28 August 1932

Paul Léon to **James Joyce**
Thanks for letter, he encloses copies of letters written according to Mr Joyce's instructions to Miss Beach, Warner Brothers and Winkler and Miss Joyce's contract, he will send the *carnet*, he has others which Mr Joyce said he did not want, weather is cooler, his family returns on Sunday, his holiday was wonderful

30 August 1932

Paul Léon to **James Joyce**
Encloses copies of two letters from Miss Beach, Léon has the impression she can be brought to print a new edition of *Ulysses*, the Japanese publisher should pay rather than the translators, encloses copy of letter from Galignani, sorry to hear details about Vogt

31 August 1932

James Joyce, Hotel Löwen, Feldkirch to **Paul Léon**, *autograph letter signed*
He is still waiting for notebook, Léon should keep the others, ask M[arsh] & P[arsons] to attend to enclosed, he has nothing to give Mr St John whom he does not remember, he will probably return to Zurich on Thursday and will then send Léon a remittance, the strain on his finances will have to go on for another six months, the Jolases will be in Paris on Friday, has Miss Beach sent her accounts, send a letter to Pinker about his account and *Ulysses*, *2p*

3 September 1932

James Joyce, [Feldkirch] to **Paul Léon**, *picture postcard of Dieppe, no postmark*
Thanks for letter, enclosure for L., is there £45 left, when does Delmas come back, Bennen's cure

8 September 1932

5

8 September 1932
postmark 7 September

James Joyce, [Feldkirch] to **Paul Léon**, *picture postcard of Feldkirch*
Goes to Zurich today, got the *carnet*, will be dragged off to Nice after a week, Léon should not end his letters with such phrases

[? September 1932]

James Joyce, [Zurich] to **Paul Léon**, *picture postcard of Zurich*
Has had eye attack, his wife is in Feldkirch, Lucia is better, will send money soon, doubts if he will see Vogt

9 September 1932

Paul Léon to **James Joyce**
Got two letters from Miss Weaver, one from Japan the other from Random House, encloses copy of letter to Pinker, understands Joyce's plans are Zurich, Nice, Paris, St Petersburg, Berlin, London, Montevideo and Zurich, '*ceterum censeo opus vestrum finiendum esse*' which he hopes nobody will find indecent, *3p*

14 September 1932

James Joyce, Carlton Elite Hotel, Zurich to **Paul Léon**, *autograph letter signed*
Did Léon get the 300, what arrangements should be made when Joyce is away from Paris, send Yeats's letter to Miss Beach, he will decline the seat in the academy, Vogt has decided to delay the operation, Léon should write to the British consul in Tokyo, can he see the man about the Albatross business, what is Pinker doing, Joyce leaves for Nice in a few days, thank Mrs Léon for her kind message

15 September 1932

Paul Léon to **James Joyce**
Enquires about Joyce's instructions re Japan and Albatross, he has had a letter from Pinker about Miss Allgood, Lane and Viking Press, Joyce should not worry about any arrangement, he has spent the 300, Léon is very distressed about Vogt

19 September 1932

Paul Léon to **James Joyce**
Has not had a reply to his last letter, the *Times* mentions Miss Allgood, did Joyce get cheque from Pinker, he saw a copy of *Ulysses* in a booksellers with an 'out of print' notice of which he informed Miss Beach, he met Kahane in the Castiglione Bar and asked him for one initial to send to Pinker, he read a complimentary review of Miss Joyce's book in the *New York Herald*

James Joyce, Hôtel Metropôle, Nice to **Paul Léon**, *autograph letter signed*
Léon should not telephone unless it is very important, the hotel has phones only on the ground floor, he got the royalties, Léon should give Miss Beach the contents of Joyce's last letter and an account of Léon's meeting with Wegner, suggests 2½% of his royalties should be paid to Miss Beach for five years, Léon should not reply to the Russian letter, thanks for money, try to get rid of Pinker, *3p*

20 September 1932

James Joyce, Hôtel Metropôle, Nice to **Paul Léon**, *autograph letter signed*
Heat and bad food have made him ill, thanks for letter, tell the Passy concierge his new address, he will return to Zurich in January, no word from Pinker, he has been asking Miss Beach about a twelfth edition of *Ulysses* for six months, the outcome of the U.S. case has nothing to do with the continental edition, the Albatross man has been sending him many messages and Joyce has agreed that he should speak with Giorgio, perhaps Joyce and Miss Beach could go in with Albatross together as Joyce does not want Miss Beach to sever her connection with the continental edition of *Ulysses*, get the first Japanese letter, return Yeats's letter as Joyce has not replied to it yet, are there any royalties as he has a lot of expenses, *3p*

25 September 1932

Paul Léon to **James Joyce**
Encloses letters and draft reply for Russians, will write to Pinker about draft, repeats instructions that Mr Joyce gave him for Albatross as he could not hear very well, important to keep Pinker out, returns letter to Rascher & Cie, will write to Cerf about film people and to Miss Beach to ask her to send royalties but will not say anything about Albatross

27 September 1932

Paul Léon to **James Joyce**
Reports on his discussion with Mr Wegner about terms of contract with Albatross for a Continental edition of *Ulysses*, Miss Beach's percentage, *2p*

28 September 1932

James Joyce, Hôtel Metropôle, Nice to **Paul Léon**, *autograph letter signed*
Received money order from Miss Beach and cheque from Pinker, he has not yet arranged to meet Albatross, asks Léon to forward Dr Jung's article to Miss Weaver after he has read it as

2 October 1932

well as a copy of his letter which should also be sent to Colum,
tell Colum Joyce got another letter from Shaw and Yeats but
did not reply, *3p*

3 October
1932

Paul Léon to **James Joyce**
Results of his interviews with Miss Beach and with Albatross,
Miss Beach pleased, terms of contract with Albatross, *2p*

5 October
1932

Paul Léon to **James Joyce**
Terms of contract with Albatross

6 October
1932

James Joyce to **Paul Léon**, *autograph letter signed on sheet of
squared paper torn from notebook*
Terms of contract with Albatross, Giorgio's comments, show
the documents to Miss Beach and allow her time to take them
in as she is confused by figures, *2p*

7 October
1932

James Joyce, Nice to **Paul Léon**, *telegram*
CONTRACTS RETURNED HOW MANY AUTHORS COPIES
AND SHOULD SIGNATURE BE WITNESSED

7 October
1932

Paul Léon to **James Joyce**
Terms of contract with Albatross, interview with Miss Beach,
Rhein Verlag has sent the initial *T*, *2p*

11 October
1932

James Joyce, Hôtel Metropôle, Nice to **Paul Léon**, *autograph
letter signed*
Wires Léon 500 francs, analogy of Pinker drawing 10% from
the *Portrait* and Miss Beach not accurate, incredible that Miss
Beach made nothing out of *Ulysses*, no publisher has a right to
money when he refuses to go on publishing, what Miss Beach
gets comes from Joyce himself, is Harmsworth in Paris, did Miss
Beach receive the book of *lettrines,* thanks for Léon's
management of the business, *3p*

12 October
1932

James Joyce to **Paul Léon**, *autograph letter signed*
Has just received enclosure, they were going ahead with the
composition before Joyce signed the contract, he refuses to
allow the English system of inverted commas and punctuation
marks to disfigure his pages, they should follow the French
system, *2p*

James Joyce, Nice to **Paul Léon**, *autograph letter signed*   15 October 1932
Got cheque, Léon should not write funny French, returns letters, he will think over Reece's proposal

Paul Léon to **James Joyce**   17 October 1932
Thanks for registered letters, what does 'no funny French' mean, Goethe's *Farbenlehre*, thanks for Joyce's kind thoughts, he had managed to pay in some money so the phone now works, he is trying to get news from Harmsworth, Miss Beach received the book, spoke with Wegner about Mr Joyce's other works

Empty envelope addressed to Paul Léon   2 February 1933 *postmark*

James Joyce, Paris to **Paul Léon**, *Valentine card signed 'J.J.'*   16 February 1933, *postmark*

James Joyce, Hotel Habis Royal, Zurich to **Paul Léon**, *picture postcard of Zurich*   10 May 1933
Greetings

[**James Joyce**, Zurich to **Paul Léon**], *carbon typescript page*   [30 May 1933]
Vogt's report on his eyes, *transcribed in Letters of James Joyce, Volume III, edited by Richard Ellmann, London, 1966*

James Joyce, Évian les Bains to **Paul Léon**, *telegram*   4 July 1933
GRAND HOTEL PRIERE AVERTIR CONCIERGE SALUTATIONS

James Joyce, [Geneva] to **Paul Léon**, *picture postcard of Zurich postmarked Geneva*   4 July 1933, *postmark*
Handwriting examined by graphologist

James Joyce, Le Grand Hôtel, Évian-les-Bains to **Paul Léon**, *autograph letter signed*   6 July 1933
Needs money, write to Miss Weaver for another £100, he has begun a cure, his wife says the place is too boring for Lucia so they will leave, he does have enough to pay the bill, *3p*

Paul Léon to **James Joyce**   6 July 1933
Encloses letters and cable, he is keeping two books received from Budgen, concierge will take care of cases till October, Léon has valise with books, Mr Joyce's financial position,

✗

encloses copy of Quinet's quotation from Mr Joyce's notebook, heatwave in Paris, Mr Joyce and his wife correct his grammar

7 July 1933

James Joyce, Le Grand Hôtel, Évian-les-Bains to **Paul Léon**, *autograph letter signed*
Léon's letter contained no money, doctors say Évian is good for Lucia but she says it is boring so they will go to Lausanne, despite his diet he has had pain, verify E.Q. piece, encloses letter from F.B., he will try to write but he has a pain coming on, he supposes the water is all right, *3p*

9 July 1933

James Joyce, Évian to **Paul Léon**, *autograph letter signed*
Léon's letter attributing Lucia's cure to Joyce led to a scene, accusations made against him, he is writing to Jaloux to cancel their lunch engagement and instead they will go to Lausanne by themselves, encloses letters for Cerf, Faber and Reece, Joyce wants to know who is 'Pegasus' and why does he treat an eminent French art critic so badly, tell Gillet that Joyce is furious with the bungling, arrange to have a cheque sent to Gillet, Léon must send more money so he can pay hotel bills, he may change hotels if he has to stay on alone, he left the hotel after the scene and will stay out till the night, he is writing in the pump room, wonders if the water is a fake as he has not had a night without pain, he is going to fast in order to have a night's sleep, he has been walking and working, if Léon refuses to write to Miss Weaver Joyce will telegraph her, Léon should keep any money he needs for his own use, he sent Léon's boy a box of chocolates, wishes Léon would not oblige him to write so much and so often, *10p*

12 July 1933

James Joyce, Grand Hôtel de Russie, Geneva to **Paul Léon**, *autograph letter signed*
Miss Weaver's disapproval of his staying at Évian forced him to give up the cure after nine days, send a cheque to Zurich, *2p*

19 July 1933

James Joyce, St Gotthard Hotel, Zurich to **Paul Léon**, *autograph letter signed*
Send an open cheque for the rest of the money and find out if Albatross or Pinker owe him anything, he will probably return to Paris on Sunday as they do not now want to take Mrs Gideon's villa, Budgen has not received *Music and Letters* or the pamphlets, his sister in New Zealand has not received the photograph, Prof. Fehr says he has not received the pamphlet

Das Wort by Rudolf Leonard, should they cable to New York for the result, *2p*

James Joyce, [Habis Royal, Zurich on notepaper of St Gotthard Hotel, Zurich] to **Paul Léon**, *autograph letter signed*   23 July 1933
Went to Habis Royal last night after a day of great pain, enclosed about Lucia is all right, Werner Laurie should be written to, use the letter to wake up Pinker and others, needs more money, asked his sister-in-law to stay in the villa but received no reply, Léon may give Joyce's news to Miss Weaver, a thunderstorm approaches, get £100 and take some for himself and send Joyce some, *2p*

Paul Léon to **James Joyce**   25 July 1933
Mr Joyce should never think he is forgotten, Léon encloses letters about Chaucer and copies of his letters to Pinker and Laurie, Léon spoke to Miss Weaver and arranged for money to be sent to Mr Joyce, notices that Mr Joyce is constantly moving, comic story about Jews

James Joyce, Geneva to **Paul Léon**, *telegram*   31 July 1933
HOTEL RICHMOND

James Joyce, Geneva to **Paul Léon**, *telegram*   4 August 1933
NOTHING RECEIVED TELEGRAPH IMMEDIATELY

[James Joyce to **Paul Léon]**, *in hand of [?Paul Léon, ?Nora Joyce]*   c. November 1933
Instructions for letters to be sent under the headings 'Parisienne', 'Reece', 'Morley', 'Miss Weaver', *2p*

James Joyce to [?], *printed calling card of James Joyce*   1934
Polla kronia, *in Greek characters*

James Joyce, Zurich to **Paul Léon**, *telegram*   15 April 1934
TELEPHONERAI CE SOIR APRES 19.00 HEURES

James Joyce, Dieppe to **Paul Léon**, *telegram*   9 July 1934
ARRIVONS 6h PRIERE PRENDRE MILLE FRANCS BANQUE FRANCO AMERICAINE

THE JAMES JOYCE – PAUL LÉON PAPERS

19 July 1934 **James Joyce**, Liège to **Paul Léon**, *telegram*
HOTEL SUEDE AMITIES

20 July 1934 **James Joyce**, Spa to **Paul Léon**, *telegram*
HOTEL BRITANNIQUE AMITIES

21 July 1934 **James Joyce**, Grand Hôtel Britannique, Spa, Belgium to **Paul**
(Belgian **Léon**, *autograph letter signed*
National Encloses cheques, if he forgot his alpaca and white jackets in
Fête) Paris Blake could send them, raining in Spa, water cures, hotel
is cheap and full, it has big reception rooms but the guest
rooms are small and the walls thin, he suspects the Victorians
eavesdropped, please send *Irish Times* and type his messages, *2p*

22 July 1934 **James Joyce**, [postmark Spa] to **Paul Léon**, *picture postcard of
Dieppe*
Ask Forel to arrange for Mrs Van Ende to send flowers with an
inscription to Lucia for her birthday

2[3] July **James Joyce**, [Spa] to **Paul Léon**, *postcard of Salon Régence in the
1934 Grand Hôtel*
Encloses cheque for £3 worth of postal orders to be sent to Eva
Joyce

23 July 1934 **James Joyce**, Grand Hôtel Britannique, Spa, Belgium to **Paul**
Léon, *autograph letter signed*
Telegrams to be sent to Lucia for her birthday from her
parents and from her brother and family, money, New York
cable, *2p*

25 July 1934 **James Joyce**, Spa to **Paul Léon**, *autograph letter signed*
Thanks for mail and letters and papers, he has the jackets so
Blake should send the suit, the concierge of r. Huysman should
be told to accept any telegram from Lucia to Giorgio on the
occasion of his birthday, has Léon asked Monro to have his
cases of books sent, encloses letter from Giorgio and Helen
and the electricity *dévis*, perhaps Gilbert could get another
electrician to send one in and they could choose between
them, 250 francs was for Miss Beach, send Giorgio a copy of
Forel's report, *2p*

James Joyce, [Spa] to **Paul Léon**, *postcard of Le Garage of the Grand Hôtel*   27 July 1934
Send money to Nyon and here, he should be ready to move anytime, rain, has Blake sent suit, he will have to sell the rest of the stock

James Joyce, [Spa] to **Paul Léon**, *postcard of the Salle de Restaurant of the Grand Hôtel*   28 July 1934
Get an estimate from another electrician and let him start when the heating men have finished and then the painters, change his address on enclosed to 7 rue Ed etc, leave incomplete list of books, reply to letters saying that Mr Joyce is away

James Joyce, Spa to **Paul Léon**, *telegram*   30 July 1934
DID LUCIA WRITE WIRE GIORGIO BIRTHDAY TYPE LETTERS

James Joyce, Spa to **Paul Léon**, *picture postcard showing Joyce standing beside a windmill*   2 August 1934
List came, encloses cheque, enquires about case of books and flat, hopes his concièrge got the identity cards, encloses reply to Reece and letter from L.G.

James Joyce, [Spa] to **Paul Léon**, *picture postcard showing the Hall and Escalier of the Grand Hôtel*   [?2] August 1934
Forgot letter, did MacSwiny get the disk Joyce left, will Léon inform the cinema people in New York of Giorgio's address

James Joyce, Grand Hôtel Britannique, Spa to **Paul Léon**, *autograph letter signed*   4 August 1934
Send Helen's and D.F's letters to the Jolases, he will send Lucia's letter to a graphologist, encloses blank cheque, the illustrations on Cerf's circular are incorrect, corrections for Irish directory, will Mrs J. find out what the Dutch printer did with Lucia's portrait, letter to H.R., is Monro sending books, *3p*

James Joyce, [Spa] to **Paul Léon**, *picture postcard of Spa*   5 August 1934
Agrees to price for shutters, refers to letter to Holroyd-Reece, does Kearsley know if any notice of the fragment in England mentions the illustrations, MacSwiney, first cheque was for Léon's own expenses, Joyce will phone about the second

6 August 1934

James Joyce, [Spa] to **Paul Léon**, *picture postcard of Spa*
Enclosure for Mrs J. and a copy of F.'s letter, there is a strike in Dublin so no papers have been published there, will send revised version of letter to R., wire more money, they may move as his wife is not well

9 August 1934

James Joyce, [Spa] to **Paul Léon**, *picture postcard of Chambre à Coucher, Grand Hôtel*
Names in Paris and Germany, no allusion in journal 'by Lady Rottenmean's husband for the bullpup fancying British in Paris', encloses letter from Helen

10 August 1934

James Joyce, Grand Hôtel Britannique, Spa to **Paul Léon**, *autograph letter signed*
List of people to whom Léon should send the *New York Herald*, write to Lane and others as the English press may contain nothing, find the address of the Italian neurologist Prof. Giglioli, worrying news from Nyon, he must see Forel as he is not willing to go on paying money for a bad result, he will write to Burns and Oates to find out about the *lettrines* and to Mrs J., he had not heard about Mrs A., *3p*

14 August 1934

James Joyce, [Spa] to **Paul Léon**, *autograph letter signed*
What Pinker should tell Lane, the U.S. appeal, *3p*

14 August 1934

James Joyce, Grand Hôtel Britannique, Spa to **Paul Léon**, *autograph letter signed*
Copies of Ver Hulst's and Reece's letters, tell Macy that Matisse has Joyce's approval, awaits Forel's reply but expects to go to Luxembourg, told Gilbert his movements, encloses cheque for Léon's holidays, copies of the *New York Herald* should also go to R. McAlmon and Miss Monnier, her superstition, *4p*

[? August 1934]

James Joyce to **Paul Léon**, *envelope of Grand Hôtel Britannique, Spa addressed to Paul Léon*
Asks for *Irish Times*, HCE is divorcing ALP that is Guinness's brewery is leaving Dublin

[? August 1934]

James Joyce, [Spa] to **Paul Léon**, *picture postcard of Appartement avec bain, Grand Hôtel*
Additional addresses

James Joyce, Luxembourg to **Paul Léon**, *telegram*
HOTEL BRASSEUR AMITIES

James Joyce, Grand Hôtel Brasseur, Luxembourg to **Paul Léon**, *autograph letter signed*
Three deaths, the lawyers should make points of the Irish Censorship list, the Hitler bonfire, and the *Index Expurgatione*, Mrs Litvinov told him *Ulysses* was banned in Russia as their government is careful about children, the only child he ever heard of reading *Ulysses* was Curran's daughter at the age of nine, no reply from Forel, his wife is under great strain, Faber should hear about Ver Hulst's letter, answer for Pinker about *New York Herald* copies for Lane, *2p*

17 August
1934

James Joyce, Grand Hôtel Brasseur, Luxembourg to **Paul Léon**, *autograph letter signed*
Got money, encloses cheque, Bailly died of brain fever, nothing from Forel, his wife knows nothing of Maple's account

18 August
1934

James Joyce, Grand Hôtel Brasseur, Luxembourg to **Paul Léon**, *autograph letter signed*
Names of people to whom copies of the *New York Herald* should be sent, can Léon point out to Cerf that the American judge has given more publicity to *Ulysses* by listing the numbers of the pages containing so called obscene material than any publisher would dare to do

19 August
1934

James Joyce, Luxembourg to **Paul Léon**, *picture postcard of Luxembourg*
More names

19 August
1934

James Joyce, Grand Hôtel Brasseur, Luxembourg to **Paul Léon**, *autograph letter signed*
His wife is nervous because they have not heard from Forel, tell the Gilberts they can join the Joyces here or at the sea, Joyce's wife wants to be back in Paris by the beginning of September, send copies of the *New York Herald* to Larbaud and Morel and to Harold Nicolson, get a statement from Nicolson about the B.B.C. ban on *Ulysses* for use by Lane's lawyer, cheque for Léon, see Stuart Gilbert about Matisse, the English press probably ignored the news, *2p*

20 August
1934

20 August 1934

James Joyce, Luxembourg to **Paul Léon**, *picture postcard of Luxembourg*
Addresses of Larbaud, Morel and Nicolson

22 August 1934

James Joyce, Grand Hôtel Brasseur, Luxembourg to **Paul Léon**, *autograph letter signed*
He leaves for Montreux, wire money, suggest the addition of the second legal report to *Ulysses* to Cerf, the judge Manton acted in an unjudicial manner by giving page references to obscene material, *2p*

[post 29 August 1934]

James Joyce to **Paul Léon**
'I told these fools by 'phone on the 15/7 to remove the *poste*. If they didn't, *tant pis*. They owe me a month's refund on the piano hire.' *annotation on letter from G. Hamm, Facteur de Pianos et Orgues, Paris to Joyce dated 29 August 1934*

7 September 1934

James Joyce, Hôtel de la Paix, Geneva to **Paul Léon**, Villa Petit Desin, Quaritier To-Suc, Hossegor, Landes, France, *picture postcard of Geneva*
Return of *lettrines* by Reece, could Ver Hulst get the book out by Xmas

9 September 1934

James Joyce, Hôtel de la Paix, Geneva to **Paul Léon**, *autograph letter signed*
No decision yet, can Brody advise re enclosed, did the Hungarian publishers pay for *Ulysses*, he sent Pugh's photographs for the *Ulysses* guidebook to Giorgio in New York, Léon should suggest cancellation of Pinker's and Lane's contracts, can they offer *Ulysses* to the OUP, *2p*

13 September 1934

James Joyce, Hôtel de la Paix, Geneva to **Paul Léon**, *autograph letter signed*
Needs money as he has to change Lucia, she behaved badly and upset his wife, he has replied to Swinnerton's letter, *2p*

9 October 1934

Empty envelope addressed to Paul Léon in hand of James Joyce

14 October 1934

James Joyce to **Paul Léon**
Ulysses for Dr Loy, Budgen's publishers have not sent his book to Prof. Fehr or to *N.Z.Z.*, Jolas is leaving, encloses U.S. letter, will not send Lucia's letter

James Joyce to **Paul Léon**
'Can't read Levy's letter J.J. Find out if Jolas sent those cigars, please. Never got them' *annotation on invoice furnished by J. Vialtelle dated 18 October 1934*

[post 18 October 1934]

James Joyce, Carlton Elite Hotel, Zurich to **Paul Léon**, *autograph letter signed*
Encloses cheque, payments for Jung, Mrs Raphael and Léon's expenses, wants return of letter from Goll, queries re Ver Hulst, cable Cerf, has Lane arranged for the proofreading of *Ulysses*, no suitable replies to their ad for a flat in Zurich, his wife does not want to go back to Paris, *2p*

20 October 1934

James Joyce, Carlton Elite Hotel, Zurich to **Paul Léon**, *autograph letter signed*
Queries re Heinke, Ver Hulst, when did the Circuit Court rule, wants a copy of the *New York Herald* to see what is on at the theatre, Jung cannot attend to the case himself, does not know how long they will stay, queries re book by Slocombe, Matisse book, did MacSwiney pick up the disk, the Sullivans, did Pinker write to Imhof about sales of his disk, *3p*

23 October 1934

James Joyce, **Nora Joyce** and **Carola Giedion-Welcker** to **Paul Léon**, *picture postcard of Restaurant "Dubeli", Lucerne, Rich. Wagner's Stammloka*

28 October 1934

James Joyce, [postmark Tells Kapelle b. Kusnacht] to **Paul Léon**, *picture postcard showing "Tell's Tod"*
Goll, has read *Irish Times* article which is the first in the Irish press for twenty years

4 November 1934

James Joyce, Carlton Elite Hotel, Zurich to **Paul Léon**, *autograph letter signed*
Encloses blank cheque, find out from Cerf whether an appeal has been lodged, pay the *garde-meubles*, did Jolas send cigars, Ver Hulst has not sent copies of the *Mime*, the fountain pen was in the lining of Lucia's fur mantle, she wants plastic surgery on her cheek, *2p*

6 November 1934

James Joyce, Carlton Elite Hotel, Zurich to **Paul Léon**, *autograph letter signed*
Encloses cheque, Giorgio and Helen are not returning, Mrs Jolas will see to the furniture and Joyce will take the family

9 November 1934

17

portraits, Giorgio is having interviews but no definite news, they have a flat and many invitations, MacSwiney is dead

12 November 1934
James Joyce, Carlton Elite Hotel, Zurich to **Paul Léon**, *autograph letter signed*
He is not well, his wife would like her warm mantle sent on, *2p*

13 November 1934
Nora Joyce, Carlton Elite Hotel, Zurich to **Paul Léon**, *autograph letter signed*
Encloses letter about fur

20 November 1934
Empty envelope addressed to Léon by Joyce

25 November 1934
James Joyce, Carlton Elite Hotel, Zurich to **Paul Léon**, *autograph letter signed on back of leaflet advertising "Dr Raebers Hohere Handelsschule"*
Cannot find notepaper, wire money, engage room in hotel, Lane and the Society of Authors should be told of the final result of the *Ulysses* case in the U.S.

27 November 1934
James Joyce, Zurich to **Paul Léon**, *telegram*
NE PARTONS PAS ATTENDEZ LETTRE SALUTATIONS

10 December 1934
James Joyce, [Zurich] to **Paul Léon**, *picture postcard of Zurich*
Books he wants

[?15 December 1934]
James Joyce to **Paul Léon**, *autograph letter signed endorsed on letter from Miss Dorothy Parker, Los Angeles*
Suffers from nervous exhaustion and colitis so cannot write, needs money and yellow drops, Léon should not telephone, Russian for the Black Sea

20 December 1934
Empty envelope addressed by James Joyce to Paul Léon, note in pencil on flap *"Please send Irish Times and yellow drops"*

25 December 1934
James Joyce, Zurich to **Paul Léon**, *autograph letter signed*
Wire money, he tore up Pinker's contract and the maid threw it out, asks about Goll and Sullivan, Léon should not telephone or mention Lucia or Joyce's work in his letters, explain to the booby in London that he is in constant worry, open his mail and send only the essential, *2p*

18

JOYCE and LÉON

James Joyce, Carlton Elite Hotel, Zurich to **Paul Léon**, *autograph letter signed*
He is writing out words and music of Irish songs to send to New York, pay his subscription to the *Irish Times*, he tore up the contract, the Black Sea, the doctors have gone away and he feels lonely

'Childermas '34'

James Joyce, Zurich to **Paul Léon**, *telegram*
AVEZ VOUS SOUSCRIT IRISH TIMES OU SONTS JOURNEAUX FELICITATIONS

8 January 1935

James Joyce, Zurich to **Paul Léon**, *incomplete autograph letter signed*
Meaning of 'porkbarrel', owner of the Elite is unsure of taking Lucia into the villa, Joyce is upset by the news that his money is gone, *annotated by Léon with meanings of words*

[c. 10 January 1935]

James Joyce, Zurich to **Paul Léon**, *telegram*
PRIERE ENVOYEZ REGULIEREMENT JOURNAUX SALUTATIONS

13 January 1935

James Joyce to **Paul Léon**
He wants a male god beginning with *C*, is *fjaellet* or *fjaellen* correct, cuttings came with depressing letter from Giorgio, arrangements for Lucia, encloses letter from Jung, got a nurse through Giorgio's aviator friend, *endorsed with typescript notes on 'portjuncula', 'fjael', 'porkbarrel' and list of names from Greek and Roman mythology beginning with 'B' and 'C', with manuscript draft in hand of Paul Léon, 4p*

[15 January 1935]

James Joyce, Carlton Elite Hotel, Zurich to **Paul Léon**, *autograph letter signed*
He wanted to know of the word *fjaell*, get him a god beginning with *C*, send *Irish Times* as he passes it on to Lucia, give his news to the Jolases and Gilbert, send his express letter to Miss Weaver, Giorgio would be very successful with Schoeck's music suite, asks about Goll and Sullivan, origin of 'porkbarrel', his brother in Trieste has been writing for money, ask Mrs Jolas to reply to Lucia's letter, what is Ver Hulst doing about the alphabet, *4p*

16 January 1935

16 January 1935, 6 pm. **James Joyce**, Carlton Elite Hotel, Zurich to **Paul Léon**, *autograph letter signed*
He has not received the power of attorney, he does not think Léon realises the situation, W. Rosenbaum Switzerland's leading criminal lawyer saw Lucia and said that she had given up the idea of a suit against Léon's brother-in-law but was suicidal, Joyce's wife was very upset, Joyce went to hear Othmar Schoeck's suite of songs for bass, he went to visit Schoeck the next day in order to get him to sign his score which Joyce could then send to Giorgio, while he was there he was summoned back because Lucia was making a scene, Lucia said she wants her aunt Eileen in Bray, no answer to his telegrams to Bray, Lucia received his wife badly today and walked out of a restaurant, the nurse resigned, his wife wants to send Lucia back to Kusnacht but she has not yet had the weekly letter from her mother after which she may change her mind, Joyce has not been able to do any work, Miss Weaver says she read about the Supreme Court decision in the papers Léon sent, Joyce did not see any papers, Schoeck is the first man Joyce has spoken to in several months, *4p*

31 January 1935, *postmark* [] **Joyce, Dublin** to **Paul Léon**, *telegram*
MRS SCHAUREK ARRIVING PARIS AMIENS STATION THIS THURSDAY AFTERNOON FOUR OCLOCK PLEASE MEET

15 September 1935 **James Joyce** to **Paul Léon**, *written on telegram form*
Wire money, received telegram from Miss Weaver re passport, he was ill and weak when Léon and Mrs Jolas phoned but was taken on a drive and is better now

20 September 1935 **James Joyce**, Savoy Hotel, Fontainebleau to **Paul Léon**, *autograph letter signed*
Encloses cheque, payments Léon should make including 15/- to Mrs Curran, he suspects that either Léon or his wife hastened Giorgio's return, will he be allowed a few days channel air, *2p*

20 September 1935 **James Joyce** to **Paul Léon**, *telegram*
PLEASE TELEPHONE SOLLICITONS [sic] CREDIT MY PARIS ACCOUNT HUNDRED POUNDS IMMEDIATELY THANKS HOPE YOU ARE BETTER GREETINGS

25 October 1935 **James Joyce** to **Paul Léon**, *autograph letter signed*
Pay telephone bill, show enclosed to Mrs Jolas

James and Nora Joyce, Paris to **Paul Léon**, *small card*   25 April 1936
Wishing Léon a happy birthnight

James Joyce, 7 rue Edmond Valentin, Paris to **Paul Léon**, *typed*   21 July 1936
letter signed
Letter authorising Léon's dealings relating to money received
from Mrs Crosby, *with credit notes from banks, 3 items*

James Joyce, Villa Connemara (ancienne Villa Maria   8 August
Madeleine), Avenue Docteur Sicard, Villers to **Paul Léon**,   1936
autograph letter signed
Sent a wire to Sullivan who is singing tonight, will Léon make
sure Obelisk return all Lucia's *lettrines*, list of people to whom
the *Nouvelles Littéraires* and prospectuses should be sent, can
Léon find out the names of those who subscribed to Kahane, *2p*

James Joyce, Casino de Deauville to **Paul Léon**, *autograph letter*   10 August
signed   1936
Phone Dr Delmas and tell him to take the things his wife sent
Lucia out of the Deauville bags and give them to her as if they
had been left at the porter's lodge, wire money, Léon's letter
came but not the sheets, *2p*

James Joyce to **Paul Léon**, *autograph letter signed*   12 August
Sheets gone, letters for Mrs J. and Mrs C., pay Kahane, needs   1936
more money for Denmark, thanks for Danish book, has not yet
got *Politiken*

James Joyce, [postmark Deauville] to **Paul Léon**, *picture postcard*   12 August
of Villers sur mer   1936
Send enclosure to Lucia

James Joyce, [postmark Deauville] to **Paul Léon**, *picture postcard*   13 August
of Deauville   1936
Send copies of *N. Litt.* to Lucia, H.W., Kahane and Mrs Jolas,
weather better

James Joyce to **Paul Léon**, *picture postcard of Villers-sur-Mer*   [? August
PS. Obelisk should be paid according to amount delivered,   1936]
they are in arrears while Joyce is in advance

James Joyce, Liège to **Paul Léon**, *telegram*   19 August
OUVREZ LETTRE HELENE SI NOUVELLES IMPORTANTES   1936
TELEPHONEZ HUIT HEURES MERCI SALUTATIONS

21

21 August 1936

James Joyce, [postmark Hamburg] to **Paul Léon**, *picture postcard of Gebr. Schubarth Vegetarisches Restaurant*
Send prospectuses, *signed James Joyce, Nora Joyce, M.C. Wegner, not in Joyce's hand*

21 August 1936

James Joyce, Hamburg to **Paul Léon**, *telegram*
HOTEL STREIT REPARTONI SAMEDI MATIN SALUTATIONI

23 August 1936

James Joyce, Copenhagen to **Paul Léon**, *telegram*
TURISTHOTEL ENVOIE ADRS HUEBSCH SALUTVAN

25 August [1936], 11 am.

James Joyce, Copenhagen to **Paul Léon**, *picture postcard of Copenhagen*
Sends cheque in case they have to leave suddenly, Albatross refuse to lend *Ulysses*, is Lucia's book out yet, wants papers, Prof. A. may visit Lucia fortnightly, he put off journalists

26 August 1936

James Joyce, [Copenhagen] to **Paul Léon**, *picture postcard of The little Sea-Nymph, Copenhagen*
Received letter, awaits text, asks for various books and articles to be sent to him

26 August 1936

James Joyce and **Nora Joyce**, Elsinore to **Paul Léon**, *picture postcard of 'Hamlets Grav', Marienlyst, Helsinger*
Asks for Huebsch's address, will send corrections to *Ulysses*

28 August 1936

James Joyce, Copenhagen to **Paul Léon**, *telegram*
CORRECTIONS TOUTES ENVOYEES VOTRE ADRESSE OUI ACHETEZ ET LIVREZ DE NOTRE PART SANS VISITE MILLE REMERCIEMENTS AVANCE VOTRE SOEUR SALU-TATIONS

[2? August 1936]

James Joyce to **Paul Léon**, *incomplete letter*
Thanks for wire, send copy of Lucia's book by airmail, Prof. Lévy Bruhl wants to see him

Sunday, 11 am. [30 August 1936]

James Joyce, Turist Hotel, Copenhagen to **Paul Léon**, *autograph letter signed*
Has received letter but not the other things he requested, arrangements to get money, A. should visit Lucia only every fifteen days till Joyce's return, A. is wasting his time reading *Ulysses* as far as Lucia is concerned, he should read *Dedalus* or

Exiles instead, Joyce will send her letter to Salzburg and will write to her about clothes, asks for *Irish Times*, returns letter with indicated reply, writes to Switzerland about his brother, Lévy Bruhl says he read *Ulysses* twice, Danish critics want to see him, persons to whom copies of Lucia's book should be sent, *3p*

James Joyce, Turist Hotel, Copenhagen to **Paul Léon**
Gift for Lévy Bruhl, has not received enough money, plans to stay a week in Germany and Léon will not be able to send him money there, Léon should send him all the money and he will buy tickets and be ready to leave, proofs can be sent to Copenhagen or to Hamburg, he got Lucia's book, send a copy to Sister Pacifique, *2p*

2 September 1936

James Joyce, [Copenhagen] to **Paul Léon**, *picture postcard of Castle of Rosenborg, Copenhagen*
Bought tickets, encloses corrections, does not know how Danish newspaper *B.T.* got hold of enclosed

3 September 1936

James Joyce, Turist Hotel, Copenhagen to **Paul Léon**, *autograph letter signed*
Plans to leave Copenhagen and go to Hamburg, Cologne, Liège and back to Paris, if Léon can get all the money to him and make arrangements with Delmas and Lane he should of course go to Strasbourg, send Lucia's book to Sister Gertrude, he has written to Lord Carlow, Mrs Jolas may show her copy to Matisse, *B.T.* note drawing attention to proposed translation of *Ulysses* into Danish is thought to be partly revenge and partly reaction, asks for *Irish Times*, thanks for what Léon has done about Lucia, *3p*

Fri. 4 September 1936

James Joyce to **Paul Léon**, *postcard*
Returned three last corrections to Lane by air, Lucia's letter enclosed, will probably leave on Monday

[?5 September 1936]

James Joyce, Copenhagen to **Paul Léon**, *telegram*
CE SOIR HAMBOURG SALUTATIONS

6 September 1936

James Joyce, Streit's Hotel, Hamburg to **Paul Léon**, *autograph letter signed*
Got wire but not letter sent to Copenhagen, his address for Lucia's doctors, he will send a letter to Lucia to A. who is to

Monday, 8 September 1936, 11.45 am.

send it to her as if it came from Paris, will *Ulysses* appear on Friday 25th, will Lane advertise it in the *Times Literary Supplement* and in the *Observer*, he will return any proofs he receives by airmail, wants *Irish Times*, asks Léon to leave the key of the Joyce's flat with Léon's concierge, money arrangements difficult owing to different regulations, hopes Léon enjoys his short stay in Strasbourg, *2p*

10 September 1936

Greta Hertz, Nora Joyce, Wilhelm Hertz and **James Joyce** [postmark Cologne] to **Paul Léon**, *picture postcard of Cologne Cathedral*
They have finished seventh bottle of wine

[?September ?1936]

James Joyce, [Liège] to **Paul Léon**, *picture postcard of Hôtel de Suède, Liège*
Ask Miss Weaver to send article on S. in *New Statesman* to Mr Mullany

[c. November 1936]

James Joyce to [?], *draft telegram endorsed in Léon's hand on letter from 'Current Controversy' dated 31 October 1936*
Plans changed, Mrs Jolas left this morning for America can you both dine eight o'clock and stay the night our flat Joyce

[c. 1937]

James Joyce to **Paul Léon**, *postscript to letter on unheaded yellow notepaper*
Get Pinker to attend to letter and to find out from Farrar and Reinhardt [sic] what Gorman is doing

[c. 1937]

James Joyce to **Madame Bertrand**, *printed calling card*
Presents his compliments

All Fools [1 April] 1937

James Joyce, Carlton Elite Hotel, Zurich to **Paul Léon**, *autograph letter signed*
Newspapers for Lucia, messages for her doctors, forward newspapers and books to Zurich, ask Monnier to send confirmation by letter, manage Gorman and Gilbert as Léon likes, he and his wife are well, *2p*

Sunday [?4 April 1937]

James Joyce, Carlton Elite Hotel, Zurich to **Paul Léon**, *autograph letter signed*
What became of the bracelet Giorgio and Helen gave Lucia for Christmas, send money, forward Monro's letters about Lane, he is looking for a job for his brother in Trieste and will go to

JOYCE and LÉON

Zug to see the head of the school there, send *Irish Times* to Mrs Jolas, cut out review of O.G.'s book and send it to Trieste, *2p*

James Joyce, [postmark Zurich] to **Paul Léon**, *postcard*
Money, send *Observer* to usual people, is there a review of O.G. book in *New Statesman* and *Spectator*, where is the book itself

Tuesday
11 am.
6 April 1937

James Joyce, Carlton Elite Hotel, Zurich to **Paul Léon**, *autograph letter signed*
Write to Monro Saw & Co and tell them to get rid of Pinker, he will not sign agreement drawn up by Pinker and Howe, what did Léon mean by his allusions to Lucia and Giorgio, he got cheque and will buy tickets, will go to opera on Friday, *2p*

7 April 1937

James Joyce, [postmark Zurich] to **Paul Léon**, *postcard*
He wrote to Monro Saw & Co as Léon wished, Helen will give Léon a message by phone, gift of Swiss wine, he should have received Gogarty's book on 1 April, H.W. is probably gone to Limehouse to address a meeting of roadmenders, likes Sava Botzaris's head of himself, send copies to Giorgio and Helen and to Lucia

9 April 1937

James Joyce, Carlton Elite Hotel, Zurich to **Paul Léon**, *postcard*
See *Times Literary Supplement*, send on mail as he will stay in Zurich, needs money, his brother and wife arrived from Trieste, saw Vogt

11 April 1937

James Joyce, Carlton Elite Hotel, Zurich to **Paul Léon**, *postcard*
Will return on Saturday, presumes *transition* has not come, the O.G. book has been bungled, keep cheque, his wife cannot always read Léon's hand

15 April 1937

Paul Léon to **James Joyce**, 7 rue Edmond Valentin, Paris VII
Léon has read reply Mr Joyce gave him to send to Monro Saw & Co, will Mr Joyce reconsider his decision, severing the connection with Pinkers will result neither in any saving nor in any simplification of the procedures for collection of royalties, Pinkers have been Mr Joyce's agents for twenty one years and their files are useful, Pinker cannot do any harm as he is not involved with negotiations with publishers, as Pinker will continue to draw commission there is no sense in dispensing with what services he can offer

4 May 1937

12 August 1937

James Joyce, [postmark Basle] to **Paul Léon**, *picture postcard of Three Kings Hotel, Basle*
Weather hot, message for his concierge, forward mail and papers

14 August 1937

James Joyce, Hôtel des Trois Rois, Basle to **Paul Léon**, *autograph letter signed*
They are leaving for Rheinfelden, thunderstorms, leave a message for Mrs Gideon telling her the Joyces's address and what she should say to Lucia about a holiday if she visits her, send a postcard to C.P.C., words and music of the *Soldiers Song*, did he write to H.W., she seems malignant, *3p*

14 August 1937

James Joyce, Hotel Krone, Rheinfelden to **Paul Léon**, *picture postcard of Rheinfelden*
Ask Kahane to send *A.B.C.* to Fr Liebetrau in Rheinfelden

15 August 1937

James Joyce, Hotel zur Kronen, Rheinfelden to **Paul Léon**, *picture postcard 'Vier Puure sind meh as vier Chung'*
Mrs G. should not tell Lucia where her parents are, is there a catalogue of the illuminated manuscripts exhibition at the Bibliothèque Nationale, words of the *Soldiers Song* should be copied for him

18 August 1937

James Joyce, Hotel Krone am Rhein, Rheinfelden to **Paul Léon**, *typed copy certified 'True copy (except as to name in Line 4 of text which we cannot read), Monro Saw & Co, 19 August 1937'*
Payments Léon should make before leaving Paris, Léon should ask his solicitors to forward whatever the publishers paid on signing the contract, *2p*

19 August 1937

James Joyce, [Rheinfelden] to **Paul Léon**, *picture postcard of Rheinfelden*
Got wire, letters, papers and books, did not get *Weekly Irish Times*

Sat 21 August 1937

James Joyce, Hotel Krone am Rhein, Rheinfelden to **Paul Léon**, *autograph letter signed*
Received cheque, pay Delmas, dictionary, take money and have a holiday, Berman's book, send book to Mme Sullivan and papers for Lucia, *2p*

James Joyce, Carlton Elite Hotel, Zurich to **Paul Léon**, *autograph letter signed*
Letters to send to Giorgio, reorder Berman's book if necessary, will write to Monro Saw & Co, ask concierge to readdress newspapers to Joyce, send photo to Griffin, Petit-Jean's address, Léon's address in Brittany, Joyce's doctor will not allow him to travel yet, he wants to go to the sea, he is getting better, wishes 1 September (H.W.'s birthday) was past, concierge should pay bill in case Lucia's piano is taken away, Léon should go to the sea, he does not mind an odd half hour of pain but objects to twenty four hours, *3p*

Fri 27 August 1937, 11 am

James Joyce, Zurich to **Paul Léon**, *endorsed on back of letter from Carola Giedion-Welcker dated 26 August 1937*
Two people were killed by lightning outside Mrs Gideon's house, there have been storms since they reached Basle three weeks ago

Sat 28 August 1937

James Joyce, Grand Hôtel, Dieppe to **Paul Léon**, *autograph letter signed*
Wire money, he is better but still too tired to write much, is Agadjanian back, find out Berman's address, *2p*

5 September 1937

James Joyce, Grand Hôtel, Dieppe to **Paul Léon**, *autograph letter signed*
Bad weather keeps them hotel bound, pay Galignani, order from him Macpherson's *Ossian*, Lennox Robinson's *The Lost Leader*, Mark Twain's *Tom Sawyer*, ask Jolas to make a digest of the plot of *Tom Sawyer* and of its sequel *Huckleberry Finn* and mark the chief points relating to the plot and the highlights of the speech, enclosure for Gorman and Petit-Jean, ask P.J. if his article has appeared in *Études Anglaises*, he has not been able to do more than twenty hours work since he left, keep the book from Budgen for him, *4p*

11 September 1937

Paul Léon to **Gerald Griffin**, *draft reply in hand of James Joyce*
Mr Joyce gave away his *Osservatore Romano* but he got one from Mrs Sullivan, please send it and the *Carmelite Review* back as they are difficult to obtain, the article in it is nothing new, Mr Joyce has a great number of friends and admirers in that quarter, he does not understand Griffin's allusion to the Irish press

[end December 1937- beginning January 1938]

11 February
1938

James Joyce, Carlton Elite Hotel, Zurich to **Paul Léon**, *autograph letter signed*
Weather bad, wishes he had money to get out, forward *Irish Times* and order other Irish newspapers of the 2nd and 3rd, show CPC's and Prof. Hogan's enclosure to Gorman and the Jolases and then send them to Giorgio in New York and also the letter from MacAlmon and a carbon copy of Gorman's part, bad news from Giorgio, got money, encloses letter for Monro Saw & Co, find out how Lucia is and make up a parcel of papers for her, *2p*

12 February
1938

James Joyce, Carlton Elite Hotel, Zurich to **Paul Léon**, *autograph letter signed*
Got [Buddha] and *Irish Times*, have copies made of enclosures and of Herbert Gorman's script to send to G.G. and to Giorgio, write to G.G. that *Ulysses* must have been placed on the *Index Expurgatione* after 1935 when Prof. Fleiner examined it, that it was not included in the holocaust of books in Berlin, that it is no longer banned in Russia and that it is issued in Japan with the Japanese censor's blanks, tell Harriet Weaver that Joyce is exhausted, that he came to Zurich but on Dr Collinson's advice will rest before seeing Prof. Vogt, in short exaggerate what he tells her, ask whether she heard the Irish broadcast assuming she was not parading in Oxford Street in favour of the Sunday morning closure of brothels, did she understand that it referred to the efforts of the amateur to whom she has given so much money, weather bad, will send money for typist, the money Gideon will get for eight lectures at Harvard, Mrs Gideon's stories of her daughter, *4p*

[1]6
February
1938, 4 pm

James Joyce, Carlton Elite Hotel, Zurich to **Paul Léon**, *autograph letter signed*
If money does not come in the morning he will have to put off people he asked to dinner, have a copy of *A.B.C.* sent to Herr Victor Sax, send a copy of Joyce's poems to Dr Othmar Schoeck, ask Lord Carlow's secretary to send two copies here, Joyce wants to give one to Vogt for his daughter, letter from Helen, messages for Mrs Jolas, Mrs S. has messages from Joyce, wants copies of *Paris-Soir* of Sunday 13th, tell Faber that he acknowledges receipt of Mr Geoffrey Faber's letter to which he will reply shortly, a friend of Tuppenycap named Steiner has asked him to have tea, book about wine, has Léon correction he sent, he is working at the *aubade* which ends the book, *2p*

James Joyce, Carlton Elite Hotel, Zurich to **Paul Léon**, *autograph letter signed*
Got money from Monro Saw & Co, does not think it will be enough, send more, has not seen Vogt

17 February 1938

James Joyce, Carlton Elite Hotel, Zurich to **Paul Léon**, *autograph letter signed*
Muddle over money, might be possible to move Lucia under Prof. Loeffler, has not seen Vogt, *2p*

19 February 1938

James Joyce, Carlton Elite Hotel, Zurich to **Paul Léon**, *autograph letter signed*
Enclosures, letter from McAlmon, suspects McAlmon's motives, suggests that Miss Weaver should write a preface, will send proof back in morning, opera libretto, *2p*

20 February 1938

James Joyce, Carlton Elite Hotel, Zurich to **Paul Léon**, *autograph letter signed*
Talked with Léon's brother-in-law, the indented side notes in the proof are now incorporated in the text, has come back from the synagogue, send Mercanton's article to Mrs G, he goes to hear a Viennese tenor

27 February 1938

James Joyce, Carlton Elite Hotel, Zurich to **Paul Léon**, *autograph letter signed*
Has had an eye attack in his right eye, encloses cheque, *endorsed in pencil in hand of Paul Léon 'On this first sad anniversary our thoughts and remembrance are with you and children James + Nora J.'*

28 February 1938

[Paul Léon] to [**?**], *written in hand of Paul Léon, French*
Report on Joyce's eyes

[10 March 1938]

James Joyce to **Paul Léon**, *written on invoice from The Galignani Library dated 31 August 1938*
'Please bring this down to 500fr. Still I don't see how it keeps so high as I don't order any books and keep paying off. Also £1 to Dublin. I have had no news of Giorgio or Helen since you left. Weather broken all the time. I hope Mrs Léon is well again. Did you ring Delmas on Sat? Salutations cordiales J.J.

[post 31 August 1938]

James Joyce, [Lausanne] to **Paul Léon**, *two picture postcards of Grand Hôtel de la Paix, Lausanne*
Thanks for letters and book, glad Mrs Léon is better, why did

1 September 1938

the girl go to see Lucia, met Giorgio and Helen in Montreux, Giorgio had to send David away, order *Irish Nights Entertainment* probably by Edmund Leamy

6 September 1938

James Joyce, [postmark Fribourg] to **Paul Léon**, *picture postcard of Estavayer-le-Lac, Fête des Costumes*
Greetings

6 September 1938

James Joyce. [Lausanne] to **Paul Léon**, *picture postcard of Grand Hôtel de la Paix, Lausanne*
Hopes Mrs Léon is out of pain, Joyce's wife says Rosina is to be paid and should prepare the flat for their return, Joyce spent the day in Fribourg with Mercanton, send more money

9 September 1938

James Joyce, Lausanne to **Paul Léon**, *telegram*
SEND TWO HUNDRED INSTEAD ONE MAY MORE SUNDAY GREETINGS

Sunday, 11 September 1938

James Joyce, Hôtel de la Paix, Lausanne to **Paul Léon**, *autograph letter signed*
Gathers that Léon is worried on account of Mrs Léon, the Joyces are going to Dijon, Joyce would like to meet Léon there, Rosina should leave the parcel at the porter's lodge, ask Faber for more page proofs as he wants to check part 7, Brauchbar has ten refugee relatives in his house, *3p*

21 September 1938

James Joyce, Hôtel du Rhin & de Newhaven, Dieppe to **Paul Léon**, *autograph letter signed*
Mrs Léon is having a good rest, money arrangements, order Irish papers of 19 and 20 September, he has to buy clothes which his wife and Rosina left out of his valise, make arrangements with Delmas, if there is no war the question of Lucia will have to be gone into, *2p*

28 September 1938, *postmark*

James Joyce, [postmark Nante-gare] to **Paul Léon**, *picture postcard of Nantes*
Phone call from Giorgio at La Baule whither they go in the morning, money arrangements, will send instructions about Lucia

28 September 1938, 5 pm

James Joyce, La Baule to **Paul Léon**, *postcard*
Hopes Léon will move to a hotel on outskirts of city, Joyce will wire him cash if necessary, send page proofs and galleys to La

Baule, Joyce will correct them with Helen, let Joyce know when Lucia leaves, give his address to concierge and Galignani, he will arrange later about key of his flat and books, will try to locate Delmas's place in La Baule

James Joyce, Adelphi Hotel, La Baule to **Paul Léon**
autograph letter signed
Thanks for letters, papers and packets, post enclosed to Lucia and the rest as arranged, hopes Mrs Léon and the boy are all right, sees some pact has been signed, phone Delmas on Sunday to say Joyce must put off his Sunday visit, type letter from Joyce's nephew so he can read it, *2p*

30 September 1938

[James Joyce to **Paul Léon]**, *[instructions for a letter to be written to Miss Weaver?]*
Mention Dr Fontaine, lectureship in Italian likely to be given to Mr Meiklejohn, flat given up, book was finished on 13 November but there are about 1000 pages of proofs to be corrected, the book does not deal with any of the social, political or economic questions of the day, he has consumed all his substance writing it, Mrs J. suspected something was wrong, she said he was in a state of exhaustion over closing pages of book, he was more excited during the recent crisis by a gramophone record of a Greek song than by the conflicts raging around him, *3p*

[c.February 1939]

James Joyce, 34 rue des Vignes to **Monsieur le Directeur du Bureau de Poste à Auteuil**, *carbon typescript unsigned, French*
Enquires about an important letter that has gone astray

28 July 1939

James Joyce, Hôtel de la Paix, Lausanne to **Paul Léon**, *autograph letter signed*
Worried about Lucia, can Léon see Denhof and Huebsch before they go, Joyce told Huebsch he thought the price of *Finnegans Wake* too high, Huebsch said the Public Library Board in Britain does not buy books above 18/-, does this mean there is no copy of *Finnegans Wake* in any public library, if Viking Press will do a cheaper edition could they at least add a sheet of corrigenda, ask Huebsch to remember Joyce to J.F. Byrne who seemed slightly unhinged when Joyce met him, Lucia talks about Byrne, *2p*

10 August 1939

[Saturday
c. 13 August
1939]

James Joyce, Hôtel de la Paix, Lausanne to **Paul Léon**, *autograph letter signed*
Thanks for letters, forward *F* and *R* letters to Harriet Weaver, hopes *Finnegans Wake* no 7 is not lost, ask Denhof for an address to which *Finnegans Wake* can be sent, if it is true that books over 18/- are banned by British Public Libraries then Faber's price of 25/- is blackmail of Joyce's admirers, they go to Bern on Monday, buy *Sunday Times* tomorrow

15 August
1939

James Joyce, Hotel Schweizerhof, Bern to **Paul Léon**, *autograph letter signed*
Giorgio and Helen arrived for the day, Joyce will stay in Bern a few days and then go to Thun, sent Léon the keys of the flat, will Léon go there and get the Joyce's lottery tickets which may have won, also get gas bill and cheque, he will need more money, tell Louis Gillet about different versions of *Anna Livia Plurabelle*, weather too warm, they will drive with Giorgio and Helen to Freibourg for dinner and will then return, he will send card for Lucia tomorrow, leave keys with the Joyce's concierge, *3p with two lottery tickets*

Friday [1?
August
1939], 7 pm

James Joyce, Hotel Schweizerhof, Bern to **Paul Léon**, *autograph letter signed*
Will not go to Thun, money arrangements, *Finnegans Wake* cannot be found in Swiss bookshops and probably not in most European countries, it is a complete wash out, Jaloux has not replied, U.S. result a fiasco, has returned books to Passy, will send letter for Lucia, hopes Léon will enjoy his holiday

Saturday [1?
August
1939], 5 pm.

James Joyce, Hotel Schweizerhof, Bern to **Paul Léon**, *autograph letter unsigned*
Ask Faber to send unbound sheets of *Finnegans Wake* so he can begin corrections, tell Louis Gillet to send press copy to a colleague who specialises in English literature, *3p*

22 August
1939

James Joyce, Grand Hôtel Monney, Montreux to **Paul Léon**, *autograph letter signed*
Wrote to manager of Lloyd's, encloses letter about *Finnegans Wake*, money arrangements, *2p*

23 August
1939
*[postmark 24
August 1939]*

James Joyce, Hôtel Monney, Montreux to **Paul Léon**, *picture postcard*
Money has not arrived, ring up Loy and find out about Lucia, will send card for her and cheques for Léon

James Joyce, Grand Hôtel Monney, Montreux to **Paul Léon**, *autograph letter signed*
Received Léon's letter of 23rd, money has not yet arrived, encloses card for Lucia, impossible to know what to do

Thursday 24 August 1939, 8.30 pm

James Joyce, La Baule to **Paul Léon**, *telegram*
PROVISOIREMT HOTEL MAJESTIC DELMAS PARTI HIER POUR PARIS SALUTATIONS

29 August 1939

James Joyce, Hôtel Majestic, La Baule to **Mrs Léon**, *autograph letter signed*
Post enclosed to Lucia, hopes they are well, if she sees Léon ask him to request Dr Delmas to cash cheque, hopes Delmas has made arrangements for transport to La Baule, *2p*

30 August 1939

James Joyce to **Paul Léon**, *telegram*
HOTEL QUI DEVAIT RECEVOIR MAISON SANTE PRIS TIERS AUCUNE PROVISION ICI DELMAS RENTRE PARIS DEMAIN SA MAISON RESTE IVRY MOMENTANEMENT JUSQUE QUELQUE SOLUTION ULTERIEURE EN ATTENDANT LUCIA SEULE ET EN DANGER COMMENTAIRE SUPERFLU AMITIES

4 September 1939

James Joyce, Hôtel Saint Christophe, La Baule to **Mrs Léon**, *autograph letter signed*
Hopes she and her family are well, post enclosed to Lucia who is trapped at Ivry, Dr Delmas has failed to keep his promises and as a result Joyce's plans to be near Lucia are in vain, she is alone in danger and probably terror in Paris, *2p*

Monday 4 September 1939, 12 h.

James Joyce, Hôtel St Christophe, La Baule to **Paul Léon**, *autograph letter signed on Hotel Majestic paper*
Lucia arrived, telephone Giorgio and tell him of her arrival, letter from Mrs Léon says Léon's brother-in-law is called in, in a further letter Joyce will tell Léon how to dispose of papers so that Joyce can get at them that is the papers that Léon has, his cheque arrived, send a copy of *Revue de Paris* of 1 September to Miss Weaver, Léon should not worry because the debt is on Joyce's side, Giorgio has asked his parents to stay with him, Joyce thinks they should all be together including Lucia, if a sanatorium could be found near Neauphe Joyce could visit her and be near her in case of trouble, will the neighbourhood of Paris be safe in the coming months, ask H. to ring him up, the Joyces have no clothes except those they wear, *2p*

Monday 11 September 1939

[17]
September
1939

James Joyce, [La Baule] to **Paul Léon**, *autograph letter signed, French*
What is Giorgio's telephone number and how is he, did Giorgio receive his letters, Joyce's daughter had a whole week of crises after her arrival here, what is the result of Léon's call up, plan to escape to New York, postcards arrive faster and it is better to type them, *2p*

24
September
1939

James Joyce, Hotel S. Christophe, La Baule to **Paul Léon**, *autograph letter signed, French*
Léon's letter of the 20th gave him much pleasure, with regard to attached letters ask this joker of a literary agent if he has any intention of paying and how much, as for the other reply affirmatively, tell his lawyers to send the monthly cheque, he leaves the choice of the Berkeley book to Léon provided it is not too dear, Lucia is not well, he has not been allowed to see her, try to see or to talk with Joyce's son, he would accept his daughter-in-law's invitation if he could find somewhere for his daughter, is Mercanton's second article in the *Nouvelle Revue Française*, give the collection to Denhof, give Joyce's address to Louis Gillet

25
September
1939

James Joyce, Hôtel S. Christophe, La Baule to **Paul Léon**, *postcard, French*
He does not have the wallet which should also contain £6 that his son gave him when he came back from London, Delmas will be in Paris from the 27th to the 29th, try to find out how much Joyce owes him, do not speak of the transfer of his daughter, Joyce received a message from his daughter-in-law, will Léon get in touch with Dr O'Brien's secretary to help her find a sanatorium for Lucia

28
September
1939

James Joyce, [La Baule] to **Paul Léon**, *autograph letter signed, French*
He does not understand anything but he supposes it is in order so he accepts

5 October
1939

James Joyce, La Baule to **Paul Léon**, *telegram*
TACHEZ CONVAINCRE MON FILS VENIR ICI AVEC LE PETIT SE REPOSER QUELQUES SEMAINES ENVOYAI LES LETTRES MA BRU AU DOCTEUR PAS DE REPONSE MAIS DIAGNOSTIC MALHEUREUSEMENT ASSEZ CLAIRE SI LEUR DEPART IMPOSSIBLE ET NOTRE PRESENCE JUGE

PAR LUI UTILE PARTIRONS PRIEZ AVOCATS TRANS-
FERER ARGENT LLOYDS BANQUE PARIS AMITIES

James Joyce, Hôtel S. Christophe, La Baule to **Paul Léon**, 6 October
autograph letter signed, French 1939
Thanks for Léon's letter and the enclosure, Joyce's wife tore up
Miss Weaver's letter so Joyce does not know what she wrote, his
wife has asked Joyce to tell Léon that she will tear up all the
other letters that he encloses, Joyce gave all his daughter-in-
law's letters to Dr Fontaine for her opinion but she has not
replied, he received a third letter from his daughter-in-law who
is at the Ritz and whose letter seems to show an exalted state,
Joyce and his wife are very worried about their son, show him
this letter because Joyce does not know whether he is still with
Léon's brother-in-law, he does not need letters to know he can
always count on Joyce, if he does not like the idea of Joyce
staying with the little boy let Joyce know what he thinks is the
best solution, *3p*

James Joyce, Hotel S. Christophe, La Baule to **Paul Léon,** 9 October
autograph letter signed, French 1939
Has received letter and telegrams from his son and from Léon,
wrote to his daughter-in-law, will Léon ask Dr Fontaine to
return the two letters Joyce sent her, his daughter has not been
well since her arrival in La Baule, she is the only person who
remembered the 35th anniversary of the Joyces's marriage, Dr
O'Brien and his friends from the Rockefeller Foundation gave
a supper in honour of the Joyces to their great surprise,
financial matters, the O'Casey book he received was not the
edition he wanted, he did not get the Berkeley, send Pelorson's
article to his publishers in London and to Curran, repeat
anything special in Miss Weaver's letter, it is impossible to hide
anything from his wife because she opens his post, she tears up
anything that looks like 'rubbish', he will send the certificate of
existence to his lawyers, he sent everything back to Gorman,
thank Giorgio for his telegram and thank Léon's brother-in-law
for what he has done to help Giorgio, ask Miss Weaver to find
out if there have been any reviews of his book in the *Sunday
Times* since the 27 September, encloses list of clothes which he
had asked his daughter-in-law to send, will Léon find out if she
did so and if not have them sent on, *5p*

12 October 1939

James Joyce, Hôtel S. Christophe, La Baule to **Paul Léon**, *postcard*
Arrangements to fetch fur coat, he is still awaiting the arrival of Mr Gunn and the promised letter from his son, the *Irish Times* should send the paper to this address, his daughter-in-law, ask Dr Fontaine to return the letters

13 October 1939

James Joyce, Hôtel S. Christophe, La Baule to **Paul Léon**, *autograph letter signed, French*
He sends back the letter for R. Kastor to whom he will write, asks Léon to get his daughter-in-law's letters from Dr Fontaine, he wants to show them to his son and also other letters he has received, they have applied for a safe conduct to Paris which will take three or four days, they will leave as soon as they get it, encloses bill from Ivry, he would like to be sure that his lawyers have lodged £100 in the bank for him, he is going to see Gunn at the hotel, Joyce's daughter is still very noisy and disturbed, Léon need not now send his wife's coat or the other things, *3p*

13 October 1939

James Joyce, La Baule to **Paul Léon**, *telegram*
OU EST ET COMMENT VA MON FILS REPONDEZ URGENCE PARTIRONS LE PLUTOT POSSIBLE PEUT ETRE DIMANCHE

19 November 1939

Paul Léon to **James Joyce**
In response to Mr Joyce's request he sends the dossier on Miss Lucia Joyce, the envelope containing cuttings about *Finnegans Wake* as returned to him by Louis Gillet and all the contracts in his possession, as the documents are important he will not leave them with the concierge but at his brother-in-law's

[2? December] 1939

James Joyce, Hôtel Lutétia, Paris to **Paul Léon**, *postcard*
Christmas greetings

5 February 1940

Paul Léon to **James Joyce**, *typed letter signed*
Encloses copies of letters he sent to America and to London after he saw Mr Joyce and the letter intended for the Tax Controller, he expects Mrs Jolas on Monday and will be glad to do anything urgent Mr Joyce wants

n.d.

James Joyce to **Paul Léon**, *printed calling card of James Joyce*
Material to send to Gorman

James Joyce to **Mrs Léon,** *small card*   n.d.
Encloses money for Léon's vacation expenses, if Joyce gives it
to him it means arguing for hours

[James Joyce to **Paul Léon]**, *fragment from letter*   n.d.
Re bill

[James Joyce to **Paul Léon]**   n.d.
Request for books to be sent to him and list returned, *with typed
and manuscript list of books with marks against 'Irish at School', 'Do
You Know Your History' and 'Sullivan's School Series-Introduction to
Geography and History', 2p*

[James Joyce to **Paul Léon]**, *fragment from letter*   n.d.
Instructions re Curran

[James Joyce to **Paul Léon]**, *fragment from letter*   n.d.
List of books 'By the same writer'

Empty envelope marked in pencil with names and addresses in   n.d.
hand of James Joyce

Miscellaneous manuscript and typescript notes and draft letters   n.d.
by Paul Léon, *42 items*

2.

CORRESPONDENCE OF JAMES JOYCE AND PAUL LÉON WITH HARRIET SHAW WEAVER

213 letters, 1930-39

22 November 1930   **James Joyce**, 192 rue de Grenelle, Paris VII to **Harriet Weaver**, *carbon typescript, unsigned, transcribed in Selected Letters of James Joyce edited by Richard Ellmann, London, 1975*

7 February 1932   **Paul Léon** to **Harriet Weaver**, Castle Park, Frodsham near Warrington, England
Mr Joyce has had a letter from Mr Pinker abandoning all claim on the Paris edition of *Ulysses* and promising to arrange for an English edition as soon as the rights question is settled, Léon has received an apology from Miss Beach for the step she took with Mr Joyce's New York lawyers and has also received her abandonment of the world rights in Mr Joyce's favour

28 February 1932   **Paul Léon** to **Harriet Weaver**
Mr Joyce has been unwell due to eye trouble, insomnia and intestinal grippe, but is feeling better now, he would like her to send the last number of the *New Statesman* to John Dulanty, High Commissioner in the Irish Free State Office, Desmond Fitzgerald, Minister of Defence and Augustus Milner, a teacher of music, and to ask the latter to return *Music and Letters*

1 March 1932   **Harriet Weaver**, 74, Gloucester Place, London W.1 to **Paul Léon**
Thanks Léon for having sent her so many letters on Mr Joyce's behalf, she has sent the copies of the *New Statesman* as requested and has asked Milner to return *Music and Letters*, she is sorry to hear that Mr Joyce was unwell, Léon's letter to Dr Borach had given better news of him, *3p*

2 March 1932   **Paul Léon** to **Harriet Weaver**
Mr Joyce is very busy dealing with four American offers for an edition of *Ulysses* and so apologizes for not writing himself, he would like her to send the last number of the *New Statesman* containing his impression of Sullivan to T.S. Eliot, F. Budgen,

Mrs Schaurek, Michael Healy, Alexander Malcolm and Constantine Curran, he is not starting a new campaign for Sullivan merely acknowledging people who have shown an interest, T.S. Eliot offered to publish Mr Joyce's last poem, Miss Beach wants a prepayment of 60.000 Frs for bringing out the 12th edition of *Ulysses*

Paul Léon to **Harriet Weaver**   3 March 1932
Thanks for her letter of 1 March, Mr Joyce wants four more copies of the *New Statesman*, the American colony in Paris has invited him to be guest of honour at a luncheon on St Patrick's Day, he has accepted the invitation on condition that he is not asked to make a speech, he foresees trouble with the American negotiations, his health is making progress

Harriet Weaver, 74 Gloucester Place, London W.1 to **Paul Léon**   12 March 1932
Returns copies of the two last sets of letters, hopes show of fireworks expected from the rue de l'Odéon not too brilliant, thanks for copy of new *transition*, sent copies of *New Statesman* as directed, *2p*

Paul Léon to **Harriet Weaver**   21 March 1932
Mr Joyce is having a hectic time and has asked Léon to thank Miss Weaver for her last letter and to forward enclosed letters and cables

Harriet Weaver, 74 Gloucester Place, London W.1 to **Paul Léon**   26 July 1932
Thanks for letters and report on Mr Joyce's eyes, had returned letters to Mr Joyce and supposes he will forward them himself to his son

Harriet Weaver, 74 Gloucester Place, London W.1 to **James Joyce**   25 August 1932
Thinks Miss Beach needs a warning but not an ultimatum as yet, encloses suggested amendments to letter by Léon to Miss Beach, does not understand Léon's paragraph about the film, *2p, with enclosed copy letters of Miss Beach to Paul Léon and of Paul Léon to Miss Beach and suggested amendments*

Harriet Weaver, 74 Gloucester Place, London W.1 to **Paul Léon**, *typed letter signed*   [c. 1933]
Thanks for his letter, she has asked Mr Joyce's solicitors to sell £100 of stock and advance half of it, she is glad the new edition of *Ulysses* is making a good start, it will be a relief to Mr Joyce

that Léon has taken over business matters from Miss Beach, news of Mr Joyce is disappointing, thanks for copy of *New Republic* containing Mr Joyce's poem

5 January 1933

Harriet Weaver, 74 Gloucester Place, London W.1 to **Paul Léon** She has asked Monro Saw & Co to sell £100 of Mr Joyce's stock immediately and forward a cheque, she is obliged to Léon for having written so fully of Mr Joyce's situation, agrees that his attitude to his daughter's illness is the right one and is glad that he clings to his work for relief, thanks for sending pages of Mr Joyce's manuscript, *2p*

7 January 1933

Harriet Weaver, 74 Gloucester Place, London W.1 to **James Joyce** Thanks for telegram of good wishes for the new year, hopes his material circumstances will improve when royalties from *Ulysses* begin to come in, hopes the intense psychic strain from which the Joyce family suffers will ease, encloses cuttings re *Two tales*, there were dozens of short notices about the Irish Academy of Letters, *2p*

[c.22 January 1933]

Paul Léon to **Harriet Weaver**, *draft telegram* If not too late please send 121 Ebury Street, Pimlico, London wreath two guineas sending cheque only leaves green brown but excluding absolutely ivy inscription To George Moore from J.J. Paris, *endorsed with notes*

29 January 1933

Harriet Weaver, 74 Gloucester Place, London W.1 to **Paul Léon**, *typed letter signed* Thanks for letters, sorry she missed his telephone calls, she ordered wreath, length of time letters take to come from Paris, she will return copy of *Hound and Horn* promptly

1 March 1933

Harriet Weaver, Hotel Galilée, Paris to **Paul Léon** Thanks for copy of letter to Miss Beach signed by directors of Albatross Press and himself

4 March 1933

Harriet Weaver, 74 Gloucester Place, London W.1 to **Paul Léon**, *typed letter signed* Hopes Mr Joyce is getting off to Zurich with Mrs Joyce and his daughter, could they not stay longer than seven days for 4,000 francs which is more than double for each of them than the amount she paid in Paris per week

Harriet Weaver, 74 Gloucester Place, London W.1 to **Paul Léon**   5 March 1933
She saw Mr Monro about Léon's queries re Mr Joyce's income, explains discrepancies, agrees that it is important for Mr Joyce to go to Zurich, *2p*

Harriet Weaver, 74 Gloucester Place, London W.1 to **Paul Léon**   6 March 1933
Stocks and shares were given to Mr Joyce so that he might be free to write, he therefore has first claim on them, can he not make this claim with regard to Zurich and his work, she is glad to hear Americans are hopeful of a favourable judgement, *2p*

Paul Léon to **Harriet Weaver**   14 March 1933
Mr Joyce still extremely nervous, he has started work on overhauling the fragments of the second part, his wishes with regard to his flat in London which should be disposed of, he wants to keep the sofa and armchair which were a gift from Harriet Weaver

Paul Léon to **Harriet Weaver**   17 March 1933
Transcribed in Letters of James Joyce, Volume III, edited by Richard Ellmann, London, 1966

Harriet Weaver, 74 Gloucester Place, London W.1 to **Paul Léon**, *typed letter signed*   18 March 1933
She gave notice to Marsh and Parsons for the breaking of Mr Joyce's lease and instructed them to let the flat for the remainder of the lease, she inspected the flat herself and rescued a drawing of Mr Joyce's son and a photograph of his daughter-in-law, she will forward copies of the *Hull Daily Mail* as directed, three cuttings have come in which Professor Vogt is mentioned, asks Léon to thank Mr Joyce for the copy of the English edition of P.P., hopes his health will improve, *2p*

Harriet Weaver, 74 Gloucester Place, London W.1 to **Paul Léon**, *typed letter signed*   20 March 1933
She was glad to receive Léon's letter of the 17th, wants to help Mr Joyce but feels powerless to do so, he seemed elusive to her on her visit to Paris, she wanted to find out Mrs Joyce's view, she always felt in a false position with regard to the rue de l'Odéon, she would like to have a full account of Dr Debray's report, asks Léon to write frankly to her, Léon is a great help to Mr Joyce, if Mr Joyce has to pay for Mr Budgen's trip to Ireland she will explain to the solicitors, the *Hull Daily Mail* has arrived, *2p*

23 March
1933

Harriet Weaver, 74 Gloucester Place, London W.1 to **Paul Léon**
Issue of the *Semaine à Paris* was that of the 17-24 May 1929, she
has posted papers containing Dr Vogt's name and also the
Birmingham Post which has an article on *The Joyce Book*, trouble
with obtaining the *Evening Standard*, thanks for copy of *Le
Phare*, thinks the photograph is excellent, hopes next news of
Mr Joyce will be better, *2p*

23 March
1933

Paul Léon to **Harriet Weaver**
*Transcribed in Letters of James Joyce, Volume III, edited by Richard
Ellman, London, 1966*

27 March
1933

Harriet Weaver, 74 Gloucester Place, London W.1 to **Paul
Léon**, *typed letter signed*
Thanks for his letter, offers to take care of Mr Joyce's daughter
herself in Paris while Mr and Mrs Joyce go to Zurich, she told
the estate agents to reduce the rent demanded for the flat in
the hope of getting a tenant, encloses newspaper cutting, *2p*

30 March
1933

Paul Léon to **Harriet Weaver**
Mr Joyce wants to be ready to leave for Zurich at a moment's
notice and would like her to tell Monro Saw & Co to sell out
£200 worth of stock

31 March
1933

Paul Léon to **Harriet Weaver**
Details of the proposed expenses for which Mr Joyce wants
£200

31 March
1933

Harriet Weaver, 74 Gloucester Place, London W.1 to **Paul Léon**
She has instructed Monro Saw & Co to sell £200 worth of stock

2 April 1933

Paul Léon to **Harriet Weaver**
Monro Saw say that Mr Joyce's monthly income will be reduced
by more than a third, this is a serious blow to Mr Joyce, reasons
for reduction, possibility of getting money from other sources,
health of Miss Joyce improved, trip to Zurich essential for Mr
Joyce's well being and his work, his immediate surroundings do
not provide enough encouragement for him, *2p*

11 April 1933

Harriet Weaver, 74 Gloucester Place, London W.1 to **Paul Léon**
Her address in Surrey, hopes Mr Joyce will be able to go to
Zurich, has not heard from the Kensington agents, *2p*

Harriet Weaver, 74 Gloucester Place, London W.1 to **Paul Léon**, *typed letter signed*   13 April 1933

Kensington agents have found a tenant for Mr Joyce's flat, she would be grateful for news of Mr Joyce, *2p*

Paul Léon to **Harriet Weaver**   16 April 1933

Mr Joyce will write to her himself about the various events that have taken place, Miss Moschos has left, Miss Joyce is better and is working under the guidance of a well known engraver, Professor Fehr from Zurich had offered to fetch Mr Joyce there, Mr Joyce has had painful attacks of colitis, German publishers planning to transfer their business to other countries because of political situation, Mr Joyce unwilling to decide go to Zurich because of his state of health and financial worries, he is brooding and does nothing to repair his own health or to get started on his work, *2p*

Harriet Weaver, 74 Gloucester Place, London W.1 to **Paul Léon**   19 April 1933

Begs for news of Mr, Mrs and Miss Joyce, will Léon tell Mr Joyce that she thinks he has been very longsuffering with her, she has been detestable

Harriet Weaver, 74 Gloucester Place, London W.1 to **Paul Léon**, *typed letter signed*   21 April 1933

Thanks for Léon's letter, Miss Hughes's letter re the London flat, sorry to hear of Mr Joyce's colitis and depression, hopes Léon will persuade him to make the Zurich journey, though she supposes he will have to sell more stock first, *2p*

Harriet Weaver, 74 Gloucester Place, London W.1 to **Paul Léon**, *typed letter signed*   25 April 1933

Thanks for letter of 21st, premonitions of new crisis with Mr Joyce's daughter most disheartening, hopes he will still go to Zurich, hitch in negotiations re Kensington flat

Paul Léon to **Harriet Weaver**   25 April 1933

Transcribed in Letters of James Joyce, Volume III, edited by Richard Ellmann, London, 1966

Harriet Weaver, 74 Gloucester Place, London W.1 to **Paul Léon**, *typed letter signed*   26 April 1933

She is distressed at latest news of Mr Joyce's condition, she has telephoned Mr Monro to sell the remaining £100 of stock, offers to pay £100 for Mr Joyce's trip to Zurich or to go to Paris herself if he does not go immediately, her own finances not good, suggests that Mr Joyce go to Zurich for the summer and give up the Paris flat, understands what Léon has said about his personal position in Mr Joyce's home and is grateful for his letters to her, *2p*

1 May 1933   **Harriet Weaver**, 74 Gloucester Place, London W.1 to **Paul Léon**
She goes to Paris tomorrow and will stay at Hotel Galilée, will ring him

5 May 1933   Statement of Mr Joyce's receipts and payments per annum in hand of Harriet Weaver

8 May 1933   **F.R.D'O. Monro,** 44 Queen Victoria Street, London EC4 to **Harriet Weaver**, 74 Gloucester Place, London W.1, *typed copy letter*
Received her letter of the 5th enclosing deed signed by Mr Joyce, surrender of shares, sale of War Stock, encloses clause of settlement dealing with raising of capital, *2p*

13 May 1933   **Harriet Weaver**, Hotel Galilée to **Paul Léon**
She has asked Messrs Monro to increase the Johannesburg stock to £500, will he tell Mr Joyce that she did not mean to treat him as if he were under tutelage, she wishes to see Léon again before leaving Paris

22 May 1933   **Harriet Weaver**, 74 Gloucester Place, London W.1 to **Paul Léon**
Thanks for good news about Zurich, hopes trip will come off and that atmosphere is now more harmonious, sends receipt from Faber & Faber for corrected episodes of *Work in Progress* which she delivered in March, *3p*

16 June 1933   **Harriet Weaver**, 74 Gloucester Place, London W.1 to **Paul Léon**, *typed letter signed*
She has asked Mr Monro to sell another £100 of stock, has had no news from Zurich since the 29th, as the Joyces returned to Paris on Saturday she gathers a decision about the operation is postponed, she is glad they enjoyed the trip to Zurich and that Mr Joyce has been able to work again, hopes Mrs and Miss Joyce will go to Ireland with Mr Byrne, *2p*

Harriet Weaver, 74 Gloucester Place, London W.1 to **Paul Léon**, *typed letter signed*
Mr Monro said he would send money direct to Mr Joyce's account at the Banque Franco-Américaine, Mr Joyce has given up communicating with her direct, the idea of going to Ireland must have fallen through as Léon says the Joyces are all at Evian, will he let her know where they go from there, why did they go to Evian, she is concerned at the way Mr Joyce is selling stock, there will soon be none left

7 July 1933

Harriet Weaver, 74 Gloucester Place, London W.1 to **Paul Léon**, *typed letter signed*
Thanks for sending her Mr Joyce's letter to read, sorry she made Mr Joyce angry with Léon, she did not know Mr Joyce went to Evian for a cure nor that he was to see two specialists in Lausanne, if Mr Joyce wants stock sold she will at once communicate with Monro Saw & Co, sends cuttings, *with annotations in hand of Paul Léon*

19 July 1933

Harriet Weaver, 74 Gloucester Place, London W.1 to **Paul Léon**
She returns letter, she has telegraphed to Mr Joyce that she hopes he will return to Evian and has written to Mrs Joyce that she hopes she will persuade Mr Joyce to continue the cure, *2p*

21 July 1933

Paul Léon to **Harriet Weaver**
Encloses letter from Mr Joyce and report on Miss Joyce's health translated from German, arranged with Monro to send money which arrived in time for the Joyces to leave Zurich on Sunday morning for Nyon, has had no further news, Mr Joyce probably needs money from the capital in trust

31 July 1933

Harriet Weaver, 74 Gloucester Place, London W.1 to **Paul Léon**
Mr Monro is on holiday so it will be several days before anything can be done about getting the Public Trustee to consent to selling stock, *4p*

1 August 1933

Harriet Weaver, 74 Gloucester Place, London W.1 to **Paul Léon**, *typed letter signed*
Returns Mr Joyce's letter and the medical report of which she retains one copy, her address over the bank holiday weekend, asks for news re U.S.A. lawsuit, hopes Léon is successfully playing Mr Reece and Mr Werner Laurie against one another

3 August 1933

11 August 1933

Harriet Weaver, 74 Gloucester Place, London W.1 to **Paul Léon**, *typed letter signed*
She is sorry that Lucia refused to remain in the Sanatorium, Mr Saw says Public Trustee sympathetic but wants full details of how £200 is to be spent on Lucia, perhaps Mr Joyce should await Mr Monro's return, she returns Mr Joyce's two letters, Dr Maier's letter and photo, Mr Joyce still too annoyed to send one for her, *2p*

16 August 1933

Harriet Weaver, 74 Gloucester Place, London W.1 to **Paul Léon**, *typed letter signed*
Mr Monro has applied to the Public Trustee who still insists on receiving an application signed by Mr Joyce with details of expenses to which he will be put on account of his daughter, Mr Joyce may find this too tiresome and fatiguing in his present condition, she is joining her brother's and sister's families in Wales till the 30th, Léon should communicate direct with Messrs Monro Saw when Mr Joyce wants to sell the last £100 of Johannesburg stock, *2p*

4 September 1933

Paul Léon to **Harriet Weaver**
Mr Joyce suffered a bad collapse last Wednesday morning which is why the Power of Attorney has not been signed, he hopes to sign it tomorrow

26 September 1933

Harriet Weaver, 74 Gloucester Place, London W.1 to **Paul Léon**, *typed letter signed*
She is very grateful for his detailed letter, hopes Mr Joyce's health will improve, if Léon ever finds Mr Joyce in a mood to listen to a message from her will he tell Mr Joyce that she is trying very hard to understand and appreciate *Work in Progress* despite her slow dull and unimaginative mind, she originally read most of the episodes in unpropitious circumstances while living in a remote spot in the north with Miss Marsden, will Léon ask Mr Joyce to sign letter to Public Trustee, *3p*

27 September 1933

Paul Léon to **Harriet Weaver**
Thanks for her letter, he tried to read it to Mr Joyce but Mr Joyce brushed it and the cutting aside, Mr Joyce wants to collect all the medical certificates relating to his daughter and send them to his solicitor in order to justify his abandonment of his British domicile for Paris, Léon did not have time to broach

the subject of the Public Trustee and is afraid Mr Joyce is determined not to enter into correspondence with him

Paul Léon to **Harriet Weaver**
Encloses correspondence which has had a bad effect on Mr Joyce who has put off his departure to Zurich

27 October 1933

Harriet Weaver, 74 Gloucester Place, London W.1 to **Paul Léon**, *typed letter signed*
Thanks for copies of correspondence re plagiarizing *Ulysses*, not surprised Mr Joyce is upset, should Mr Golding's book be sent to anyone else

28 October 1933

Paul Léon to **Harriet Weaver**
Mr Joyce asked him to return Mr Golding's book, he seems nervous

4 November 1933

Harriet Weaver, 74 Gloucester Place, London W.1 to **Paul Léon**
Thanks for Mr Golding's book and the two papers, hopes Mr Pinker will soon send news of the suppression of the threatened English piracy of *Ulysses*, now that Léon applies direct to Mr Joyce's solicitors for the sale of stock he should keep a careful account of the amounts applied for as the firm's cashier is a little careless, *4p*

7 November 1933

Harriet Weaver, 74 Gloucester Place, London W.1 to **Paul Léon**
Thanks for *Work in Progress* manuscript, article on Mr Joyce in November *Bookman*, *3p*

7 December 1933

Paul Léon to **Harriet Weaver**
Thanks for her letter, the fragments in manuscript sent to her do not contain the present work, he sent her the *New York Herald* with the good news, she must excuse him for not keeping her au courant but he has seen Mr Joyce rarely and his visits have often been short and curt, gave the news to Albatross and the rue de l'Odéon

9 December 1933

Harriet Weaver, 74 Gloucester Place, London W.1 to **Paul Léon**
Thanks for *New York Herald*, she saw news in *Times* and telegraphed congratulations to Mr Joyce, *2p*

13 December 1933

Paul Léon to **Harriet Weaver,** *incomplete*
Will she excuse him for not writing before, since Mr Joyce's

9 January 1934

return he has seen him rarely but the correspondence on his account has grown enormously, Mr Budgen's book postponed because the chemists Boots refused to include it in their list, Mr Joyce has withdrawn his authorisation for his biography from Mr Gorman, Mr Joyce thinks people think his domestic events and the defection of his friends have brought his work to an end, a deputation from Faber & Faber came to Paris to see Mr Joyce about *Ulysses*, Monro Saw sent Mr Joyce a copy of a letter from Faber signed by T.S. Eliot asking about the copyright and publishing history of *Ulysses*, if she receives such a letter Mr Joyce would like her to show him a copy of her reply before sending it, American decision brought letters and telegrams from persons not heard from for years, Mr Joyce annoyed at an interview given by Miss Beach, American decision brought Léon into conflict with Mr Reece and Mr Wegner, Mr Joyce phoned Harold Nicolson who was in Paris to give a lecture, Mr Alen [sic] Lane made a formal offer for an option on an edition of *Ulysses*, *2p, rest of letter missing, pencilled draft of this letter in hand of Paul Léon on verso of letter from Monro Saw & Co dated 1 January 1934, see p. 125.*

12 January 1934	**Harriet Weaver**, 74 Gloucester Place, London W.1 to **Paul Léon**, *typed letter signed* She has already been in communication with Mr Eliot, she inspected the files in the office of Monro Saw and gave Mr Eliot particulars, Mr Eliot told her he would be loath to let Mr Joyce down by entering on a lawsuit unless his firm was prepared to put up the strongest possible defence, she supposes Léon will have heard by now from both Albatross and Faber and in the event of a withdrawal by both will have given the option to Mr Lane, she is planning a short visit to Paris, *2p, with 2 copy notes enclosed*
1 March 1934	**Harriet Weaver**, 74 Gloucester Place, London W.1 to **Paul Léon** Her address in Cumberland, she would be glad to see the documents of which Léon spoke on the telephone and of news, *2p*
11 March 1934	**Paul Léon** to **Harriet Weaver** How Mr Joyce has been affected by the departure of Miss Joyce for the Sanatorium at Nyon, a feeling of emptiness in the house, the public has not been prepared to receive the new development of his genius, describes the evening in Mr Joyce's honour at the Coupôle, newspaper reports inadequate, Mr Joyce realises

he is cut off from literary circles, literary and social solitude has affected his health, he must reestablish connections with the literary world and he must be enabled to complete *Work in Progress,* he should take an unfurnished flat, the political situation might force him to go to England, his own and his daughter's health, Mr Joyce feels abandoned by all his friends, he has broken his links with the rue de l'Odéon but was annoyed to find that Miss Beach seemed to know all about his personal affairs, his financial worries, he will not write letter to Public Trustee, Miss Weaver should write directly to Mr Joyce saying she has not forgotten him and that she will always assist him, some misunderstanding between herself and Mr Joyce, she should also send over his books in storage in London, it would be a good thing if she would induce Miss Monnier to bring out a cheap edition of the French *Ulysses,* some friends going on a motor trip will take Mr Joyce to Zurich, Mr Joyce would like Miss Weaver to be present at a reading of *Work in Progress, 6p*

Paul Léon to **Harriet Weaver**
News of appeal against Judge Woolsey's decision in favour of *Ulysses*

14 March 1934

Harriet Weaver, 74 Gloucester Place, London W.1 to **Paul Léon**, *typed letter signed*
She has written to Mr Joyce as Léon suggested but is doubtful that her letter will carry any weight, she will arrange with Monro Saw for the exchange of Mr Joyce's Canadian stock for some more saleable stock of her own, Mr Joyce should sign letter to Public Trustee, *2p*

17 March 1934

Harriet Weaver, 74 Gloucester Place, London W.1 to **Paul Léon**, *typed letter signed*
Thanks for his letter, Mr Joyce had written to her at intervals since March but without giving details of his daughter's illness until the last letter in which he told her of the last day at Nyon, she will write to Mr Joyce and urge him to return to Paris, the financial situation is serious, if Mr Joyce remains obdurate in refusing to write to the Public Trustee she will have to exchange some of her own stock for the Canadian Pacific stock, but this will lead to a reduction in her own income and render her less able to help in the future, she would be grateful if Léon will keep her informed, *2p*

5 October 1934

7 October
1934

Harriet Weaver, 74 Gloucester Place, London W.1 to **Paul Léon**, *typed letter signed*
She wrote to Mr Joyce urging his return to Paris using the arguments of work, of his having a flat in Paris, and that by leaving Miss Joyce now her parents will have more strength to help her in the future, she did not use the argument of the expense of keeping up three establishments, *2p*

10 October
1934

Paul Léon to **Harriet Weaver**
Thanks for her letters, difficult to persuade Mr Joyce to leave his daughter after the bad experience in Prangins, success will depend on effects of Dr Jung's cure

6 November
1934

Harriet Weaver, Westwick, Warwick's Bench, Guildford to **James Joyce**
She came down for weekend after she finished Nijinski book, she hopes Dr Jung will soon give a more reassuring opinion so that Mr Joyce will be able to return to Paris and his work, the example of Lucia's clairvoyance is extraordinary and her letter makes it hard to picture the violent scenes which have occurred, there have been no press notices of Lucia's designs, Miss Weaver had much affection for her father but treated him callously in his later years as she did in other cases one of which Mr Joyce may know, she admires Mr Lane's enterprise in setting up a press to print *Ulysses*, what is Professor Vogt's latest report on Mr Joyce's eyes, *4p*

13 November
1934

Harriet Weaver, 74 Gloucester Place, London W.1 to **Paul Léon**
Thanks for letter giving Mr Joyce's message about the discovery of his daughter's pen and for sending *N.Y. Herald* with account of presentation of special copy of *Ulysses* to Columbia University, hopes Léon's strong letter to Mr Joyce will have some effect, she also has written to him, *2p*

11 December
1934

Harriet Weaver, 74 Gloucester Place, London W.1 to **Paul Léon**
Has he any news of Mr Joyce, she has heard nothing, *2p*

20 December
1934

Harriet Weaver, 74 Gloucester Place, London W.1 to **Paul Léon**, *typed letter signed*
She received a letter from Mr Joyce enclosing MS of the piece he is working on, he said that when he told Lucia five weeks ago that he had decided to return to Paris there was a repetition of the fire episode at Prangins so he stayed on but

did not go to see her for a month, Lucia told him of a nightmare that had been worrying her, impossible to urge him to leave at the moment but she is glad to know he is working, she encloses newspapers, value of C.P.R. stock has not depreciated by as much as she thought, she has written to Mr Joyce who wants her to write to Lucia too, *2p*

Harriet Weaver, 74 Gloucester Place, London W.1 to **Paul Léon**, *typed letter signed*
She is sorry for delay in answering his questions, Monro Saw say they still have £50 and a further £500 of the Johannesburg stock, if Mr Joyce still declines to enter into correspondence with the Public Trustee it will be necessary to sell the Canadian stock, news Léon sent is gloomy, hopes Mr Joyce's colitis attacks will not recur, *2p*

4 January
1935

Harriet Weaver, 74 Gloucester Place, London W.1 to **Paul Léon**, *typed letter signed*
She returns Mr Joyce's letter and hopes it will be possible for the Joyces to return to Paris bringing Lucia with them to a sanatorium nearer Paris, she gathered the *Ulysses* case was finally won from the *N.Y. Herald Tribune* of the 13th October which Léon sent her

22 January
1935

Harriet Weaver, 74 Gloucester Place, London W.1 to **Paul Léon**
Thanks for telegram telling her of Mr Joyce's safe arrival in Paris with his family, *2p*

1 February
1935

Harriet Weaver, 74 Gloucester Place, London W.1 to **Paul Léon**
She is writing to invite Lucia suggesting that her aunt should accompany her to London, *3p*

7 February
1935

Harriet Weaver, 74 Gloucester Place, London W.1 to **Paul Léon**
She has written full reports daily to Mr Joyce at Léon's suggestion, Mr Joyce's sister also wrote daily till she left London, Mr Joyce asked her not to telephone directly to his own flat but to Léon's at 8pm but this is a difficult time as Lucia would be in the room, if it is necessary to telephone she will ring Léon after 10pm, *3p*

25 February
1935

Harriet Weaver, 74 Gloucester Place, London W.1 to **James Joyce**, 7 rue Edmond Valentin
Went with Lucia to the doctor in Harley Street, has typed an

26 February
1935

51

account of the interview, Lucia insisted on trying to obtain an earlier appointment with Sir H. Gillies but was unsuccessful, Miss Weaver thought of fixing the appointment with Dr Rott for a day early next week when Mr Joyce's sister will be back, *4p*

27 February 1935

Harriet Weaver, 74 Gloucester Place, London W.1 to **Paul Léon** She sends this letter care of Léon as it might alarm Mrs Joyce too much, Léon had better read it before showing it to Mr Joyce, she will telegraph tomorrow with news of Lucia's safe return, she hopes

27 February 1935, 11.30am

Lucia Joyce to **Harriet Weaver**, *telegram* VERY SORRY ABOUT YESTERDAY GOT LOST HOPE YOU ARE WELL WILL PROBABLY COME TODAY OR TOMORROW HAVE YOU ANY NEWS I HAVE WET FEET

27 February 1935, 3.15pm

Harriet Weaver, 74 Gloucester Place, London W.1 to **James Joyce** Lucia has not been back since the previous day, she sent enclosed telegram from Baker Street which Miss Weaver received at 12.50, Miss Weaver found out Lucia spent the night at a hotel nearby, she went off at 2pm the previous day refusing to let Miss Weaver go with her, Miss Weaver's efforts to find her, Mr Joyce's sister has been contacted and will cross from Dublin tonight, hopes to telegraph Mr Léon tomorrow to announce Lucia's safe return, Miss Weaver thinks her attitude irritated Lucia, *4p*

28 February 1935, 8.55am

Harriet Weaver to **Paul Léon**, *telegram* RETURNED EIGHT LAST EVENING TIRED AFTER VIST [*sic*] TO UNCLE REGARDS

28 February 1935, 15.05pm

Harriet Weaver to **Paul Léon**, *telegram* MRS SCHAUREK RETURNS TOMORROW WILL GIVE MESSAGE REGARDS

2 March 1935, 8.10am

Harriet Weaver to **Paul Léon**, *telegram* MRS SCHAUREK ARRIVED WRITING MR JOYCE CARE OF YOU REGARDS

2 March 1935

Harriet Weaver, 74 Gloucester Place, London W.1 to **Paul Léon** Perhaps he would ring up Mr Joyce and read enclosed if Mrs

Schaurek has not yet written, she has not seen Mrs Schaurek since morning, writing express makes little difference, *2p*

Harriet Weaver, 74 Gloucester Place, London W.1 to **James Joyce**
Mrs Schaurek arrived and has been with Lucia, she will write, *2p*

2 March 1935, 5 pm

Harriet Weaver, 74 Gloucester Place, London W.1 to **Paul Léon**
Encloses note for Mr Joyce, asks for news of him and of Mrs Joyce, *2p*

4 March 1935

Harriet Weaver, 74 Gloucester Place, London W.1 to **James Joyce**
Misunderstanding with Lucia cleared up, Lucia tired after three days racketing about, *2p*

4 March 1935, 2.30 pm

Harriet Weaver, 74 Gloucester Place, London W.1 to **Paul Léon**
Thanks for £3 for Mrs Schaurek's expenses, she did not intend to incriminate Mr Joyce's sister, notes non-necessity of addressing Mr Joyce care of Léon, *2p*

5 March 1935

Harriet Weaver, 74 Gloucester Place, London W.1 to **James Joyce**
She wishes he would write to his sister, they wish he would send 10/- to Lucia, they are planning to take her away from London to a farm near Lewes in Sussex, Lucia wished to see a mental specialist in London so an appointment has been made with Dr Bernard Hart, appointment with Sir H. Gillies cancelled as Lucia not feeling well, Lucia has not yet been told about Sussex, *2p*

7 March 1935

Harriet Weaver, 74 Gloucester Place, London W.1 to **Paul Léon**
She has written to Mr Joyce agreeing with all the points Léon raised except Miss Walker's salary, Lucia had a violently hysterical crisis yesterday but is calmer today, Dr Macdonald says the crises will recur but will become milder, she returns photographs of Mrs Joyce, *2p*

9 March 1935

Harriet Weaver, London to **Paul Léon**, *telegram*
WE WILL NOT TELEPHONE REGARDS

9 March 1935, 5.56pm

Harriet Weaver, 74 Gloucester Place, London W.1 to **Paul Léon**
Please tell Mr Joyce that she gave Mrs Schaurek money for fares

19 March 1935

to Dublin and sufficient for their expenses in Ireland for the first few days, she does not want to be refunded, mystery of telegram cleared up, her address in Sussex, *2p*

1 April 1935   **Harriet Weaver**, as from 74 Gloucester Place, London W.1 to **Paul Léon**
Thanks for letter and enclosed MS, she will arrange with Monro Saw to advance £100 immediately if the American royalties do not arrive

3 April 1935   **Harriet Weaver**, 74 Gloucester Place, London W.1 to **Paul Léon**, *typed letter signed*
She wrote to Mr Joyce, Mr Joyce's stock has depreciated further, she will arrange an advance if necessary so the selling of the stock may be postponed, *2p*

5 April 1935   **Harriet Weaver**, 74 Gloucester Place, London W.1 to **Paul Léon**, *typed letter signed*
She happened to have £300 of capital repaid lately and put it into a deposit account in case of emergencies, she will forward £250 of this to Mr Joyce for the payment of the debts due, will Léon write direct to Mr Monro about his queries re deduction of the monthly payment, she wishes Lucia would vent her feelings on someone other than her father and will suggest this to her, Lucia often talked about suicide to her aunt, Miss Weaver suggested to Mr Joyce that she should go over to Dublin to find out what the situation really was, *2p*

15 April 1935   **Harriet Weaver**, 74 Gloucester Place, London W.1 to **James Joyce**
Apologises for having failed with Lucia, she did not intend to compare Lucia with Mr Joyce's sister, corrects a misunderstanding, she is sorry Lucia's visit to Ireland is a failure, she blames herself, *3p*

15 April 1935   **Harriet Weaver**, 74 Gloucester Place, London W.1 to **Paul Léon**
She has made an appointment with Mr Monro, Léon's news is gloomy, she is afraid of upsetting Mr Joyce by writing to him, she advised Mrs Schaurek to write fully to Mr Joyce, Mr Joyce is trying to handle Lucia by correspondence, *2p*

Harriet Weaver, 74 Gloucester Place, London W.1 to **Paul Léon**, *typed letter signed*   16 April 1935
She saw Mr Monro who found there was a mistake in the figures and has agreed to pay £40 per month, Canadian National Railways were deducting income tax from their dividends which will be repaid to Mr Joyce, Mr Monro's advice as to which stock should be sold first, hopes Mr Pinker mistaken as to royalties and numbers of copies sold, will Léon tell Mr Joyce that she has not sent his sister any money in Ireland, *2p*

Harriet Weaver, 74 Gloucester Place, London W.1 to **Paul Léon**   20 April 1935
Returns copy of Léon's letter to Pinker, she is sorry there should be this trouble with him

Harriet Weaver, 74 Gloucester Place, London W.1 to **Paul Léon**   21 June 1935
She is glad that Mr and Mrs Joyce are coming to London next Thursday, she had a letter from Mrs Schaurek on June 12 saying Lucia was better, she has posted *Irish Press* of June 13 to Mr Joyce, it is a pity sale of the depreciated Canadian stock has to begin, she will be visiting her friend Miss Dora Marsden in Liverpool on the day the Joyces arrive, *4p*

Harriet Weaver, 74 Gloucester Place, London W.1 to **Paul Léon**   24 June 1935
Address of Royal Palace Hotel, thanks for two sheets of manuscript

Harriet Weaver, 74 Gloucester Place, London W.1 to **Paul Léon**   29 June 1935
Thanks for letter and *Revue Universelle* with the article on Mr Joyce, she received a letter from Mrs Schaurek about Lucia's improvement, apologises if she gave away the secret of Mr and Mrs Joyce's visit to London to Mrs Joyce's uncle and his niece in her reply, will Léon let her know if another day is fixed for the journey, she will be in Guildford next week, *2p*

Harriet Weaver, 74 Gloucester Place, London W.1 to **Paul Léon**   5 July 1935
She will visit Guildford tomorrow only, address and phone number at which she can be contacted, she will remain indoors on Sunday until Mrs Jolas contacts her, dreadful disappointment for Mr and Mrs Joyce, *2p*

Harriet Weaver, 74 Gloucester Place, London W.1 to **Paul Léon**, *typed letter signed*   17 July 1935
She wrote to Lucia inviting her to visit Sussex, she went to considerable trouble to find accommodation there, Mrs Curran

told her Lucia had gone to a nursing home outside Dublin, will Léon let her know whether Mr Joyce may want her to take Lucia somewhere, her plans for August and September, *2p*

22 July 1935   **Harriet Weaver**, 74 Gloucester Place, London W.1 to **Paul Léon**
Thanks for his long letter, Mr Curran told her he had written a long letter to Mr Joyce, she will mention Sussex to Lucia again, she suggested that she should go over to Paris to Mr Joyce in April but he did not appear to want it, if he does not object now she would be glad to make the trip, the whole situation is bewildering, *4p*

17 August 1935   **Harriet Weaver**, 74 Gloucester Place, London W.1 to **Paul Léon**
Thanks for three letters and photographs of Mrs Joyce and for arranging despatch of Lucia's *Lettrines*, she is not now sending daily reports to Mr Joyce, she has arranged to call on a stalwart mental nurse should Lucia have a violent outburst rather than send her to a nursing home, she has told Mr Joyce that she wrote to Mrs Schaurek about the disposal of the clothing and she also told him that she will cease corresponding with Mrs Schaurek, she is glad to hear Mr Joyce is working regularly now, *2p*

20 August 1935, 11.22am   **Harriet Weaver**, Reigate to **James Joyce**, *telegram*
PASSEPORT [sic] RECEIVED KINDEST REGARDS

29 August 1935   **Harriet Weaver**, 74 Gloucester Place, London W.1 to **Paul Léon**
Thanks for his last letters which she has answered direct to Mr Joyce, she has received the £10 for the salary of the new nurse, she encloses note of thanks from steward for £1 *[enclosed]*, strain has been reduced by presence of a second nurse, doctor's opinion is that Lucia should live in a quiet place and be "policed" by a capable nurse, Miss Walker suggests that they take a bungalow, she has asked some nurses to come for interview, *2p*

9 September 1935   **Harriet Weaver**, 74 Gloucester Place, London W.1 to **Paul Léon**
Thanks for letter, cheque and birthday greetings, sends statement of expenditure and receipts *[enclosed 2 items]*, a new nurse started last Wednesday who will accompany them to the country, she will give Léon the address of the bungalow near Reigate when arrangements are fixed, Lucia needs more clothing, has an appointment with the oculist and is tired of her imprisonment in the flat, *2p*

Harriet Weaver, 74 Gloucester Place, London W.1 to **Paul Léon**
Thanks for his letter, passport has not yet reached her, she will try to find out what Lucia did with her copy of *Pomes Penyeach*, shocked at news of Mr Joyce, afraid her letter to him may have been harsh but the doctor has emphasized to her that Lucia must be rigorously "policed", the new nurse has fallen off, worry about her friend Miss Dora Marsden another neurotic victim, Lucia has not been improving, *4p*

13 September 1935

Harriet Weaver, 74 Gloucester Place, London W.1 to **Paul Léon**
Address of bungalow in Surrey

13 September 1935

Harriet Weaver, Loveland's Cottage, Loveland's Lane, Lower Kingswood, Surrey to **James Joyce**
Encloses letter from Mr Curran, Mr and Mrs Curran will ensure that the passport is safe, Lucia tired after the journey down, Lucia showed Miss Weaver her father's letter, Miss Weaver touched by the kind things Mr Joyce said about her, Lucia's visit to Dr Macdonald, they will probably move on to Sussex in a month, sorry to hear from Mr Léon how ill Mr Joyce had been but glad that he had improved since going to Fontainebleau, *2p*

18 September 1935

Harriet Weaver, Loveland's Cottage, Lower Kingswood, Surrey to **Paul Léon**
Thanks for cheque for £10, encloses statement of accounts and receipts *[enclosed 6 items]*, she wrote to Mr Joyce at Fontainebleau, all is still going smoothly, expenses of coming down here small, *2p*

26 September 1935

Paul Léon to **Harriet Weaver**
The letters Lucia wrote to her father have worried him, he has asked Léon to ask Miss Weaver to arrange for Dr Macdonald to see Lucia and to ask Dr Macdonald if he has any objection to Mrs Jolas visiting Lucia, Léon is anxious about Mr Joyce who refuses to see him and speaks to him only over the phone

2 October 1935

Harriet Weaver, Loveland's Cottage, Lower Kingswood, Tadworth, Surrey to **Paul Léon**
Thanks for £10, as Lucia is much better they will dispense with the second nurse and hire a domestic servant instead which will free Miss Walker to look after Lucia, Miss Weaver will bear all the household expenses and leave Mr Joyce to pay the nursing and other medical expenses, clothing etc, Miss Walker's salary,

7 October 1935

Miss Weaver wrote to Mr Desmond Flower of the *Sunday Times* informing him that Mr Joyce was willing for a page of his MS to be put on exhibition, to which publishers does Mr Joyce wish her to show Lucia's alphabet, Lucia has been resting, *3p*

28 October 1935

Harriet Weaver, Loveland's Cottage, Lower Kingswood, Tadworth, Surrey to **Paul Léon**
Thanks for his letters, she wrote to Mr Joyce to explain to him that Dr Macdonald said Lucia would have ups and downs, Lucia writes letters only when in her difficult moods, if Mr Joyce were to allow Miss Weaver to open Lucia's letters before sending them she might be able to explain them, Lucia's moods very changeable, both Miss Weaver and Miss Walker think Lucia much better than when she arrived in London, she is sorry Léon is still worried about Mr Joyce's health, is there any news of his son, details of expenditure, *3p*

8 November 1935

Harriet Weaver, Loveland's Cottage, Lower Kingswood, Tadworth, Surrey to **Paul Léon**
Thanks for £10, she wrote to Mr Charles Morgan on lines suggested, glad Mr Joyce somewhat better

5 December 1935

Harriet Weaver, Loveland's Cottage, Lower Kingswood, Tadworth, Surrey to **Paul Léon**
She has written two letters to Mr Joyce one dealing with the question he had asked Léon to bring up of corporal chastisement, best times to telephone, encloses details of expenditure, received letter from Monro Saw about selling stock, *2p*

14 December 1935

Harriet Weaver, Loveland's Cottage, Lower Kingswood, Tadworth, Surrey to **Paul Léon**
Dr Macdonald came down and arranged for Lucia to go to Saint Andrew's Home at Northampton, she received £50 from Monro Saw, encloses letter from Mr Speed

29 January 1936

Harriet Weaver, 74 Gloucester Place, London W.1 to **Paul Léon**, *typed letter signed*
She has received letters from Messrs Monro, she is very worried about the financial situation, if she has to subsidize Mr Joyce from her own resources they will be exhausted in less than ten years, she also has to support Miss Dora Marsden, could someone pull strings to get Mr Joyce the Nobel prize, what to do with the Canadian Pacific stock, it has not been paying

dividends for three years and she has been making up the deficit to Mr Joyce though he does not know this, her expenditure on Mr Joyce's account, Dr Macdonald's charges seem exorbitant, *2p*

Harriet Weaver, 30 Grange Road, Eastbourne, Sussex to **Paul Léon**

1 February 1936

She will send the *Irish Times* of 24 January to the addresses he gave when she returns to town, Léon should not mention the financial worry to Mr Joyce now that he has eye trouble, glad to hear from Mrs Jolas that he had been working steadily on the book aided by Léon, sorry to hear of trouble in Léon's family, perhaps Léon could mention the transfer of the Canadian Pacific stock, *2p*

Harriet Weaver, 74 Gloucester Place, London W.1 to **Paul Léon**, *typed letter signed*

7 February 1936

She has arranged the transfer of the C.P.R. stock, she will sell her stock when Mr Joyce needs money, the Nobel prize was Mrs Jolas's suggestion, Mrs Jolas also said there was still an offer from America for the filming of *Ulysses*, Mr Joyce must economize, she cannot herself economize any further unless she parts with her flat, she blames herself for not having made the capital more inaccessible to Mr Joyce, it should have been available only for needs not for luxuries, she should have protected him from himself, she resented Dr Macdonald's casual attitude, she regards the Northampton hospital as admirable, she is always encouraging towards Lucia, the hospital bill, *2p*

Harriet Weaver, 74 Gloucester Place, London W.1 to **Paul Léon**, *postcard*

13 February 1936

Her address in Sussex

Paul Léon to **Harriet Weaver**

18 February 1936

Mr Joyce asked him to tell Miss Weaver that it has been decided to take Lucia out of St Andrew's Hospital and bring her to Paris, the hospital accounts, Léon is also directed to write to Monro Saw for £200, Mr Joyce did not realise that the transfer of stock meant any sacrifice on Miss Weaver's part and will not go ahead with it, Léon has to write to Monro Saw asking for another transfer to sell on the open market, Mr Joyce will do his best to write to Miss Weaver this week

19 February 1936	**Harriet Weaver**, 30 Grange Road, Eastbourne to **Paul Léon** Thanks for his letters, she has written to Dr Rambaut, payment to the hospital, will Léon ask Mr Joyce to allow her to visit him in Paris in order to clear up the misunderstandings between them which cannot be cleared up by correspondence, Lucia's passport is locked up in her flat and also some of Lucia's clothing and her photograph of her nephew, she wrote to the Nonesuch Press that she would show them the illuminated alphabet on her return to town, she will probably return to town on Friday, *4p*
21 February 1936	**Harriet Weaver**, 74 Gloucester Place, London W.1 to **Paul Léon** Encloses letter from Dr Rambaut *[enclosed]* of St Andrew's Hospital, she presumes Mrs Jolas will collect Lucia, Lucia needs a larger suitcase, she would have liked to have seen Lucia on her way through London but may be allowed to see her if she goes over to Paris, *2p*
22 February 1936	**Harriet Weaver**, London to **Paul Léon**, *telegram* PASSPORT REACHED NORTHAMPTON BILL PAID REGARDS
23 February 1936	**Harriet Weaver**, 74 Gloucester Place, London W.1 to **Paul Léon**, *typed letter signed* Encloses receipt and letters from Dr Rambaut and accountant at St Andrew's Hospital *[letters enclosed]*, confusion re bills, Lucia's copy of *Pomes Penyeach* missing, she put Lucia's photograph of her nephew in a suitcase, arrangements with Mrs Jolas, Miss Weaver will not go to Paris this weekend but on March 6th or 13th if Mr Joyce is agreeable, *2p*
25 February 1936	**Harriet Weaver**, 74 Gloucester Place, London W.1 to **Paul Léon** Will Léon ask Mr Joyce how she is to reply to enclosed letter from Francis Meynell *[enclosed]*, Mr Joyce does not wish her to let *Lettrines* out of her keeping, will he allow them to remain at Nonesuch Press for a day if she takes them in and fetches them herself
28 February 1936	**Harriet Weaver**, 74 Gloucester Place, London W.1 to **Paul Léon**, *typed letter signed* The number of her house will be changed to 101, she will insure the *lettrines* for £120 for the 24 hours of their stay with Nonesuch Press, agrees that it is advisable to postpone her visit to Paris

Harriet Weaver, 101 Gloucester Place, London W.1 to **Paul Léon**, *typed letter signed*
Hopes Léon is better, she received the *lettrines* safely back and encloses letter that came with them *[enclosed]*, she has invited Miss Beach who is coming to London on a business trip to stay with her, she herself would still like to go to Paris though she understands it is unlikely she would be allowed to see Lucia, she sent copies of *John O'London's Weekly* to Mr Joyce and others, will Léon inform Mr Joyce of the alteration of her address which she likes as 101 has meaning, the wheel goes round and starts again

10 March 1936

Harriet Weaver, 101 Gloucester Place, London W.1 to **Paul Léon**
Is Mr Joyce still too antagonistic towards her to send a message, if so it would be useless for her to go to Paris, Mrs Jolas wrote that both she and Lucia had the grippe, that Lucia had been moved to a nursing home and that Lucia wanted to go to a community of nuns, *3p*

22 March 1936

Harriet Weaver, 101 Gloucester Place, London W.1 to **Paul Léon**
Thanks for letter, she thinks the American edition of *Ulysses* with the Matisse drawings should be kept back in case Mr Joyce decides to give it to someone else, as Mr Joyce does not want to see her and does not care if misunderstandings are not cleared up she will regard the idea of her trip to Paris as cancelled, she hopes for Lucia's recovery, *2p*

30 March 1936

Paul Léon to **Harriet Weaver**, *manuscript draft and carbon typescript*
He told Mr Joyce she did not intend to come over at present and thought he might change his mind about the Matisse edition of *Ulysses*, Mr Joyce replied that she was not missing much, Lucia is at a critical stage, she is in a mental home outside Paris and receives no visits except from her father, Mr Joyce refused Lane's offer to publish *Ulysses* in an edition of 3,000 with royalty of £1,350, Mr Joyce wants *Ulysses* published on 1st October in an ordinary edition, he thinks Matisse's illustrations would make the condemnation of the book easier, *3 + 1p*

[c. April 1936]

Harriet Weaver, 101 Gloucester Place, London W.1 to **Paul Léon**
Asks for news of Lucia and of Mr Joyce, Mr Monro reported to her that Léon had said Mr Joyce had urgent decisions to make

5 May 1936

with regard to Lucia, Mr Kahane wrote last week for the *lettrines*, *2p*

11 May 1936

Harriet Weaver, 101 Gloucester Place, London W.1 to **Paul Léon**, *typed letter signed*
Thanks for letter and enclosed correspondence, hopes all will go well, she wishes to join with Mr Joyce in the birthday present he has planned for Lucia and to contribute half the cost of publishing the alphabet, she is not surprised that Lucia assaulted the nurses at Vésinet as she knows Lucia hates confinement, Dr Agadjanian's description of the illness corresponds with what she herself observed, sometimes Lucia spoke very angrily against her and at others would be very friendly, she is afraid Lucia will become bored, she is anxious to know how Lucia gets on and what is the result of her brother's operation, *2p*

11 May 1936

Harriet Weaver, 101 Gloucester Place, London W.1 to **Paul Léon**
Encloses 2500 francs for the alphabet and two pound notes

26 May 1936

Mrs Paul Léon to **Harriet Weaver**
Mr Joyce asked her husband to write to Monro Saw & Co for £100 to be raised by selling Canadian Pacific stock, her husband is laid up

27 May 1936

Harriet Weaver, 101 Gloucester Place, London W.1 to **Paul Léon**, *typed letter signed*
She instructed Mr Monro to realize £100 for Mr Joyce by selling Canadian Pacific stock, she agrees that it would be advisable for Mr Joyce to sign a letter to the Public Trustee, she thinks it extraordinary that Mr Joyce would pay for his son's operation, he should send only ten or twelve copies of the *Chaucer Alphabet* to begin with as she is not a good saleswoman, it would be well to evade the ten percent commission charged by the Obelisk Press, she will look at the correspondence in the office of Messrs Monro, her address in Yorkshire, Léon's help and friendship must have been of the greatest support to Mr Joyce, *2p*

15 June 1936

Harriet Weaver, 101 Gloucester Place, London W.1 to **James Joyce**
Sorry Mr Monro had not sent £50, details of financial transactions, the powers of the Public Trustee, she herself is not ruined yet but has become careful of every penny, she does not think it a mistake to spend money in the hope of curing

Lucia but she does think that the treatments of Drs Ischlondsky and Macdonald were not a success, hopes Lucia will not get bored at Ivry before Dr Agadjanian's treatment has had an effect, calamity pursues Mr Joyce with his son ill and his brother exiled from Italy, her friend Miss Marsden is in a state of apathy in a sanatorium following a severe nervous breakdown, Miss Weaver does not think she will recover or finish her four books, Miss Weaver has sent out notices of Lucia's book and could probably dispose of another ten or twelve, she encloses Dr Goulden's prescription for the spectacles, tomorrow is Bloom's day and her youngest sister's birthday, *6p*

Harriet Weaver, 101 Gloucester Place, London W.1 to **Paul Léon**   15 June 1936
She wrote to Mr Joyce today explaining misunderstanding with Mr Monro, she has explained the powers of the Public Trustee to Mr Joyce, she has sent out the dozen notices of Lucia's book and could dispose of ten or twelve more, she has not yet had any replies, *2p*

Paul Léon to **Harriet Weaver**   12 July 1936
Lucia is progressing well at Ivry, Dr Agadjanian thinks it is not a case of dementia praecox, Dr Macdonald's injections must have had a good effect, the printers brought out one copy of Lucia's book for her birthday, this reminded Mr Joyce of how the first copy of *Ulysses* was sent to him for his birthday sixteen years ago, Viscount Carlow wants to bring out a fragment of *Work in Progress* with *lettrines* by Lucia, Mr Joyce received an invitation from the PEN club for their congress in Buenos Ayres which he refused but he has made up his mind to go to Denmark, *Ulysses* will come out before the end of September, the corrections of the proofs are as far as p500, Lane has realized that *Ulysses* is a commercial proposition and will print 1,000 copies, Mr Joyce has received an offer from Everyman's Library to publish a volume of his selected verse and prose, Mr Joyce asked Léon to tell her that Sullivan has been reengaged at the Opéra, Mr Joyce had a visit from a Soviet emissary about a Russian translation of *Ulysses*, Léon refused to meet this gentleman, Mr Joyce also had a visit from Stephen [*sic*] who wanted him to become a member of the Irish Academy and take up the mantle of literary head of Ireland, *2p*

15 July 1936

Harriet Weaver, 101 Gloucester Place, London W.1 to **Paul Léon**, *typed letter signed*
The only subscription she has obtained for the *Chaucer A.B.C.* is from Mr Eliot, she herself will subscribe for two copies, will Léon let her know the date of publication so she may send the instalment she promised, will Mr Joyce allow her to send birthday greetings to Lucia, she fetched the two parcels of the corrected Parts I and III which Mrs Léon brought over, she was glad to hear from Mrs Léon that Mr Joyce seemed better but was sorry that things are not going well with Lucia, Mrs Léon delivered the other parcel to Mr Eliot, *endorsed with handwritten list of names*

30 July 1936

Harriet Weaver, 101 Gloucester Place, London W.1 to **Paul Léon**, *typed letter signed*
Arrangements to pay her half of the second instalment of 5000 francs to the publishers of the *Chaucer A.B.C.*, her address in Scotland whither she is going to see her friend Dora Marsden, *2p*

29 August 1936

Harriet Weaver, 101 Gloucester Place, London W.1 to **Paul Léon**, *typed letter signed*
Thanks for his letters, she is glad that Lucia is well, Lucia was always better when she could be out of doors for many hours a day, she is sorry to hear of the isolation in which Mr and Mrs Joyce have been living and especially of the break with Mrs Jolas, she had not heard of what had happened beyond the failure of the experiment of Lucia's becoming a member of Mrs Jolas's household, she sent Mr Joyce's article on Sullivan in the *New Statesman* to Mr Mulanny, she will send Mr Curran's subscription for Lucia's book, it is good news that the English edition of *Ulysses* is well subscribed, *2p*

31 August 1936

Harriet Weaver, 101 Gloucester Place, London W.1 to **Paul Léon**
Encloses Mr Curran's subscription for Lucia's book

[September 1936]

Harriet Weaver, 101 Gloucester Place, London W.1 to **Paul Léon**, *typed letter signed*
Received a subscription from Mr Herbert Hughes for Lucia's book and names of three persons to whom prospectuses might be sent, Miss Weaver has received copies 3 and 4 of the edition, she will present one to her niece Rosemary Weaver who met Lucia and got on well with her, if Mr and Mrs Joyce are back

from Denmark she hopes they are better, Mr Joyce sent her a Danish paper saying he was negotiating for a Danish translation of *Ulysses*, *2p*

Harriet Weaver, 101 Gloucester Place, London W.1 to **Paul Léon**, *typed letter signed*
She received the five copies [of Lucia's book] and the batch of circulars, how she has disposed of the five copies, names of people to whom circulars should be sent, *2p*

18 September 1936

Harriet Weaver, 101 Gloucester Place, London W.1 to **Paul Léon**, *typed letter signed*
This letter is supplementary to the one she sent this morning and is confidential, she has bought £2330 of Mr Joyce's Canadian Pacific Railway stock, if and when it rises again she will sell out and make over the balance to the good to Mr Joyce, she has done this without Mr Joyce's knowledge as Mr Joyce did not wish it when she proposed it to him a few months ago for fear she should lose, she hopes that if Mr Monro gets a fresh power of attorney he will be able to sell the stock without Mr Joyce's knowledge

18 September 1936

Paul Léon to **Harriet Weaver**
Thanks for her letters, the last few weeks before the publication of *Ulysses* have been very stressful, last week John Lane found he did not have sufficient paper to print the signed copies, the details are in the correspondence with Monro Saw, *Ulysses* will appear on October 3rd, announcement will appear in the *Times Literary Supplement* on 1st October, Mr Joyce wishes her to send copies to various addresses, he has sent her five more copies of the *Chaucer A.B.C.*, Mr Joyce wishes her to take a copy to the British Museum and give it with a circular to the Keeper, he would like them to send an acknowledgement to Miss Joyce, c/o The Obelisk Press, *2p*

22 September 1936

Paul Léon to **Harriet Weaver**
Ulysses will appear on 3rd October, he has arranged for a copy to be delivered to her by hand on Saturday morning, Mr Joyce wishes her to find out from Faber and Faber what happened to the *Chaucer Alphabet* he sent to Mr Eliot, Mr Joyce wants Mr Eliot to use his influence to have the *Alphabet* mentioned in the *Times Literary Supplement*, two more addresses to which the notice in the *Times Literary Supplement* should be sent

24 September 1936

29
September
1936

Harriet Weaver, 101 Gloucester Place, London W.1 to **Paul Léon**, *typed letter signed*
She has received the five copies of the *Chaucer A.B.C.*, the batch of circulars and Léon's three letters, she left a copy of the *Chaucer A.B.C* at the British Museum, the copy sent to Sir Francis Oppenheimer has been returned as per enclosed letter *[enclosed]*, Faber and Faber say Mr Eliot's copy is being kept till his return from America, she told Mr Eliot's secretary that she would try to obtain a review copy for the *Times Literary Supplement*, she feels honoured that arrangements have been made to have a copy of *Ulysses* delivered to her by hand, she received Léon's letter saying Mr Joyce wants her to lend this copy to Mr Monro over the weekend in case of trouble on Monday, she will send copies of the notice in the *Times Literary Supplement* if it appears to the names on the list, Mr Kahane returned the *lettrines, 2p*

1 October
1936

Harriet Weaver, 101 Gloucester Place, London W.1 to **Paul Léon**
She will send copies of the *Times Literary Supplement* tomorrow to the twenty nine names Léon gave her, Mr Monro read her the latest correspondence on *Ulysses* from which she gathered something of the difficulties they have had, *2p*

2 October
1936, 8.42
am

Harriet Weaver, London W.1 to **Paul Léon**, *telegram*
ADVERTISEMENT IN TIMES LITERARY SENDING AIRMAIL MR JOYCE REGARDS

[? October
1936]

Harriet Weaver, 101 Gloucester Place, London W.1 to **Paul Léon**, *postcard*
Good article in today's *New Statesman*, to whom would Mr Joyce like her to send copies and also of the *Star* and the *Morning Post*, there was a run on last week's issue of the *T.L.S.*, she is going away for the weekend

8 October
1936

Harriet Weaver, 101 Gloucester Place, London W.1 to **Paul Léon**, *typed letter signed*
She has ordered further copies of the *Times Literary Supplement* and will send them to the names on the new list, she received a cutting of the *Star* and has ordered two dozen copies six of which she will send to Mr Joyce, Mrs Gideon's address, will Léon thank Mr Joyce for his telegram on Saturday, misprints in *Ulysses, 2p*

Harriet Weaver, 101 Gloucester Place, London W.1 to **Paul Léon**, *typed letter signed*
Thanks for his letter, she is sorry to hear of Mr Joyce's collapse, the extract Léon promised from a biography of George Moore was not enclosed, she has sent to Mr Joyce and to Léon all the press notices of *Ulysses* that she has received and lists those she has sent to various other people, would Mr Joyce like her to send any to anyone else, a copy of *Ulysses* is on show in the window of her bookshop, she has read through the correspondence in Mr Monro's office, *2p*

21 October 1936

Paul Léon to **Harriet Weaver**
Thanks for her letter, asks her not to send cuttings to anyone except Mr Joyce and himself, cutting from *Daily Express* of October 20th, incomprehensible number of misprints and discrepancies from Albatross edition, trouble with Pinker about Danish translation of *Ulysses*, Mr Joyce is not well and Léon does not know why

23 October 1936

Harriet Weaver, 101 Gloucester Place, London W.1 to **Paul Léon**
She is sorry to hear Léon's bad account of Mr Joyce, did a letter of hers pain him, she would like to go over to Paris but Mr Joyce might not want her there, will Léon give Mr Joyce her kindest regards and her thanks for the batch of manuscript of the new piece he is working on, she hopes he will feel less nervous now that three doctors have told him there is nothing wrong with him except nerves, *Ulysses* has the central place of honour on Lane's stall at the *Sunday Times* book exhibition, she is going for the weekend to her sister in Surrey, she sends two copies of the *Daily Express* of October 31, *2p*

5 November 1936

Paul Léon to **Harriet Weaver**
Mr Joyce has asked him to forward pages from a fragment due to appear in *Transition*, Mr Joyce started feeling unwell about five weeks ago, he went to about four doctors who all told him he was in good health and his feeling unwell was caused by his nerves, Léon was summoned by phone at midnight by Mrs Joyce about a fortnight ago because Mr Joyce was suffering from a terrible anguish, since he returned from Copenhagen he hardly goes out and sees nobody, about five days ago he started to prepare a fragment for *Transition*, he appears in bad shape

5 November 1936

9 November
1936

Harriet Weaver, 101 Gloucester Place, London W.1 to **Paul Léon**
Thanks for his kind enquiry, she has recovered from her journey across the channel, she has arranged for a copy of the English edition of *Ulysses* to be sent to Judge Woolsey, she encloses press cuttings of notices of the English edition, the placards in London are devoting much space to the England v Australia test match, she hopes the conducting of the newly christened Russian general towards his début will go smoothly, *2p*

12 November
1936

Harriet Weaver, 101 Gloucester Place, London W.1 to **Paul Léon**
What will her half share of the final payment to the Obelisk Press amount to

18 November
1936

Paul Léon to **Harriet Weaver**
Thanks for her letters, the loss of his brother-in-law prevented him from replying immediately, he thinks she should visit Paris and that Mr Joyce would like to see her as what he wants to tell her could only be expressed orally, Mr Joyce says his situation is so black that nobody would want to see him, ill luck is pursuing his children, the lack of success of his daughter's book has disgusted him, the almost complete silence which met the British publication of *Ulysses* especially in Ireland has added to Mr Joyce's estrangement, he is working very hard but his physical strength is greatly taxed, the third payment for the book is due the day after tomorrow, *2p*

19 November
1936

Harriet Weaver, 101 Gloucester Place, London W.1 to **Paul Léon**
Arrangements to send 5,000 francs to Mr Joyce, half for the publishers and the other half as an advance on £60 due to Mr Joyce when she sells some Canadian Pacific Railway stock which has risen slightly, she hopes to cross early next week and will go to Hotel Galilée, *2p*

21 November
1936

Harriet Weaver, 101 Gloucester Place, London W.1 to **Paul Léon**
She has sent copies of the *T.L.S.* as directed, she is arranging to travel to Paris on Monday, she is sorry to hear of the loss of Léon's brother in law, *2p*

10 January
1937

Harriet Weaver, 101 Gloucester Place, London W.1 to **Paul Léon**, *typed letter signed*
Apologises for delay in sending verifications, she will ask Mr Monro not to deduct the £24 which she paid for the final instalment of Lucia's book from the profit of the resale of the

Canadian Pacific stock, has Mr Jolas recommended Mr Joyce for the Nobel Prize, she hopes Mr Joyce is well and working, *2p*

Harriet Weaver, 101 Gloucester Place, London W.1 to **Paul Léon** She sends pp 47-52 of the *Mime of Mick, Nick and the Maggies*

28 January 1937

Harriet Weaver, 101 Gloucester Place, London W.1 to **Paul Léon**, *typed letter signed* Thanks for his letters, she will send to Mr Joyce *The Novel and the People* by Ralph Fox and Philip Henderson's *The Novel Today*, Oliver Gogarty's *As I was going down Sackville Street* will not be published until the spring, she has posted the three Irish newspapers of yesterday's date, she is sorry to hear Mr Joyce is worrying, Mrs Stephens said she would write to Mr Joyce whose birthday she and Mr Stephens had remembered, *2p*

9 February 1937

Harriet Weaver, London to **Paul Léon**, *telegram* PLEASE DISREGARD SOLICITORS INCOME STATEMENT TILL HEARING FURTHER REGARD

11 February 1937

Harriet Weaver, 101 Gloucester Place, London W.1 to **Paul Léon** Thanks for his letter conveying Mr Joyce's message, she is glad to hear that Lucia is doing so well, she hopes Mr Joyce does not collapse in his effort to finish *WiP* by February 2nd, she would like to know what is the present position of the trade edition of *Ulysses*, she is going to Scotland to join her friend Miss Marsden, *2p*

8 August 1937

Harriet Weaver, 101 Gloucester Place, London W.1 to **Paul Léon** Will Léon thank Mr Joyce for the telegram he sent her on her birthday, she appreciated the fact that he took her holiday address with him to Zurich, she hopes the oculist gave a good report of his eyes, that Mr Joyce's brother has found a post and that there is further good news of Lucia, is there any news of the trade edition of *Ulysses*, *2p*

24 September 1937

Harriet Weaver, 101 Gloucester Place, London W.1 to **Paul Léon**, *typed letter signed* She is glad to hear of Lucia's wonderful improvement, sorry that Mr Joyce is unwell, regrets she did not send a list of errors she noticed in the English edition of *Ulysses* months ago, she thought the trade edition would be reset from the text used for the *de luxe* edition and not from the edition itself, many of the

19 October 1937

errors have been repeated, the errors in the *Oxen of the Sun* episode have been corrected, *2p*

28 October 1937

Harriet Weaver, 101 Gloucester Place, London W.1 to **Paul Léon**
She read *English Studies, Études Anglaises,* and *Il Convegno* with interest, she is glad that the proof correction of Parts I and III of *WiP* is nearly finished and that Mr Joyce hopes to send most of Part II to the printer next month, only one press notice of the unlimited edition of *Ulysses* - in *John O'London's Weekly*, *2p*

2 November 1937

Harriet Weaver, 101 Gloucester Place, London W.1 to **Paul Léon**, *postcard*
She will post the three journals to Mr Joyce today

20 December 1937

Harriet Weaver, 101 Gloucester Place, London W.1 to **Paul Léon**
She is going to stay with her sister at Guildford till the New Year so will Léon hold back the pages of corrections and additions to Part II, she is sorry to hear Mr Joyce is still working at such tremendous pressure, *2p*

11 January 1938

Harriet Weaver, 101 Gloucester Place, London W.1 to **Paul Léon**
Will Léon send her now the pages of corrections and enlargements of Part II, will Mr Joyce succeed in finishing by February 2nd, *2p*

20 January 1938

Harriet Weaver, 101 Gloucester Place, London W.1 to **Paul Léon**
Thanks for first batch of latest additions to *WiP*, will he convey her thanks to Mr Joyce for the gift

24 January 1938

Harriet Weaver, 101 Gloucester Place, London W.1 to **Paul Léon**
Thanks for second batch of corrections and additions to *WiP*

2 February 1938

Paul Léon to **Harriet Weaver**
He will probably go to visit his brother-in-law who has had an operation at Lausanne, Dr Collinson said that Mr Joyce had a retinal congestion and advised him to stop work and go to see Vogt in Zurich, Mr Joyce is in a state of exhaustion partly due to difficulties and delays with the publishers, he gave Mr Joyce the O'Reilly clan paper, Mr Joyce applied to her in roundabout fashion because he wanted to avoid any direct contact with the *Irish Times* office, Léon thinks Mr Joyce is as reluctant to ask Mr Curran to do things for him in connection with his work as he is to ask Miss Weaver, Mr Joyce has both her cable and Mr

Curran's beside his bed with the usual six or seven others, Mr Joyce's son had to leave suddenly for America a fortnight ago because his wife's father was dying, Mr Joyce is sorry that the volume brought out by Lord Carlow was not ready by the appointed date, *2p*

Harriet Weaver, 101 Gloucester Place, London W.1 to **Paul Léon** 9 February 1938
Thanks for his letter, will he let her know Professor Vogt's report after Mr Joyce's return to Paris, hopes it will be possible to get *WiP* out by 4th July, she posted to him newspapers and cuttings but did not send duplicates to Mr Joyce, *2p*

Harriet Weaver, 101 Gloucester Place, London W.1 to **Paul Léon**, *typed letter signed* 24 May 1938
She has corrected the new fragment of *WiP* in *transition* by comparing it with the latest corrected typescript sent to her, please thank Mr Joyce for the manuscript pages enclosed with Léon's letter, she is sorry to hear of Mr Joyce's eye attack and gripe since his return from Zurich, she would like to hear news of Lucia, *2p*

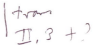

Harriet Weaver, 101 Gloucester Place, London W.1 to **Paul Léon** 29 May 1938
Encloses page 15-16 previously 49-50 of *Transition* 26 with insertion for verification of missing words which are "you're marchadant too forte so don't start furlan your ladins till you've learned the lie of her landmage!"

Harriet Weaver, 101 Gloucester Place, London W.1 to **Paul Léon**, *postcard* 2 June 1938
Thanks for returning page

Harriet Weaver, 101 Gloucester Place, London W.1 to **Paul Léon** 1 July 1938
Thanks for packet of proofs, typescript and pages of manuscript.

Harriet Weaver, 101 Gloucester Place, London W.1 to **Paul Léon** 11 July 1938
Thanks for packet sent by Léon on behalf of Mr Joyce, she is glad to see it includes a few sheets of Part IV in manuscript, hopes this concluding part of book will go well in spite of the work being done concurrently correcting the proofs of the earlier parts, *2p*

Harriet Weaver, 101 Gloucester Place, London W.1 to **Paul Léon** 20 July 1938
Thanks for first corrections of *Transatlantic Review* piece of *WiP*,

71

she is forwarding five copies of *Irish Times* of 11 July to Mr Joyce
and one to Mr Griffin

27 July 1938

Harriet Weaver, 101 Gloucester Place, London W.1 to **Paul
Léon**, *typed letter signed*
She has found the bit on St Patrick that she typed for Mr Joyce
when he was at Bognor, there were four bits, the sheets of Part
II Léon spoke of were not enclosed, she hopes Mr Joyce is not
overstrained

17 August
1938

Paul Léon to **Harriet Weaver**
He thinks *Work in Progress* will be finished by October, Part I is
nearly set in page form, Part II is in galleys with some thirty or
forty pages left over half of which are in typescript, Part III is
complete in galleys, over half of the epilogue-prologue Part IV
is typewritten, Léon fears Mr Joyce will collapse when the work
is finished especially if the publishers make difficulties, he fears
that Mr Joyce will be attacked by the Left for being in the
service of capitalist art, the German and Italian translations of
Anna Livia have been witheld for fear of attracting the hostile
attention of the authorities in Germany and Italy, nobody visits
Lucia except her father who goes to the Sanatorium every
Sunday afternoon, Mr Joyce's daughter-in-law collapsed and is
in a sanatorium in Switzerland, he encloses parts of Mr Joyce's
manuscript, Mr Joyce does not remember four lots copied in
Bognor, he has the O'Connor, Kevin and St Patrick parts, will
she send on any others, it is difficult for Mr Joyce to take a
holiday as his daughter insists on seeing him every Sunday, *2p*

18 August
1938

Paul Léon to **Harriet Weaver**
After he finished his letter yesterday Mr Joyce rang up and they
had dinner together, Mrs Joyce very depressed on account of
Lucia, Mr Joyce seems well, Léon hopes he has persuaded them
to take a holiday, Mr Joyce showed him a letter from the
Austrian writer Hermann Broch whom he succeeded in getting
to England, Mr Joyce has also used his influence with the
French Foreign Office to get four other Austrians into the
U.S.A. and Holland, this activity throws a new light on his
attitude

19 August
1938

Harriet Weaver, 101 Gloucester Place, London W.1 to **Paul
Léon**, *typed letter signed*
Thanks for pages of manuscript and letter, sorry to hear such

depressing news, hopes Mr Joyce will not be upset by criticism of his book by the young generation of the Left, she is not surprised that Mr Joyce arranged the escape of the Austrian writers, she has posted to Mr Joyce the fourth Bognor piece which is Tristan and Isolde, she is going away for a short holiday soon, *2p*

Harriet Weaver, 101 Gloucester Place, London W.1 to **Paul Léon** Thanks for his letter, hopes his wife will make a satisfactory recovery from her illness, sorry news of Mr Joyce's daughter-in-law still poor, it must have been disappointing for Mr and Mrs Joyce not to have seen their son when they were so near Lausanne, *2p*

16 September 1938

Harriet Weaver, 101 Gloucester Place, London W.1 to **Paul Léon** Thanks for manuscript and typescript of *WiP*, she will take it all to her sister's house in Surrey, she is glad that Mr and Mrs Joyce and Léon's wife and son have left for the country, it must be a nerveracking time for Léon in Paris, *2p*

27 September 1938

Harriet Weaver, 101 Gloucester Place, London W.1 to **Paul Léon** Mr Joyce telegraphed her on the evening of November 13th that he had finished *Work in Progress* that night, she hopes the proof correcting is finished and that Mr Joyce did not have a collapse from the intense pressure, will the book be published on February 2nd, she hopes there is good news of Mr Joyce's daughter and daughter-in-law, she wonders how Mr Joyce is placed financially now, hopes Léon is well and that Mrs Léon has recovered, thanks for the copy of *Études de lettres*, *2p*

5 December 1938

Paul Léon to **Harriet Weaver**, *autograph letter signed* Mr Joyce had a sudden collapse in the Bois de Boulogne, the doctor attributed it to overwork and lack of sleep but Mr Joyce continues to work, 355 pages have been finally revised, Léon wonders at Mr Joyce's preoccupation at this time of weighty and tragic events, Mr Joyce spoke of taking a teaching post in some Capetown University when the book was finished in order to rectify the financial situation but appears now to have abandoned the idea, *2p*

14 December 1938

Harriet Weaver, 101 Gloucester Place, London W.1 to **Paul Léon** Thanks for his letter, Mr Joyce's collapse understandable as due to overwork, strain and lack of sleep, she hopes Mr Joyce

21 December 1938

will rest but doubts that he will do so while there are still hundreds of pages of proofs to go through, Léon's forecast of the reception of the book is depressing, people are preoccupied with political and social problems, she herself is worried by the menacing political situation which she thinks was brought about by the disastrous British government, it is well that the Capetown project fell through, Léon is very kind in what he says about the small help she has given from time to time but it is infinitesimal compared to what Léon has done, she will be glad to have any news of Mr Joyce which he may be able to send, *2p*

30 December 1938

Harriet Weaver, 101 Gloucester Place, London W.1 to **Paul Léon**
She has received six registered envelopes of proofs and a copy of the U.S.A. Matisse edition of *Ulysses*, she is afraid she has offended Mr Joyce in some way as for the first time in twenty three years he has not sent her Christmas greetings nor has he written her name on the copy of *Ulysses*, she hopes Mr Joyce has been resting, *3p*

24 January 1939

Harriet Weaver, 101 Gloucester Place, London W.1 to **Paul Léon**
Thanks for sending her the ends of sections III and IV of Part II of *WiP*, hopes Mr Joyce has recovered from his collapse

24 January 1939

Harriet Weaver, 101 Gloucester Place, London W.1 to **Paul Léon**
She has received four further packets, mostly corrected galley proofs of Part III

31 January 1939

Harriet Weaver, 101 Gloucester Place, London W.1 to **Paul Léon**
Thanks for further batch of corrected proofs

4 February 1939

Harriet Weaver, 101 Gloucester Place, London W.1 to **Paul Léon**
She has received corrected galley proofs of Part IV, some Ms pages and proof of title page which lets her into the secret of the name, she likes it

14 February 1939

Paul Léon to **Harriet Weaver**
Encloses manuscript proofs which turned up in the course of dismantling Mr Joyce's flat which he is due to leave in mid-April, he is giving away most of his books and furniture, one of the rooms already empty, after page 355 they stopped receiving the second revise in order to save time, two copies of the first revise were sent from the printers, one went back corrected to

Faber and Faber and the second stayed with Mr Joyce, there are hardly any corrections by him and whatever writing there is on it is in the hands of Mr Gilbert, Mr Joyce's son, Mr Jolas or of Léon, Léon does not know when Miss Weaver will get a copy of the book, Mr Joyce got a bound copy for his birthday but the American publishers are delaying publication, Mr Joyce has tried to force their hand by having the French press notices of his birthday and his book cabled to New York as front page news and by trying to arrange for another publisher to take the book, the American publishers are very slow, they have cabled back expressing a sudden eagerness but Léon does not know what will happen, the three broadcasts planned from French stations for March have also been postponed, Mr Joyce believes that great harm has been done to his work before its appearance on the American market, this situation is a complete anticlimax for Mr Joyce after his seventeen years work, he does not like to talk about it, today he is ill in bed and running a temperature, he cannot leave Paris for he has to wait for the sheets of the limited edition which he has to sign, *2p*

Harriet Weaver, 101 Gloucester Place, London W.1 to **Paul Léon**   19 February 1939
Thanks for corrected galleys Mr Joyce found of Part IV, Episode IV and for Léon's letter, she is sorry to hear of the hold up in the American edition, hopes Mr Joyce will soon have the relief of hearing that the drastic action taken on February 3rd has been effective and that publication will take place, she will be honoured if Mr Joyce sends her the advance copy with corrections though not in his own hand, *2p*

Harriet Weaver, 101 Gloucester Place, London W.1 to **Paul Léon**   13 March 1939
She received Mr Joyce's notes for certain episodes of *Ulysses*, some corrected typescript of *Haveth Children Everywhere*, and two packets of older corrected proofs of *WiP*, she is sorry the difficulties over publication have not lessened, *2p*

Paul Léon to **Harriet Weaver**   17 March 1939
Thanks for her letter, his excuses for not having warned her that the rest of the sheets and proofs were to be taken by his wife, encloses cutting from the Paris *New York Herald* about Mr Joyce's agent who absconded with some royalties, Mr Joyce's royalties due on March 1st have not yet reached him, Pinker gets commission on all Mr Joyce's books merely to keep out of the way, all agreements are done by Messrs Monro which

involves communications and phone calls which irritate Mr Joyce

2 April 1939

Paul Léon to **Harriet Weaver**
Miss Joyce's health is unchanged, Mr Joyce continues his visits on Sundays but does not talk about them, Mr Beckett also visits her weekly, if there is an emergency the doctor has told Mr Joyce the patients will be transferred to La Baule, the doctor does not think Miss Joyce's health as good as last year, Mr Joyce has taken a small flat at 34 rue de Vignes, the news of his daughter-in-law is worse, the child has been removed from their flat, Mr Joyce's son has been obliged to suspend work on a projected concert, the sheets for the limited edition of *Finnegans Wake* have not left London for the U.S., a provisional publication date in May has been extracted from the New York publishers by Mr Joyce refusing to sign the sheets of the limited edition otherwise, Monro Saw will collect the royalties for Mr Joyce's publications, Mr Joyce feels that his seventeen years work is being wrecked by the incompetence of his publishers, a novel called *The Reincarnation of Finn MacCool* has just been published which he regards as harmful, the jacket had to be sent back because of a glaring mistake, the sale of some of Mr Joyce's manuscripts to public institutions in the U.S. has created a situation for Mr Joyce where he may find himself confronted with publications of texts never intended for publication, Léon does not think Miss Weaver has got all the manuscripts but whatever is left will have to be packed with the books and papers destined for the new apartment, Léon is sure Mr Joyce received Miss Weaver's telegrams and good wishes, *2p*

5 April 1939

Harriet Weaver, 101 Gloucester Place, London W.1 to **Paul Léon**
Thanks for his letter, sorry to hear such gloomy news, hopes publication of *Finnegans Wake* will not be postponed from May, she had not heard of the sale of Mr Joyce's manuscripts, everything seems to conspire against him, hopes Léon and his family are well, *2p*

28 April 1939

Harriet Weaver, 101 Gloucester Place, London W.1 to **Paul Léon**
Thanks for his letter telling her of Mr Joyce's new address and enclosing a copy of the letter Léon was sending to the person in the U.S. who wanted to publish parts of the earliest manuscript of *Portrait of the Artist,* she hopes the negligence over the consular invoice will not mean postponement of

publication from May 4th, she received an advance copy from Faber and Faber, *2p*

Harriet Weaver, 101 Gloucester Place, London W.1 to **Paul Léon**   13 June 1939
Léon will receive from Mr Joyce a typed copy of Mr Joyce's epilogue to Ibsen's *Ghosts,* Giorgio called and brought with him a card for Miss Weaver from Mr Joyce that had been misdirected, Mr Joyce sent her a batch of American press notices, does Léon wish her to continue sending to him as well as to Mr Joyce copies of the English press notices as it seems he is getting them direct, *2p*

Harriet Weaver, 101 Gloucester Place, London W.1 to **James**   14 July 1939
Joyce
She returns further batch [of press notices], the U.S.A. is outdoing England, she has only two or three notices to send, she has crossed out a couple of lines in the galley, she is sorry that the BBC turned down his son's voice though passing others of a lower standard, *2p, annotated in pencil by Paul Léon 'for Mr Gorman which please return after perusal' 'East Dean=265= Auldicus' delight Barking Gap Eastlog'*

Harriet Weaver, 101 Gloucester Place, London W.1 to **Paul Léon**   17 August
Thanks for letter from Mr Gorman and the publisher of his   1939
biography and for the further pages of corrected typescript of *Finnegans Wake* that he found

Paul Léon to **Harriet Weaver**   n.d.
Money to be sent from Monro Saw

3.

GENERAL CORRESPONDENCE OF JAMES JOYCE AND PAUL LÉON WITH FAMILY, FRIENDS AND ACQUAINTANCES

arranged in alphabetical order of corrrespondent, 370 letters with enclosures, 1931-40

ALTER
7 December
1932

.1 **Stefan Alter** to **James Joyce**
Sorry not to have received a reply to his letters, asks for explanation of *Ulysses* published by Rhein Verlag

AVOUT
10 July 1933

.2 **Bernard d'Avout**, Administrateur, Imprimerie Darantière, Dijon to **James Joyce**
Sorry to have missed M. Joyce when he called at the printers ten days ago, his regret at not being able to undertake a new impression of *Ulysses* as Albatross are issuing it in a completely new format, hopes M. Joyce will not forget him if he has any manuscript for printing, *annotated in hand of James Joyce 'Ask Baron D'Avout to call on you. A cheap French edition should be arranged. A.M. cannot sit on Ulysses for the rest of her life.'*

BAILLY
17 November
1934

.3 **René Bailly**, 42 rue du Marais to **James Joyce**
Thanks for news of Miss Joyce, apologises for not having returned borrowed book, *2p*

[193?]

[René Bailly to **James Joyce]**, *page 3 of letter only*
Invitation to Villers

BAX
21 March,
11 May 1933

.4 **Anthony Bax** Paris to **James Joyce** and **Paul Léon**
His interest in Joyce's work, he does not understand *Ulysses*, he is not related to Arnold Bax, *2 letters*

BELLAING
c.January
1935

.5 **D.W. Bellaing**, École des Sciences Politiques, Paris to **James Joyce**
Asks for a few lines for their student review, met Mr Joyce at the home of Madame Bailly and met Mrs Joyce last year, *2 letters*

GENERAL CORRESPONDENCE

.6 **Paul Léon** to **A. Medcalf**, 25 Claude Road, Glasnevin

He has forwarded to Mr Curran a copy of the will of the late John S. Joyce, Mr Joyce would like to have a list of his father's personal effects and would like to know when his sisters last saw their father before he was taken to hospital and whether his father knew that the usual small Christmas presents had been sent

BERGAN/
MEDCALF/
CHARLES
5 January
1932

Albert E. Medcalf to **Paul Léon**

He has written to Mr Joyce with particulars required

7 January
1932

Paul Léon to **Alfred Bergan**, 2 Claude Road, Glasnevin

Mr Bergan is co-executor of the late Mr John Joyce's will, does he consent to act in that capacity, Léon appends a list of books and other papers which should be in the late Mr Joyce's possession

12 January
1932

Alfred Bergan to **Paul Léon**

Consents to act, will Léon forward will to his solicitor David H. Charles, a daughter of Mr Joyce took away a valise with letters and documents, Mr Joyce asked him to see to certain matters before his death

15 January
1932

Paul Léon to **Alfred Bergan** and **David H. Charles**

Forwards will, his client anxious to know what matters the late Mr Joyce confided to Mr Bergan, *with Charles's letter of acknowledgement, 21 January 1932*

19 January
1932

Alfred Bergan to **Paul Léon**

Encloses copies of replies from Local Government Board and Insurance Company re monies due to John Joyce from his pension and his insurance policy, rent due to his landlord, *6p*

27 January
1932

Paul Léon to **A. Medcalf**

Mr James Joyce wishes to inform him that Mr Alfred Bergan is acting as executor of his father's will

28 January
1932

Paul Léon to **Alfred Bergan**

Has communicated contents of letter of 27th to Mr Joyce, Léon has written to Mrs Schaurek about the books which she admitted were with her

4 February
1932

31 March 1932

Alfred Bergan to **Paul Léon**
Probate has been passed, details of payments due

11 April 1932

Paul Léon to **Alfred Bergan**
Returns account of expenses which Mr Curran sent, most of the items have been paid by Mr Joyce, will he communicate the verbal matters which Mr John Joyce transmitted to him direct to Mr James Joyce

24 May 1932

David Charles to **James Joyce**
Encloses cheque, executor's account and vouchers, *9p*

2 June 1932

James Joyce, 2 avenue Saint-Philibert, Paris to **David Charles**
Acknowledges cheque and accounts

2, 10 June 1932

Paul Léon to **Alfred Bergan**
Re Mr John Joyce's verbal instructions and his wishes for his tombstone, *2 letters*

14 June 1932

Alfred Bergan to **Paul Léon**
Thanks for present, deceased wished only his and his wife's name on tombstone

28 November 1932

Paul Léon to **Alfred Bergan**
Mr Joyce apologizes for not having answered before, he approves of inscription mentioned in Bergan's letter

1 December 1932

Alfred Bergan to **Paul Léon**
Asks for approval for draft inscription

6 December 1932

Paul Léon to **Alfred Bergan**
Encloses final text of inscription

12 December 1932

Alfred Bergan to **Paul Léon**
Has handed inscription to sculptor

4 February 1932[?3], 6 March 1933

Alfred Bergan to **Paul Léon**
The sculptors have erected the headstone which he has inspected, he encloses photographs, he has not yet received *The Criterion, 2 letters*

GENERAL CORRESPONDENCE

Paul Léon to **Alfred Bergan**
Mr Joyce is pleased with tombstone, he has been indisposed lately

14 March
1933

Alfred Bergan to **James Joyce**
Thanks for copy of *New York Herald* containing a reference to the admission of *Ulysses* to the United States

18 December
1933

.7 **R.I. Best**, National Library of Ireland, Kildare Street, Dublin to [ ] **Wright**
The Library has two copies of the anonymous *Oxmantown and its environs*, Dublin, 1845

BEST
5 October
1935

.8 **Bibliothèque Nationale** to **Paul Léon**
Books by James Joyce held by the Bibliothèque Nationale, thanks for the illuminated work by Lucia Joyce, acknowledgement of books by Joyce received, *3 letters and list*

BIBLIO-
THÈQUE
NATIONALE
7, 28 March,
15 April 1933

.9 **H.P. Boland**, 3 Merton Road, Rathmines, Dublin to **Paul Léon**
Encloses receipt for the subscription of James Joyce to the Parnell Grave Memorial Fund

BOLAND
15 December
1938

.10 **Paul Léon**, Paris to **Monsieur E. Borack**, [*sic*] 21 Bellerive strasse, Zurich, *French*
Mr Joyce is sorry not to have written to Borach but he has been overburdened with work, he will go to London before going to Zurich where he expects to be around June, Mr Joyce cannot use his binoculars in the theatre and wishes Borach to ask Professor Vogt's advice on how to use them or to suggest an alternative

BORACH
9 March 1931

Georges Borach, Bellerive 21, Zurich to **Paul Léon**, *French*
Thanks for Léon's letter of the 23rd and regrets that an article on Goethe is not obtainable from Mr Joyce, he would like a copy of the issue of *transition* devoted to Mr Joyce and also the exact date of his birthday, the Swiss TSF stations are planning a Joyce evening, Borach has agreed to speak on the works of Joyce, he would like Léon to send him any of Joyce's poems

29 February
1932

81

that have been set to music and the poem Joyce has written recently on the birth of Stephen James, Clement-Janin has published an article about the facsimile of the 9th edition of *Ulysses* in the journal *Candide*, he expects to receive in a few days the issue of *Omnibus* containing his own article *Gespräche mit Joyce*

29 June 1932

Georges Borach, 21, Bellerive, Zurich to **Paul Léon**
Recommends Prof. Dr Hans W. Maier for Lucia, he does not know of any sanatorium where the sisters do not wear uniform

5 July 1932

Georges Borach, Zurich to **Paul Léon**, *picture postcard of Val Toscolano, French*
He received Léon's letter of the 4th, he has reserved a room in the Hôtel Elite for the Joyces

7 July 1932

George Borach, Carlton Elite Hotel, Zurich to **Paul Léon**, *autograph letter signed, French*
Mr Joyce wants Léon to telephone Mr Colum and tell him to telephone Mlle Barney immediately, she has not sent back the proofs of the *lettrines T* and *N* which Mr Joyce wants to get as quickly as possible to show to a silk merchant who is one of his old friends, these *lettrines* demonstrate Miss Joyce's talent, she has already done some textile designs, a telegram yesterday gave news of her arrival at Feldkirch, Mr Joyce will see Prof. Vogt after a few days rest and will then go to Lucerne, Léon should arrange to have money sent to him, Mr Joyce would like to have the *lettrines* by Monday morning as his meeting is on Monday afternoon

18 July 1932

Georges Borach, 21, Bellerive, Zurich to **Paul Léon**, *picture postcard of Goldiwil Hotel, Jungfrau, French*
Refers to Léon's last letter to Mr James Joyce dated 15 July, Mr James Joyce wants Léon to send to Borach the *lettrine*, the prescription, the cheque and the issue of *transition* with the caricature of Mr Joyce

20 July 1932

Georges Borach, 21, Bellerive, Zurich to **Paul Léon**, *French*
Confirms his postcard of the 18th, he received the cheque for Mr Joyce, will Léon have the kindness to talk to the oculist, thanks him for the caricature in *transition*, encloses an article by Ivan Goll, there are a lot of storms this summer in Zurich which

is unfortunate for Mr Joyce but the news from Feldkirch is good, he spends pleasant hours with Mr Joyce, Professor Vogt hopes to operate on Mr Joyce in the autumn

Paul Léon to **Georges Borach**, *French*
Mr Joyce has asked him to send cuttings from the Lyon newspapers about Sullivan's performance in *William Tell*, he has heard that *William Tell* will be put on at the Stadttheater in Zurich but thinks that it is Schiller's *William Tell*, if it is Rossini's who is the German tenor and could not Sullivan have the part, finally Mr Joyce would like to know what is the first stage of the treatment offered by Doctor Liebmann, this is for Miss Beach

12 February 1933

Paul Léon to **Georges Borach**, *French*
A copy of *Pomes Penyeach* has been sent to Mademoiselle Hélène Vogt from Mr Joyce with an accompanying letter, Borach's letters to Miss Beach and Miss Weaver have not had any success, Mr Joyce wants to go to Zurich but cannot go alone

1 March 1933

Georges Borach, Schuls to **Paul Léon**, *picture postcard, French*
The Hotel Habis telephoned his office in Zurich for a forwarding address for Mr Joyce, can Léon supply it

9 September 1933

.11   **Kay Boyle**, Hotel Kaiser, Kitzbühel, Tirol to **James Joyce**
Request for a short story to number 300 words for inclusion in a collection, *2p*

BOYLE
24 April 1934

.12   **Edmund Brauchbar**, Zurich to **Gustav Zumsteg**, Paris
Encloses letters for Mr Joyce, Zumsteg is to find out what Mr Joyce will do for Brauchbar's relatives, Mr Joyce is under an obligation to Brauchbar

BRAUCHBAR
13 May 1938

.13   **D.G. Bridson**, Manchester in correspondence with **James Joyce**, **Paul Léon** and **Sylvia Beach**
Review of *Shem and Shaun* by Bridson published in the *New English Weekly*, publication of *Work in Progress* and *Pomes Penyeach*, Bridson is glad that Mr Joyce read and liked his review, he saw the Everyman notice and thought that some of the T.S.E. section had been taken from a review of his own, plans to review other works by Joyce, *review enclosed*

BRIDSON
5, 30, [?]
January 1933

BROWN
26 March
1935

.14 **Pauline Brown**, Hotel du Col[ ], Champs Elysées, Paris to
Paul Léon
Mrs Joyce asked her to send her address to Léon, the Matron of
the 'Anglo American' will know where she is at any time should
she be required for Miss Joyce, *with note of her address*

BUDGEN
[1933]

.15 **Frank Budgen**, Ormond Hotel, Ormond Quay, Dublin to
Paul Léon
Encloses letter for Mr Joyce, has received cheque

[?1933]

Frank Budgen, New Ormond Hotel, Dublin to **Paul Léon**
Encloses letter for Mr Joyce, he is leaving Dublin today,

25 May 1933

Frank Budgen to **James Joyce**
Nothing Joyce can do for him in Zurich, would Joyce like to see
Paul Suter while he is there, he received the photograph of the
portrait of Lady St Leger but it was badly damaged in the post,
he is writing another page or two for the chapter on *Work in
Progress* in his book, he had already at Joyce's suggestion
expanded his chapter on Circe, Miss Weaver has suggested he
call, *2p*

29 May 1933

Air Express receipt for airmail of book to Frank Budgen in
London made out to Paul Léon

14 June 1933

Frank Budgen to **James Joyce**, *postcard*
Thanks for Zurich material, wants to return books, photo and
manuscripts but does not know where to send them, publishers
are anxious to have manuscript and he is working hard on it

23 June 1933

Frank Budgen, 207 Junction Rd, London N19 to **James Joyce**
Details for his chapter on Zurich and for the page on the tenor
voice, he is being pressed to finish his manuscript in time for
publication in the Autumn, will Joyce look at the typescript
rather than the proofs, he is shirking getting in touch with
Taylor who is in Chapter 1, Mr Dufay's book very dry, should he
mention Lady St Leger's name, *3p*

2 July 1933

Frank Budgen to **James Joyce**, *postcard*
Asks for information for his book, manuscript due in a week

Frank Budgen to **Paul Léon**, *postcard*   18 July 1933
Thanks for *Der Katholik*, has not yet received the pamphlets Léon
mentioned, his manuscript has to be delivered in three days

Frank Budgen, 207 Junction Road, London N19 to **James Joyce**   19 July 1933
Thanks for Joyce's letter, he is working hard on his manuscript
which is due on Saturday, details of the text, he will send Joyce
a typescript or proof, *6p*

Frank Budgen, 207 Junction Road, N19 to **James Joyce**   12 September 1933
Thanks for Joyce's reply, pleased Joyce liked the book, kind of
Gilbert to read the proofs, will see Joyce in Paris, *2p*

Frank Budgen, Chez Professor Fleiner, Alle Vigne, Ascona   22 September 1933
Thanks for Joyce's notes but they arrived too late, he will keep
them for reference and may be able to work some of them in,
he got in most of the notes he took in Paris, he and Suter paid
a visit to [Uehluger], if he gets duplicate proofs of the drawings
he will send them to Joyce, *2p*

Frank Budgen to **James Joyce**, *picture postcard 'Al Porto d'Ascona'*   25 September 1933
Thanks for cuttings

Frank Budgen, Ascona to **James Joyce**   28 September 1933
Encloses copy of letter from Jonathan Cape, the proofs of the
drawings give a very poor idea of the originals, he expects the
page proofs in a week, he encloses a letter for the Odyssey
Press, the photograph of the portrait of Joyce came also, *2p*

Frank Budgen, Ascona to **James Joyce,** *postcard*   1 October 1933
Will return via Paris, his address in Zurich will be c/o Professor
Fleiner, page proofs should arrive in a few days, Faber rang up
Graysons

Frank Budgen, 207 Junction Rd, London N19 to **James Joyce**   18 August 1934
He has been trying to get in touch with an acquaintance who
once worked for Burns & Oates, Joyce should sue Burns & Oates
for losing Lucia's *lettrines*, the Matisse drawings, his publishers
are not likely to issue a cheap reprint of his book, he is repairing
the damage to Miss Weaver's paintings caused by a fire while she
was away, he may go to Paris for a week's holiday, *4p*

26 June 1935

Frank Budgen, 245 Camden Road, London N VII to **Paul Léon**, *postcard*
Will Léon forward his change of address to Mr Joyce

30-31 March 1939

Frank Budgen, 39 Belsize Square, NW3 to **Paul Léon**
His book was remaindered, he does not know how to get hold of a copy, *1p*

BURTON
7 August
[19?33], n.d.

.16 **Basil Burton**, London to **James Joyce** and **Paul Léon**
Thanks to Mr Joyce for birthday card, request for list of criticism of *Ulysses*, *2 letters, letter to Joyce annotated in hand of James Joyce 'Can't read this'*

BYRNE
23 February
1933

.17 **M. Alice Byrne**, La Bergerie, Portarlington to **Paul Léon**
She has sent his letter on to her husband in New York

c. June 1933

[James Joyce to **J. Kingsley Martin]**
Draft letter in hand of Paul Léon introducing J.F. Byrne 'my friend and schoolfellow' to J. Kingsley Martin, editor of the *New Statesman*

22 June 1933

Paul Léon, Paris to **J.F. Byrne**, Heaton's Oxford Hotel, 10 Euston Square, London NW1
Mr Joyce has asked Léon to inform Mr Byrne that two parcels have been sent to him one containing his slippers and the other books including copies of *transition*, Mr Joyce will send a copy of the *New Statesman*, Mr Joyce found a 100fr note in his pocket which he believes Mr Byrne put there, he has used the money to make a recording of himself reading *Anna Livia Plurabelle* to be sent to Mr Byrne's daughter as a present, Mr Byrne can hear the disk at the Imhof Gramophone Cy, the record is a HMV record

22 June 1933

J.F. Byrne, Ardmay Hotel, Woburn Place, London WC1 to **James Joyce**
Mr Christiansen, acting editor of the *Express* took his story but has not yet reached a decision on it, he has abandoned efforts to reach Dulhunty

23 June 1933

J.F. Byrne, PS, New Oxford Street, London WC1 to **James Joyce**
He has received a letter from Léon and a letter from Joyce

including a letter of introduction to Slocombe, a letter from Mme Jolas to Joyce and a marked copy of the *Paris Herald*, however he has decided to quit trying to put his parable across, he will cross to Ireland tonight, his daughter will thank Joyce for his record

Scrap of paper signed 'J.F. Byrne' and recounting a humourous anecdote

n.d.

.18   **Arnold Tunstall**, President, Cambridge University English Club to **James Joyce**
Invitation to lecture, *with reply from Paul Léon refusing invitation on behalf of Mr Joyce who never lectures.*

C.U. ENGLISH CLUB
10 September, 1 November 1934

T.R.M. Creighton, Cambridge University English Club to **James Joyce**
Invitation to lecture, *annotated in hand of James Joyce: 'My wife read me 7 lines of this. I can't read the rest. Reply*
   J.J. at present in C. Thanks very much. Never speaks to anyone. Greatly appreciates. (Ulysses [comes out in London] on 25. ix. P.S.)

24 August 1936

.19   **Clark Tourist Co** to **James Joyce**
Refers to Mr Joyce's call at their office to cancel the three Paris to London tickets not used the previous Sunday

CLARK TOURIST CO
20 April 1932

James Joyce, Hotel Belmont, 30 rue Bassano, Paris to **Clark Tourist Co**, 11 rue Castiglione, Paris, *carbon typescript unsigned, French*
Asks for a refund for the three Paris to London tickets which he has been unable to use owing to his daughter's attack of nerves at the station, encloses a medical certificate, they are staying in a hotel in Paris and have given up the idea of living in England, he has lost the deposit and advance payment of rent on his flat in London

22 April 1932

Paul Léon to **Clark Tourist Co**
On behalf of Mr Joyce he thanks them for the trouble they have taken and for cheque

27 April 1932

19 May 1932   **Clark Tourist Co** to **James Joyce**
                Further refund

COLUM   .20   **James Joyce** to **Padraic Colum**, Pachamak, New York,
[? February   *carbon typescript of telegram*
1932]   Thanks Beach contract annulled world rights now mine any
                     offers therefore should be sent me

[c. 24   **James Joyce** to **Padraic Colum**, c/o Murray Crane, 820 Fifth
February   Avenue, N.Y.C., *carbon typescript of telegram*
1932]   Call cables Pachawan Two offers Bennett Cerf and Morrow
               Hobson have you any others must decide as soon as possible,
               impression of typescript copy of first stanza of Ecce Puer on verso

28 November   **Padraic Colum**, The Panhellenic, 3 Mitchell Place, First Avenue
1933   and 49th Street, New York to **James Joyce**
               Encloses cutting, hopes Judge Woolsey will give a favourable
               decision

4 June 1936   **Padraic Colum** to **James Joyce**, *telegram*
               ADDRESS WILL BE SIX CIRCLE STREET NORWALK
               CONNECTICUT GOOD WISHES TO ALL

CRAIG   .21   **Maurice James Craig**, 24 rue Franklin, St. Germain-en-
12 June 1938   Laye, Seine-et-Oise to **James Joyce**
               He and Scott wish to express their gratitude to Mr Joyce for having
               received them, he has written today to Mr Sam Henry enquiring
               about 'The Lord in his mercy', comments on *Ulysses*, *3p*

CURRAN   .22   **Paul Léon** to **Constantine Curran**
5 January   Mr Joyce has received a letter from Mr Medcalf asking him to find
1932   the will of the late John S. Joyce, his father, there are two wills in
               the possession of Giorgio Joyce, Léon forwards a copy of the
               second will, will Curran let him know what steps should be taken,
               with copies of 2 wills of John S. Joyce, dated 13 March and 22 May 1915

9 January   **Constantine Curran**, 15 Garville Avenue, Rathgar, Dublin to
1931[2]   **Paul Léon**
               Steps he advises Léon to take, *2p, with pencilled annotations in
               hand of Paul Léon*

Paul Léon to **Constantine Curran**
Steps he is taking, encloses list taken down at Mr Joyce's
dictation containing titles of books and of letters to his father
which should have been in his father's rooms, he is also writing
to Mrs Schaurek to enquire for them, should they be found
they should be deposited immediately with Curran, encloses
draft in settlement of disbursements which Curran has
incurred, *2p*

Constantine Curran to **Paul Léon**
Advice about solicitors, money he has expended including
money given to Mrs Schaurek, Mr Medcalf says he gave a valise
containing documents to Mrs Schaurek but there were no
books among them, Curran has obtained the valise from Mrs
Schaurek and encloses a list of its contents, the correspondence falls entirely within the twelve years that John S.
Joyce lived in Mr Medcalf's house, it will be difficult to find
anything from an earlier period, encloses note of John S.
Joyce's insurance policy and loan numbers, he can find no
books except an uninscribed copy of *Exiles*, Mr Charles Joyce
may have the copy of *Ulysses* in London, Mrs Schaurek says she
lent the gramophone disc to Mr Desmond Fitzgerald, Minister
for Defence, the correspondence includes many letters from
Mr Michael Healy of Galway to whom Mrs Joyce should write, a
Mr William Dwyer, solicitor, Roscrea got permission from John
S. Joyce to retain two of James Joyce's letters and it is possible
he may have some knowledge of the missing books, the letters
from Mr Michael Healy and from Sister M. Gertrude from New
Zealand made continual allusion to Mr James Joyce, Curran
will keep the letters safely until he gets further instructions,
16p, with 7 receipted bills

Paul Léon to **Constantine Curran**
The late Mr Joyce's will is in the hands of David Charles,
solicitor, Mr Bergan has written that he had verbal instructions
from the late Mr Joyce, Mr James Joyce is very grateful to
Curran for all his kindness, he has been very depressed since
the death of his father, Léon is writing to William Dwyer, Mr
Joyce would like him to send the letters of his sister and of his
uncle in law Mr Healy, Mr Joyce cannot understand what could
have happened to his books

14 February 1932

Paul Léon to **William Dwyer,** Solicitor, Roscrea, Ireland
Asks whether he knows anything about the inscribed copies of his books which Mr James Joyce sent to his father John Joyce

20 February 1932

William Dwyer to **Paul Léon**
He occasionally visited John Joyce, he understood that the inscribed copies of Mr James Joyce's books were taken by some members of his family

2 January 1934

Paul Léon to **Constantine Curran**
Mr Joyce thanks him for his letter which he will answer in a few days, Mr Joyce would like to have a double bench erected on Whitworth Road opposite Claude Road but does not want anyone to know he is paying for it

8, 17 January 1934

Constantine Curran to **Paul Léon**
He has been in touch with the Corporation, suggested siting of the bench, *2 letters*

22 January 1934

Paul Léon to **Constantine Curran**
Mr Joyce agrees with his proposal

14 August 1934

Constantine Curran to **James Joyce**
Plans for his trip to the Continent, hopes the Joyces will enjoy Spa, thanks for *New York Herald* giving good news from Court of Appeals, encloses Latin verses on the *vin de S. Patrice* by Osborn Bergin, *5p*

11 April 1935

Paul Léon to **Constantine Curran**
Thanks for kindness to Lucia, Curran will receive a copy of *Pomes Penyeach* with *lettrines* painted by Lucia

7 May 1935

Constantine Curran to **Paul Léon**
Excuses his not having acknowledged *Pomes Penyeach* sooner but his mother died, comments on poems, has not seen Lucia recently but Mrs Schaurek reassured him about her, *2p*

13 May 1935

Constantine Curran to **Paul Léon**, *telegram*
LUCIA COMFORTABLE IN TEMPORARY NURSING HOME

17, 23, 27 July 1935

Paul Léon to **Constantine Curran**
Thanks for his care of Mr Joyce's daughter, arrangements to bring her to London, cost of her treatment, *3 letters*

Receipt made out to C.P. Curran by H.R.L. Rutherford, Farnham House, Finglas for the care of Lucia Joyce	22 July 1935

Helen Curran to **James Joyce**
Lucia's passport sent to Miss Weaver, she has settled matters with the landlady in Bray and has rescued Lucia's clothes, *Pomes Penyeach* is in the hands of Paddy Schaurek, Lucia sold most of her jewellery, letter and telegram

10, 16 September [1935]

Helen Curran to **Miss Weaver**
Her search for Lucia's passport, glad to hear Lucia's progress is satisfactory

16 September [1935]
12 January 1936

Paul Léon to **Constantine Curran**
Encloses cheque on Mr Joyce's behalf for AE fund, Mr Joyce would like Curran to take up again the matter of erecting a bench in memory of his father

Constantine Curran to **Paul Léon**
Will get information from Dr Munro, encloses letters from Dublin Corporation about the seat which Mr Joyce wishes to have erected, *with 4 letters enclosed, 8p*

17, 26 April 1936

Paul Léon to **Constantine Curran**
Thanks for Dr Munro's communication, it would be desirable for the doctor in the mental hospital where Miss Joyce stayed in Dublin to write to Dr Delmas, Mr Joyce approves of the site for the bench

30 April 1936

Constantine Curran to **Paul Léon**
Encloses Dr Rutherford's letter, *3 items*

'Saturday' [May 1936?]

Constantine Curran to **Paul Léon**
Performance of *Exiles* to take place on 24 May, he will see that the principals get bouquets with Mr Joyce's cards before curtain rises, the Peacock Theatre, his plans for a motor trip to the Continent, photos Léon took at Hôtel Savoy, performance of *Exiles* postponed, his meetings with Herbert Gorman and Louis Gillet, he is sending on music, *4 letters, 13p*

30 April, 24 May, 2 June, 20 August 1937

Constantine Curran to **Paul Léon**
Radio Éireann broadcast on Joyce, he is contributing the personal sketch and Professor Hogan is doing the critical

31 January [1938?]

estimate, *Irish Beekeeper* and book on 18th century Dublin both sold out, his daughter Elizabeth is in Paris, *2p and newsclipping*

3 May 1939

Constantine Curran to **Paul Léon**
Thanks for copy of *Finnegans Wake*, what will Mr Joyce do now, *4p*

15 May 1939

Constantine Curran to **James Joyce**
Thanks for *Finnegans Wake* which he finds difficult, *2p*

2 February 1938

Texts of talks broadcast by Radio Éireann on the occasion of Joyce's fifty sixth birthday:
'Personal sketch' by Constantine Curran, *4p, 2 copies*
'Biographical sketch' by Herbert Gorman, *2p, 3 copies one signed by Gorman*
'Critical appreciation' by Professor Jeremiah Hogan, *4p, 2 copies*

DENHOF
5 June 1935
4, 14 October 1939

.23   **Maurice Denhof**, 'La Résidence', Place de l'Église, Le Mont-Dore to **[Paul Léon]**, *letter and postcard, French*
His new address, he would be glad to receive Mr Joyce's book, how is Mr Joyce

DILLON
24 October 1932

.24   **E.J. Dillon**, 12 Calle Pomaret. Sarria, Barcelona to **James Joyce**
Enquires after Joyce's eyesight, he should consult Dr Barraquer in Barcelona

DODDS
5 June 1935

.25   **E.R. Dodds**, The University, Edmund Street, Birmingham to **James Joyce**
He is preparing a short memoir of his friend Stephen MacKenna, Spicer Simson the sculptor told him that MacKenna had once introduced him to Mr Joyce and suggested that Dodds should apply to Mr Joyce for information about MacKenna

DYER
Christmas 1934

.26   **James and Louise Dyer** [to **James Joyce**]
Christmas card

.27 **Oliver Edwards**, University of London to **James Joyce**
Asks permission to publish letters of James Joyce to W.B. Yeats in connection with the publication of *The Countess Cathleen* in Italian in 1912, *2p*

Paul Léon to **Oliver Edwards**
Mr Joyce has no objection to the publication of his letters to Mr Yeats but would like to see them before publication, quotes part of Joyce's Italian translation of *The Countess Cathleen*, Mr Joyce was the only student who refused to sign the protest against the play, Mr Yeats did not help with the publication of *Dubliners* though Ezra Pound did

15 May 1935

Oliver Edwards, University of London and Llysydolau, Radyr, Glamorgan to **Paul Léon**
Could his wife have an interview with Mr Joyce in order to ask him about his aquaintanceship with Mr Yeats, she will bring copies of Mr Joyce's letters with her, does Mr Joyce have any copies of Mr Yeats's letters, he has sent copies of Mr Joyce's letters to Mr Yeats direct to Mr Joyce, *2 letters*

25 May, 29 September 1935

Oliver Edwards, Llysydolau, Radyr, Glamorgan to **James Joyce**
Encloses copies of three letters written by Joyce to Yeats in 1912 from Trieste, refers to letters written in 1915 about the Literary Fund which Frank Budgen mentions in his book, *with 3 copy letters enclosed from James Joyce to W.B. Yeats dated 19 September 1912 [transcribed in Letters of James Joyce edited by Stuart Gilbert, London 1957], and 16, 25 December 1912 referring to The Countess Cathleen and Dubliners, 5p*

30 September 1935

Oliver Edwards, Llysydolau, Radyr, Glamorgan to **Paul Léon**
Mr Yeats is sorry about Mr Joyce's loss of his copy of the collected poems, he has asked Mr Joyce to accept an autographed copy of the latest edition with his compliments and is grateful for Mr Joyce's offer to autograph the title page of *Ulysses*, Edwards has seen a copy of a letter from Joyce to Lady Gregory written probably in November 1902 and would like to publish it but does not know the whereabouts of the original, *3p*

2 November 1935

.28 **John W. Elmes** to **James Joyce**
Sends copy of Judge Woolsey's decision on *Ulysses*, *with acknowledgement by Paul Léon, 2 letters*

ERNEST-
CHARLES
27 December
1939,
16 April 1940

.29   **J. Ernest-Charles**, Avocat à la Cour, 34 Rue Singer, Paris
to **James Joyce** and to **Paul Léon**, *French*
Asks for his fee, thanks Léon for loan of book by Joyce, Mr
Joyce has not replied to his letters, *2 letters*

ERNST
3 September
1937

.30   **Morris L. Ernst**, Greenbaum, Wolff & Ernst, 285 Madison
Avenue, New York to **James Joyce**
Sends two copies of *To the pure*, he is happy to have had the
chance of dining with Mr Joyce, would appreciate an inscribed
copy of *Ulysses*

FELLOWES
25 July 1934

.31   **Daisy Fellowes**, Les Zoraïdes, Cap Martin to **James Joyce**
Thanks for the copy of his new book which Mr Joyce has sent
her, she was longing for it ever since Mlle Behrens [*sic*] read
extracts at the Coupôle, the illustrations are very attractive

FERNANDEZ
3 January
1938

.32   **Emile Fernandez et Madame** to **Mr and Mrs Joyce**, *calling
card, French*
Good wishes for 1938

FISCHER
17 October
1932

.33   **Fritz Willy Fischer**, Salzburg to **James Joyce**, *German*
Refers to Mr Joyce's visit to his father Professor Adolph
Johannes Fischer, his portrait of Mr Joyce

FLEINER
6 September
1934

.34   **Fanny Fleiner**, Ascona to **James Joyce**
Their mutual friend Frank Budgen has told her that Mr Joyce is
anxious for information about a malady which her husband
described, recommends Professor H. Otto Naegeli for diseases
of the blood, also recommends Johannes Kohl for a psychical
treatment for Mr Joyce's daughter, *3p*

8 January
1935

Professor F. Fleiner, Paris to **Paul Léon**, *German*
They must return to Zurich, cannot carry out Léon's request
with regard to Miss Joyce

FLORENCE,
MAYOR OF
26 March 1932

.35   **Comitato fra gli Enti di Alta Cultura, Città di Firenze** to
James Joyce, *copy letter*
Invitation to give a lecture

James Joyce to **Gherardesca,** Mayor of Florence, *carbon typescript*   [April 1932]
of telegram
Ringrazio dispaccio lettera giunse venerdi resposi domenica mi
scusi recardo ossequi

James Joyce to **Sen. conte Giuseppe Della Gherardesca, Mayor**   9, 10 April
of Florence, *3 draft typescripts, transcribed in Letters of James Joyce,*   1932
Volume III, edited by Richard Ellmann, London, 1966

.36   **Dr Geo. A. Geist**, St. Paul, Minnesota to **James Joyce** and   GEIST
Paul Léon   15 December
Offers to send to Mr Joyce his musical setting of Mr Joyce's   1937, 13
poem *Alone, 2 letters*   April 1938

.37   **Carola Giedion-Welcker,** [Zurich] to **Paul Léon**, *German*   GIEDION-
Professor Vogt's opinion on Joyce's eyes, book for Professor   WELCKER
Vogt's daughter, hopes the operation in New York has gone   [May 1933]
well, photographs, *2p*

Carola Giedion-Welcker, Stein A./Rhein to **Mr and Mrs Joyce**,   24 [? 1934?]
picture postcard
Thinks of them both

Carola Giedion-Welcker to **James Joyce**   6 November
Thanks for cards from Arcachon, has spoken to Mr Lichtensteiger   1936
about the Zuger affair, will write to Direktor Keller

Carola Giedion-Welcker to **James Joyce**   26 August
She did not see Lucia in Paris, they wish to see Mr Joyce, she   1937
will try to get *Review* for him, *endorsed with letter from James Joyce to*
Paul Léon dated 28 August 1937, see p. 27

Carola Giedion-Welcker to **James Joyce**   8 December
Thanks for Joyce's letter of 6 December, she will have as many   1937
Brissago cigars as possible brought to Paris, sorry Lucia is not
well, her difficulty in coping with her own daughter's illness,
she has nearly finished the book

Carola Giedion-Welcker to **James Joyce**   20 December
She tried to telephone Joyce and Giorgio in Paris on her return   1939
from America in August 1939, an effort is being made to

procure for Joyce the Eliot Norton chair at Cambridge [U.S.A.] now held by Stravinsky, however she fears Joyce would be unwilling to go to America, her husband is still in Cambridge finishing his book

GILBERT
21 August
1934

.38 **Stuart Gilbert**, 7 Rue Jean du Bellay, Paris to **Paul Léon**
Encloses a copy of the 'chart' taken from the proofs of his book, M. Matisse will not find much to help him in it

[2 August
1937]

S[tuart] G[ilbert], "Plyie d'Or", Mont à l'Abbé, Jersey to **James Joyce**, *picture postcard of Mont Orgueil Castle, Gorey, Jersey*
Hopes Joyce received a copy of 'Night and Day', invites him to Jersey

GILLET
3 June, 6 July
1933

.39 **Louis Gillet**, Institut de France, Musée Jacquemart-André, Chaalis to **James Joyce**, *French*
Joyce is right to stay a while in Zurich, he will find the preface for the *Alphabet* at rue Galilée, Gillet would have been happy to do the preface for nothing but his need of money leads him to ask for 1000 or 1200 francs, when the volume appears can he publish his text in French perhaps in *Nouvelles Littéraires*; he has not heard any news from Joyce, is worried that Joyce did not get his letter or preface, he is going to the country on the 13th, *2 letters, 6p*

16 July 1933

[?], London to **Louis Gillet**, 17 Rue Buonaparte, Paris, *carbon typescript unsigned, French*
Gillet's letter reached him in Paris just as he was leaving, the *Alphabet* should be published in the autumn, there should be no problem with Gillet's publishing his preface in French, publication in *Candide* would be good publicity

1933

The Alphabet of Miss Lucia Joyce, 2 typescripts, one corrected for the printer, *4 x 2p*

L'Alphabet de Lucia Joyce, typescript with ms additions and annotations, *5p, on verso of p.5 in hand of Paul Léon: 'Yeats, Riversdale, Rathfarnham, Dublin, Congratulations and many happy returns James Joyce'*

Louis Gillet to **Sylvia Beach**, *French*   11 May 1934
Asks her to put him down for a copy of *The Mime of Mick*
published by the Servire Press

.40   **Herbert Gorman**, 1084 Kensington Terrace, Larchmont   GORMAN/
Estates, Union, N.J., U.S.A. and c/o Farrar & Rinehart to **James**   FARRAR &
Joyce   RINEHART
Reasons for his long silence, hopes to finish his biography of   10 October,
Joyce by early spring and to see Joyce in Europe about it;   29 December
arrangements to meet Joyce in Europe, his book on Mary   1932
Stuart has been successful, Farrar & Rinehart are making
elaborate plans for the biography, he gave the French notice of
Lucia's work on Joyce's poems to the *New York Evening Post*,
encloses clippings of reviews of his book on Mary Stuart, *2
letters, with 2 newsclippings*

Herbert Gorman, 330 East 43rd Street, New York to **Paul Léon**   1 April 1933
Re Frank Budgen's proposed book on Joyce, Léon's letter to
Pinker has been forwarded to him and he takes up the points in
numbered order, he himself has no intention of abandoning his
biography, reasons for deferral of his trip to Europe, hopes to
publish in Spring 1934, disapproves of Budgen's book which may
steal his thunder, he would not give Budgen any material, *2p*

Paul Léon to **Herbert Gorman**   16 April 1933
Writes to appease Gorman's worries, intended to inform him of
Budgen's book not to seek any collaboration, Budgen deals
with the composition of *Ulysses* during Mr Joyce's stay in Zurich
a period of which Budgen has first hand knowledge, glad that
Gorman expects his own book to be a success

Herbert Gorman, 43 Manchester Street, Manchester Square,   7 November
London to **James Joyce**   1933
Surprised to hear from Pinker that Joyce has withdrawn his
authorisation for the biography, delays due to circumstances
beyond his powers, wants to hear from Joyce direct, *2p*

Paul Léon to **Herbert Gorman**   22 November
Transcribed in Letters of James Joyce, Volume III, edited by Richard   1933
Ellman, London, 1966

25 November
1933

Herbert Gorman to **James Joyce**
Denies that he gave the chart to Random House, the chart was
not given to him for the biography nor was it given
confidentially, he showed it privately to some friends but does
not know who gave it to Random House, he does not know
whether he will write the biography as he has not had a direct
withdrawal of permission

25 November
1933

Herbert Gorman to **Bennett A. Cerf**, *two copy letters*
Received a letter from Paul Léon accusing him of giving Cerf a
privately drawn up plan re *Ulysses*, wants to know from whom
did Cerf receive the plan

[?1 June
1939]

Herbert Gorman, c/o Farrar & Rinehart to **James Joyce**
Encloses four chapters of the biography for perusal and
correction, Farrar & Rinehart want to publish in July, wants
four more illustrations, proposals for frontispiece and cover,
news of his family, praises *Finnegans Wake*

[June 1939]

James Joyce to **Farrar & Rinehart**, *draft telegram*
Chapter four incorrect misleading two vital points require
therefore entire typescript except last pages if purely critical
before giving authorisation publication

[June 1939]

James Joyce to **Farrar & Rinehart**, *draft telegram*
Have no typescript your book whatsoever except chapters two
four nine ten which leave by Queenmary with photographs
important corrections send me double galleys of which will
promptly return one set revised consider your unexpected
haste after prolonged silence inexplicable kindly note Léons
address twenty seven not twenty one

6 June 1939

Paul Léon to **Herbert Gorman**, *carbon typescript and manuscript
draft in hand of Paul Léon, transcribed in Letters of James Joyce,
Volume III, edited by Richard Ellman, London, 1966*

7 June 1939

Herbert Gorman to **James Joyce**, *telegram*
BOOK BEING TYPESET WILL MAIL COMPLETE PROOFS
YOU HAVE ENTIRE TYPESCRIPT EXCEPT LAST CHAPTER
PLEASE RUSH RETURN MANUSCRIPT WITH CORREC-
TIONS

Adelaide A. Sherer, Managing Editor, Farrar & Rinehart to **James Joyce**
Despatch of two sets of proofs of Chapters I-IX

Paul Léon to **Farrar & Rinehart**
Encloses batch of galleys, his letters to Mr Gorman unanswered, had not heard from Mr Gorman for nine months until typescript of several chapters of his biography arrived with letter announcing imminent publication, many errors in galleys and typescript, text corresponds to book which Mr Gorman published on Mr Joyce seventeen years ago, they know nothing of what Mr Gorman has written about Mr Joyce's mature life, what are the plans for publication, when will they receive the complete text embodying corrections

Herbert Gorman to **Paul Léon**
Léon did not receive his letter acknowledging the first thirty five galleys, incorporation of corrections, publication planned for October, his present text does not correspond to the work he wrote seventeen years ago, sorry that various obstacles have made him seem procrastinating

John Farrar to **Paul Léon**
Enthusiastic about Mr Gorman's manuscript, the publication of the biography will help the sales in America of *Finnegans Wake*, progress of the printing and correction of the galleys

.41   **Georg Goyert**, 7. Bottermannstr.7, Witten-Ruhr to **James Joyce**, *German*
Received a letter from Herr Borach asking him to type his letters to Joyce, he himself hates typewritten letters but understands that Joyce has difficulty reading handwritten ones, when he has finished with *Anna Livia* he would like to try translating *Tales told*, he would like a copy of the other editions of the fragments, thanks Mr Joyce for his work on Goyert's version of *Anna Livia*, he regrets not having taken part in the meetings of the Paris Collective

Georg Goyert, 7. Bottermannstr.7, Witten-Ruhr to **James Joyce**, *German*
Thanks for Mr Joyce's letter, he will ask Brody for a copy of

Tales told, he does not mean he is completely finished with *A.L.P.*, he never liked Jung's article on *Ulysses*, he awaits the notice about Miss Joyce with great interest

3 July 1933

Georg Goyert, 7. Bottermannstr.7, Witten-Ruhr to **James Joyce**, *German*
Thanks for all the work and trouble Mr Joyce and the Collective have taken in going through his translation of *A.L.P.*, he is now working on *Tales told*, he had to return his Black Sun Press copy to Mr Borach and so would like to borrow a copy from Mr Joyce, he heard that Mr Joyce had been in Zurich and that the Professor is to some extent satisfied with him

6 November 1934

Georg Goyert, 7. Bottermannstr.7, Witten-Ruhr to **James Joyce**, *German*
Thanks for Mr Joyce's letter, he was afraid that he had lost all contact with Mr Joyce as he had no reply to several letters which he now hears Mr Joyce never received, the tragic fate of Mr Borach has shaken him even though he did not know him personally, he is sorry to hear that Miss Joyce's health is so bad, he has had trouble with his own son Klaus, his work on *A.L.P.* and *Tales told*, asks Mr Joyce for a copy of *The Mime of Mick, Nick and the Maggies* with a dedication

GRIFFIN
1 February, 6, 17, 22 August, 5 October, 20 December 1937

.42 **Gerald Griffin**, 42, Ashburnham Mansions, Chelsea, London to **Paul Léon**
Tribute in the *Osservatore Romano* to *Ulysses* and *Work in Progress*, asks D'Annunzio to autograph Joyce's copy of *La Città Morta*, thanks Léon for sending issue of *transition* and various articles on Joyce, the Dublin Puritans will be shocked that the official organ of the Vatican praised Joyce, miscellaneous queries re Joyce's work, *5 letters*

[c. 1 January 1938]

[Paul Léon to **Gerald Griffin]**, *draft letter in hand of James Joyce*
Mr J. gave away his O.R. he says. After a lot of vain searching I got a copy from Mrs S. wife of the Franco-Irish tenor. Please send it back along with the *Carmelite Review* as I need both for my files. The O.R., as I know from experience, is quite unobtainable at any Kiosk, bookshop or agency, lay or religious, in Paris. It was not obtainable at the Pontifical Pavilion.
The article in it is nothing very new. There are several long articles in French reviews of more or less the same class. They

are usually appreciative. In fact he has a great number of friends and admirers in that quarter too.

I am afraid I miss the point you raise about the Irish press. I can recall only an allusion or two to Mr J. among their files. I think they were about his eyesight and copied from the popular press of Gt.Br.

PS   Mr J gave me this Xmas no. for you which I add in as he thought it might interest you

Gerald Griffin to **Paul Léon**
Files of *Weekly Irish Times* kept in Dublin and in the British Museum annexe at Hendon, he received the copy of the Irish broadcast on Mr Joyce too late to make a reference to it in his book, *3 letters, letter dated 21 January 1938 endorsed with draft reply in Léon's hand*

21, 26 January, 20 April 1938

.43   **Michael Healy** in correspondence with **Paul Léon**
Payment for year's subscription to the *Irish Times* for Mr Joyce, *2 letters*

HEALY
3, 22 January 1934

Michael Healy to **Paul Léon**
Thanks for Léon's letter of 31 January and £4 enclosed, apologies for not replying sooner to Léon's letter of the 19 March, information on the book *Irish Flora*, encloses two copies of the *Register of Prohibited Publications* which Léon wrote for on the 17 August, acknowledges receipt of book, *4 letters, Healy's letter of 28 August annotated in Léon's hand:*
'With deep gratitude and affection from Nora and Jim
Sincerest sympathy Giorgio and Helen Joyce'

3 February, 10 April, 28 August 1934, 9 July 1935

.44   **Anna Herzog** to **[?James Joyce]**, *French*
Re visa for Hermann Broch, *4p*

HERZOG
9 July 1938

.45   **Olga [Howe]**, 32, Curzon Street, London W1 to **Paul Léon**
Asks Léon to induce James Joyce to give a manuscript or first edition for auction at a P.S. League charity auction under the auspices of the Queen, *with memorandum marked 'Private and Confidential' on proposed Evening Auction at Bridgewater House and leaflet on The Personal Service League (for assisting the unemployed with clothing in the distressed areas)*

HOWE
12 October 1933

19 November 1933

Paul Léon, Paris to **Olga [Howe]**
He could manage to have an inscribed copy of *Ulysses* sent to her as he is anxious to have sales of *Ulysses* recorded in England, neither he nor Mr Joyce has a first edition of *Ulysses*

HURST 6 November 1931

.46 **H.N. Hurst**, Box 44, Stellenborch, Cape Province, S. Africa to **James Joyce**
Would like the exact time of Joyce's birth on the 2 February 1882, he is interested in the relation of literature and astrology, gives the position of the planets on Joyce's birthday, *2p, annotated in Léon's hand: 'Excuse/ Born 6 a.m. in Dublin 2 Fev 1882/ Whos Who James Stephen/ copy of essay'*

27 April 1932

Paul Léon to **H.N. Hurst**
Mr Joyce begs to be excused for not having replied sooner owing to the death of his father and other worries and his intensive work, the exact date of his birth is 2 February 1882 at 6 o'clock in the morning, *Who is Who* gives the same date and place of birth for James Stephen, Mr Joyce would like a copy of Hurst's essay

INCOR- PORATED SOCIETY OF AUTHORS 24 April-25 May 1934

.47 **Paul Léon** and **James Joyce** in correspondence with **D. Kilham Roberts** and the **Incorporated Society of Authors, Playwrights and Composers**
Léon heard from Mr Allen Lane that the Society would like to have Mr Joyce as a member, Mr Joyce appreciated the leader in *The Author*, prospectus, subscription and application form, request from D. Kilham Roberts for a contribution by Joyce to an anthology and his apology for the fee offered, thanks for Mr Joyce's subscription to the Fighting Fund, *8 letters, with prospectus*

GUGGEN- HEIM 13 December 1935

.48 **John Simon Guggenheim Memorial Foundation/Henry Allen Moe**, 551 Fifth Avenue, New York to **James Joyce**
Robert M. McAlmon has given Mr Joyce as a referee in his application for a fellowship

JOLAS 23 July, 7, 28 August 1932

.49 **Maria Jolas**, 544 East 86th Street, New York to **Paul Léon**
Does not understand what was wrong with her check but the equivalent amount will be cabled next week so Mr Joyce can count on it; news of herself and Eugene, she spoke to Dr

Berman by telephone, Berman has not written to Mr Joyce and his plans to go to Europe are uncertain so Joyce should not wait for him in Paris, *Transition* is successful in America; Mr Joyce's letter reached them just in time for the September issue of *Transition, postcard and 2 letters, 5p*

Eugene Jolas, 9 Rue Borghèse, Neuilly-sur-Seine to **Paul Léon**   24 October 1932
Has a cold, apologizes for missing Léon, wants details of Japanese protest

Paul Léon to **Eugene Jolas**   17 October 1932
Jolas's letter misdated 24 October, has a cold himself, encloses a copy memorandum for the Japanese which he received from Mr Joyce this morning

Eugene Jolas, Modern Hotel, St Gervais-les-Bains, Hte Savoie to **James Joyce**   18 December 1933
Encloses letter from Thomas H. Ussell a New York publisher who wants to reprint part of *Work in Progress*, he was happy to hear of Woolsey's decision, he will certainly attend Joyce's *Bal de la Purée*, wishes them all a happy Christmas, *2 letters, 3p, endorsed with address of Michael Healy, 16 St Mary's Terrace, Taylor's Hill, Galway*

Maria Jolas, Utelle to **Paul Léon**   17 August [?1934]
Encloses documents to return to Joyce as she fears the Joyces may have left Spa, will Léon read her letter and see if what she advises is wise, Forel is an ass

Maria Jolas, Cherbourg to **Paul Léon**, *French*   [?November ?1935]
Cheques drawn on Paris and New York for Joyce, Léon should not let himself be discouraged in his friendship for Joyce who needs faithful friends, thanks to Léon and to Lucie for their care for her this long winter, *3p*

Maria Jolas, 'on board Cunard White Star', Cherbourg to **Mr and Mrs James Joyce**   28 November 1935
Thanks for telegram and best wishes for a pleasant evening

Maria Jolas, École Bilingue de Neuilly, 60, Rue Borghèse, Neuilly-sur-Seine to **Paul Léon**   15 May 1936
Encloses list of addresses which Mr Joyce asked her to forward to him, her husband sends his remembrances

29 December 1937	**Maria and Eugene Jolas**, [Feldkirch] to **Mr and Mrs James Joyce**, *picture postcard* Best wishes for the New Year
3 May 1939	**Eugene Jolas**, 58 rue Borghèse, Neuilly-sur-Seine to **James Joyce** He is in the midst of *Finnegans Wake*, sends his best wishes for its success
30 June [?1939]	**Maria Jolas**, [?Neuilly-sur Seine] to **James Joyce** She is leaving Paris apprehensive of what the summer may bring, wants Joyce and Mrs Joyce to know that she is a steadfast friend
JOYCE, George and Helen 15 March 1935	.50 **George and Helen Joyce**, 168 West 86th Street, New York to **James Joyce** Scenario of *Ulysses* proposed by Louis Zukofsky, thanks for music and songs, *2p*
20 September 1935	**George Joyce** to **James Joyce**, Hotel Savoy, Fontainebleau, *telegram* Sailing September 25
5 April 1938	**George Joyce**, Hotel Cameron, 41 West 86th Street, New York to **James and Nora Joyce** Thanks for getting hold of their propriétaire, Mme Vincent, Helen and Stephen are well, he had an audition at Columbia
[c. 1938]	[**?George Joyce** to **?James Joyce**], *copy telegram* Temporary address Park Lane Hotel doctors insist no cause for worry present separation best possible step conducive to recovery
JOYCE, John 3 June 1934	.51 **John Joyce**, Beach House, Beach Rd, Clacton-on-Sea to **James Joyce**, c/o George Joyce, 9 Rue Huysmans, Paris VIe He is Joyce's nephew, wants a job
JOYCE, Stanislaus 24 March 1937	.52 **Stanislaus Joyce**, Via Cesare Battisti, Trieste to **James Joyce** Sent Joyce three [presritz], his friend Finlayson copied Joyce's letters and was in direct correspondence with Gorman, refers to Oliver St John Gogarty's *As I was going down Sackville Street*, signed 'Stannie'

.53   **Dr. C.G. Jung**, Küsnacht-Zurich, Seestrasse 228 to **James Joyce**, Hotel Elite, Zurich, *copy letter, transcribed in Letters of James Joyce, Volume III, edited by Richard Ellmann, London, 1966. With issue of Europäische Revue, September 1932, containing article by Jung entitled 'Ulysses: ein Monolog', pp.547-68, annotated on front cover 'with the author's compliments'*

JUNG
[August 1932]

.54   **John P. Kaestlin**, The Union Society, Cambridge; St. John's College, Cambridge and Reform Club, Pall Mall, London to **James Joyce** and **Paul Léon**
He wishes to write an article on Joyce's poetry for a literary magazine in Cambridge entitled *Contemporaries and Makers* of which he is editor, arrangments to meet Léon, alterations he has made to his article resulting from Léon's criticisms, answers Léon's query about an article in the *Cambridge Review*, asks for Léon's help in getting a job, *7 letters, 17p*

KAESTLIN
March-November 1933, 26 April 1937

.55   **Robert Kastor** to **Mr and Mrs Giorgio Joyce**, 9 Rue Huysmans, Paris
Re contract for American edition of *Ulysses*, encloses letter from Cerf explaining changes to the original contract drawn up by James B. Pinker & Son and amended by Paul Léon, financial arrangements are exactly as Mr Joyce wished, every day's delay in signing jeopardizes Mr Joyce's rights in the U.S.A., *3p and copy letter enclosed, 4p*

KASTOR
23 March 1932

Paul Léon to **Robert Kastor**
Encloses contract and other documents, Mr Joyce asks that correspondence should be sent to Léon while he is away from Paris, money should be sent to Pinker, congratulations on successful termination of negotiations

5 April 1932

Robert Kastor to **Paul Léon**
Contracts etc have been delivered to Mr Cerf and check mailed to Mr Pinker

14 April 1932

Robert Kastor to **Paul Léon**
Bennett Cerf says he has written to Léon giving him the status of the trial on *Ulysses*, Cerf has a great deal invested in *Ulysses*, Kastor is strongly of the opinion that Mr Joyce should consent to the inclusion of the chart [showing parallels between

6 September, 8 November 1933

episodes in the *Odyssey* and *Ulysses*] in the American edition, *2 letters*

22 November 1933

Paul Léon to **Robert Kastor**
The chart is a piece of literary criticism which does not belong in the text of *Ulysses* itself, the introductory letter from Mr Joyce to Mr Cerf should suffice to authenticate the edition, suggests account of legal proceedings against *Ulysses* should be added to the text in order to compete with pirated editions

7 December 1933

Paul Léon to **Robert Kastor**
Has just received cable from Cerf containing good news about *Ulysses* case, thanks for Kastor's aid and help, *2 copies*

7 December 1933

Robert Kastor to **James Joyce**
Acknowledges Joyce's cable of thanks following victory in Federal Courts, encloses newspaper clippings

24 September 1934

Paul Léon to **Robert Kastor**
Asks Kastor to act as intermediary between Mr George Joyce and the film people in discussions about filming of *Ulysses*, Mr Joyce's views, Mr George Joyce has with him a scenario of *Anna Livia Plurabelle* written by Stuart Gilbert, *2p*

6, 15 October 1934

Robert Kastor to **Paul Léon**
Kastor and Mr Cerf think it will be difficult to sell the film rights of *Ulysses*, the movie magnates would hesitate to touch it because of campaign for 'cleaner pictures', encloses copy letters from two film companies, little interest in filming of *Anna Livia Plurabelle, with two copy letters enclosed*

23 October 1934

Paul Léon to **Robert Kastor**
He had in mind the definite proposal that had been made for the filming of *Ulysses*, Mr Joyce would not be pleased if he knew that *Ulysses* had been circulated on the market

26 February 1935

Seymour Stern, Hollywood, California to **Robert Kastor**, *copy letter*
Apologizes for failure to answer Kastor's letters of 29 December and 11 February, there is no possibility of getting the scenario of *Anna Livia Plurabelle* produced as a film

GENERAL CORRESPONDENCE

Robert Kastor to **James Joyce**   9 June 1939
Encloses newspaper clippings re sentence of Eric S. Pinker,
happy to hear of Giorgio's opportunity at the B.B.C., their
anxiety about Helen's progress

Robert Kastor to **Paul Léon**   14 February
Does Léon have marriage contract between Helen and George   1940

.56   **Sydney Kellner**, New York to **Shakespeare & Company**   KELLNER
He is compiling a bibliography of James Joyce   23 June 1932

.57   **Dr Alfred Kerr**, 3, rue de Villejust, Paris to **James Joyce**   KERR
Reminds 'Maître Joyce' of their conversation a few months ago   15 November
in Rue Galilée, encloses clipping about *Ulysses* from *Figaro* and   1934
asks if there is an abridged edition of *Ulysses* available in
England, *with newsclipping enclosed*

.58   **Koninklijk Kabinet van Schilderijen (Mauritshuis Musée**   KONINKLIJK
Royal de Tableaux) to **James Joyce**, *French*   KABINET VAN
In reply to Mr Joyce's letter the Museum does not sell   SCHILD-
photographs of Vincent Van Gogh   ERIJEN
                                                                 13 August 1935

.59   **Paul Léon** in correspondence with **Harold J. Laski**   LASKI
Attempt to get Sir Frederick Pollock's opinion on *Ulysses* which   14, 20
Sir Frederick feels too old to do   November
                                                                 1934

Harold J. Laski, London School of Economics and Political   5 May 1938, 10
Science, to **Paul Léon**   July 1939
Query re Warburton, will send letter to Léon for transmission
to Levy-Bruhl, plans to go to Paris, cannot discover any volume
on medieval civilisation by anyone named Laistner, *2 letters*

.60   **Alexis Léon** to **Paul Léon**, *picture postcard of Utelle*   LÉON, Alexis
Thanks for letter, he wanted to earn money to buy stamps   [1935]

.61   **Lucie Léon,** Bonville Hotel, Eype, Dorset Coast to **Paul**   LÉON, Lucie
Léon, *Russian*   [c. August
She is leading a vegetable life, told Alexis off, Léon should stay   1938]

107

as long as he can in Lausanne or St Palais, sends her regards to the Joyces

Lucie Léon to **Paul Léon**, *picture postcard of Dieppe, Russian*
She is resting, they [the Joyces?] are taking good care of her

.62   **James Joyce**, 42 rue Galilée, Paris VIII to **W.K. Magee**, *carbon typescript unsigned*

Dear Magee,

I am writing to know whether you can give me any information about George Moore's funeral. I read your name in the list of mourners published in the *Morning Post* but apparently no other man of letters was either present or represented and none of his Irish friends and colleagues seems to have taken any part in the proceedings. As you know I made the acquaintance of George Moore only a few years before his death and I hope that I behaved towards him during the three or four visits I paid him with the respect due to his age personality and achievements. At his suggestion I tried here to have his *Aphrodite in Aulis* translated into French. I spoke to my own publisher here and also to Louis Gillet, the litterary [sic] editor of the *Revue des Deux Mondes* and a friend of Moore's and also to the principal French translator of *Ulysses* an old friend of mine and an excellent English scholar. But all this was of no avail, and the time of crisis was also unfavourable to a limited *de-luxe* edition which seemed the only solution. Of course I was unable to be present at the funeral but on learning of his death I telephoned to London and had a large chaplet wreath of cistapala and burberry leaves green and brown mixed with an inscription to him and my name. It seems strange that although this was sent to his house long before the funeral no mention of it is made among the floral tributes cited by the press. It has been suggested to me that this list was handed to the press by his family who.... and finish the sentence for yourself. I know nothing about his family and care less. I simply wished to pay a tribute to his memory; perhaps you can enlighten me.

I hope all is well with you and yours. Since I saw you I have become a grandfather. A little poem by me appeared in the December *Criterion* and if you care to see it I will send it to you.

With best wishes and kind remembrance
sincerely yours.

C.D. Medley, Field Roscoe & Co., 36, Lincolns Inn Fields, London to **W.K. Magee**, 14 Leigham Vale Road, Bournemouth, Hants.
Received his letter and the letter from Mr James Joyce which he enclosed, sorry that Mr Joyce did not receive any acknowledgement of his wreath, agrees with Mr Joyce that the attendance of literary men at the funeral was very disappointing only Charles Morgan and David Garnett being there, *2p*

9 February 1933

C.D. Medley, Field Roscoe & Co., 36, Lincolns Inn Fields, London to **James Joyce**
Mr Magee sent him Joyce's letter about George Moore's funeral, regrets that Mr Joyce did not receive any acknowledgement of the noble wreath he sent, a good many artists attended the funeral but no literary men apart from Mr Magee, Charles Morgan and David Garnett, *2p*

10 February 1933

Paul Léon to **W.K. Magee**, c/o Messrs Macmillan & Co, London
Mr Joyce wants Magee's private address in Bournemouth as he wants to send him something

18 November 1936

.63 **Sherry Mangan, The March of Time**, London to **Paul Léon**
Sorry he could not see Mr Joyce before he left Paris, thank Mr Joyce for his gift of the Chaucer *A.B.C.*

MANGAN/ MARCH OF TIME 20 June 1939

.64 **Henri Matisse**, Hotel Lutétia, 43 Boulevard Raspail, Paris to **James Joyce**, *French*
He has finished the illustrations for *Ulysses*, he would like to know what Joyce's reaction is to his work, he hopes to meet him soon

MATISSE 30 November 1934

.65 **Dr Heinrich Meng**, Basel to **James Joyce**, *German*
Will Mr Joyce let him know if he will join the Freud committee

MENG 29 February 1936

MERCANTON
15 October
1935

.66   **Jacques Mercanton**, Hôtel Dacia, Boul. St Michel 41, Paris to **James Joyce**, *French*
He is writing to Mr Joyce on the advice of Miss Sylvia Beach to whom he has confided his wish to make some studies of Mr Joyce's work which he would like to make known in French Switzerland, he would like to discuss *Work in Progress* with Mr Joyce, *2p*

14 February
1937[?8]

Jacques Mercanton, Primerosa, Lausanne to **James Joyce**, *French*
Thanks for the hours Mr Joyce allowed Mercanton to spend with him in Lausanne and for the newspapers he gave him, *2p*

4, 14 March
1938

Jacques Mercanton, Primerosa, Lausanne to **Paul Léon**, *French*
Has received Léon's letter, asks Léon to tell Mr Joyce that he will receive twelve copies of the newspaper with the article on Miss Joyce's book at the beginning of next week, the Hôtel Elite of Zurich should have sent on his letter of thanks to Mr Joyce for the newspaper containing his article, sorry he missed Léon whose telephone message was wrongly transmitted; asks Léon to make his excuses to Mr Joyce for the delay in sending the newspapers, *2 letters, 4p*

16 August
1938

Jacques Mercanton, Lausanne to **Paul Léon**, *French*
Thanks for the Irish newspaper Léon sent him quoting the name of Mr Joyce, the terms available at the Hôtel de la Paix, he would like to make a window display in a bookshop in the town of the works of Mr Joyce to coincide with the publication of *Work in Progress*

10 March, 11,
25 April, 1, 3,
31 May, 4 June
1939

Jacques Mercanton, Via della Robbia 56, Florence to **Paul Léon**, *French*
Article he has written on *Finnegans Wake* to be offered to Jean Paulhan of the *Nouvelle Revue Française*, the second part of it to be edited and offered to M. Thiébaut of the *Revue de Paris*, thanks for Léon's hospitality in Paris, hopes Mr Joyce has settled in the Rue des Vignes, asks Léon to send a copy of the song 'Finnegans Wake', Thiébaut rejected his article, would Mr Joyce like to glance at his article on *Ulysses* and *Don Quixote*, *6 letters and 1 postcard, 8p, with article entitled 'Ulysse et Don Quichotte', signed 'Jacques Mercanton, Janvier 1938/9'and letter of rejection from M. Thiébaut*

Jacques Mercanton, Via della Robbia 56, Florence to **James Joyce,** *French*   23 June 1939

Thanks for the newscutting of the song 'Finnegans Wake', he does not know what would be its French equivalent, praises *Finnegans Wake*, he is still trying to get the second part of his article published, has Joyce any plans which will bring him to Switzerland this summer

Jacques Mercanton, Via Leopardi 17, Viareggio to **Paul Léon**,   30 June 1939
French

Léon's letter has reached him, he wrote immediately to Francini in Florence, he will copy the song for M. Gillet, thanks for Léon's efforts on behalf of his article

.67   **Myrsine Moschos**, Hôtel Morot et de Genève, Dijon to   MOSCHOS
Paul Léon   7 October
Recommends the medical establishment of Dr Richard   1934

.68   **J. Mullany**, Fair Green, Dundalk, Ireland to **James Joyce**   MULLANY
Encloses cutting re John Sullivan *[not enclosed]*, news of his   9 March 1938
family, wants Mr Joyce's recommendation for a job, *endorsed in hand of James Joyce 'ring me up re this. The paper is for Giorgio' and notes of draft reply in hand of Paul Léon*

.69   **Paul Léon** to **The National Geographic Magazine**, The   NATIONAL
National Geographic Society, Washington   GEO-
Their subscriber Mrs James Joyce asks whether they have   GRAPHIC
published an article on the life of the natives in the Bismarck   MAGAZINE
Archipelago and in the Solomon Islands, if so will they send it to   6 June 1938
her, *with circulars inviting James Joyce to become a member of the Society*

.70   **Paul Léon** to **Harold Nicolson**, 4, King's Bench Walk,   NICOLSON
Temple, London   21 August
Sends report published in *New York Herald Tribune* of decision   1934
in favour of Mr Joyce against the U.S. government appeal re
Ulysses, it may carry weight in Great Britain, asks Nicolson to
give a written statement of his experience with the B.B.C. when
they gave way to his insistence on lecturing on *Ulysses* and
permission to use the statement

24 August
1934

Harold Nicolson, Sissinghurst Castle, Kent to **Paul Léon**
Advises against publicity, it would be better to attempt private persuasion at the Home Office, the B.B.C. incident would not be of much value, offers to interview the Home Office privately, *2p*

Ó FAOLÁIN
1 December
1936

.71 **Seán Ó Faoláin**, Killough House, Kilmacanogue, Co Wicklow to **James Joyce**
Asks for three poems for three guineas for inclusion in an anthology of Irish verse mainly for schools

O'SULLIVAN
[Easter,
1935]

.72 **Seán O'Sullivan**, [Paris] to **James Joyce**, *postcard*
Mr Con Curran of Dublin is anxious to have a drawing of Joyce, asks to call on Joyce when Joyce returns on Saturday, a drawing would take about an hour, *annotated in Léon's hand 'To be back middle of next week'*

[1935]

Seán O'Sullivan, 51 Talbot Road, Bayswater, London to **James Joyce**
Asks for a sitting, *2p*

15 August
1935

[Seán O']Sullivan, 4 Monmouth Place, London to **James Joyce**, *telegram*
COULD YOU SIT FOR DRAWING WEEKEND IF I COME OVER

[1935]

Seán O'Sullivan, 18B Sydney House, Sydney Parade Ave, Sandymount, Dublin to **Mrs Joyce**
Thanks for her hospitality and the delightful evening spent with her husband and M. Léon, *endorsed with annotations in hand of Paul Léon*

PARTRIDGE
2, 13 July, 22
September
1934, 11 July
1935

.73 **Robert Partridge**, Librarian, Passmore Edwards Public Library, 236 Kingsland Road, London to **James Joyce** and **Paul Léon**
Asks Joyce to autograph his copy of *Ulysses* for use in an exhibition, delighted that Mr Joyce will present the library with an autographed copy of *Ulysses*, thanks for gift, would also like *Et tu, Healy, The Day of the Rabblement* and musical programme linking Joyce's name with that of John McCormack

.74 **Georges Pelorson**, 8 bis Boulevard de Courcelles, Paris to **James Joyce**, *French*
Marcel Thiébaut of the *Revue de Paris* has asked him to write an article on *Finnegans Wake*, could he see Joyce about it or perhaps have dinner with the Joyces and the Jolases

PELORSON
4 July 1939

.75 **Antonio Aita, P.E.N. Club de Buenos Aires** to **James Joyce**
Invitation to the Fourteenth International Congress of P.E.N., *with reply from Paul Léon on behalf of James Joyce refusing, 2 letters*

P.E.N.
24 March, 10 August 1936

Henri Membré, Quinzième Congrès Internationale de la Fédération P.E.N., Paris to **James Joyce**, *French*
Thanks Joyce for accepting the invitation to the Congress, asks him also to join the three day visit to Chartres and the castles of the Loire

8 June 1937

.76 **Paul Perles**, Vienna to **James Joyce**
Mr Brauchbar of Zurich has told him Mr Joyce will help them to go to America, answers Mr Joyce's questions

PERLES
29 May 1938

.77 **Peter A. Pertzoff** to **Sylvia Beach** and **James Joyce**
Bibliographical queries, sends a copy of his thesis, *2 letters*

PERTZOFF
11 November 1932, 6 June 1933

.78 **Armand M. Petitjean,** Les Vallières to **[Sylvia Beach]**
Introduces himself, he is nearly 20, he wants to meet Mr Joyce, *2p*

PETITJEAN
23 April 1933

Armand M. Petitjean, Les Vallières to **James Joyce**
Does not see why Mr Joyce should deny him the right of speaking to him

24 October [1933]

Armand M. Petitjean writing from various addresses to **Paul Léon**, *French*
His efforts to secure publication of his essay on the significance of Joyce in *The Criterion* and elsewhere, *2 letters and 1 card*

27 January, 26 March, 23 July [193?]

Armand M. Petitjean, Las Palmas, Canary Islands to **[?James Joyce]**, *picture postcard of Roque Benlaiga, Gran Canaria*
'In the country of the Canaris, the sweetie tirds'...quotes Apollinaire

6 August [193?]

PORGET,
30 August
1938

.79   **[Suzy M. Porget]** to **Paul Léon**, *French*
Letter of thanks for book dedicated to her by Mr Joyce

POUND
*[postmark
unclear '-33 -
2.17']*

.80   **Ezra Pound**, [Rapallo] to **James Joyce**, 2 Avenue St Philibert, Paris, *postcard, typed*
Dear but eternally naive Jhamez: DO you suppose those young men ASKED me whether I wd. be a consultant or whatever "edtr"? I imagine they are too young to KNOW who infamied before they left college. However I am forwarding 'em yr/ opinion. They have obliged me by eliminating other putrid matter, and perhaps will not again open their pages to S.R. (than who no one cd/ be more fitting as commenter on Shaw and Harris.

Yr interpretation of my interpretation of the term "morality" is hightly incorrect. I was considering things of the spirit, not LOW questions of commerce. Besides/ what evidence have we that the Irish OUGHT to be moral?

The convegno is by the way one of my particular abominations/

AND so forth. Rossi, as I indicated in p/s is quite simpatico, but there is NO cash in these transactions.

Lebwohl

[Signed] E.P.

28 April 1933

Farrar & Rinehart to **James Joyce**
They send copies of Ezra Pound's *A Draft of XXX Cantos* and *The Cantos of Ezra Pound*

14 April
[1935-39]

Ezra Pound, Hotel Italia, Via 4 Fontane, ROMA to **James Joyce**. 7 rue Edmond Valentin, Paris
Eminent Illustrious & Egrigious = [vita] focundus ac potens.

Thanks for noble effort to enlighten the Florentine seignory =.

[Zumattez ou act Cauda] has already asked me to stand on me head in his tent at the coming Tuscan circus. Do you think the Pod. wd. lend me a high hat & suitable regalia for the occasion.

Love to Nora

ever

E.P.

PRESCOTT
26 April 1936

.81   **Joseph Prescott** to **James Joyce**
Asks if he may write to Mr Joyce about a problem

.82 **Thomas W. Pugh**, 6 Churchill Terrace, Ballsbridge, Dublin to **James Joyce**
Encloses photos *[not enclosed]*, thanks Mr Joyce for the copy of *The Mime of Mick, Nick and the Maggies*, details of the photographs

PUGH
23 August
1934

.83 **France Raphael**, Paris to **Paul Léon** and **James Joyce**, *French*
Payments due to her, *5 letters, with receipt dated 22 November 1934*

RAPHAEL
11 April-6
November
1935

.84 **Kenneth Reddin**, 21 Upper Fitzwilliam Street, Dublin to **James Joyce**,
Reminds Mr Joyce of the days when he and Paddy Tuohy used to call to 2 Square Robiac, asks Mr Joyce to accept a copy of his novel *Somewhere to the Sea*, congratulations on completion of *Work in Progress, letter and postcard*

REDDIN
3 March
1936, 11 May
1939

.85 **Paul Léon** to **H. Romanova**, Literature of the World Revolution, Central Post Office Box 850, Moscow, *typescript unsigned, transcribed in James Joyce by Richard Ellmann, Oxford University Press, 1982, p.630. With copy of letter to which this is a reply written in pencil in hand of Paul Léon*

ROMANOVA
[late
September
1932]

.86 **Royal Academy Illustrated** to **James Joyce**
Offers copy of reproduction of Mr Joyce's portrait published in the *Royal Academy Illustrated*

ROYAL
ACADEMY
ILLUS-
TRATED
20 June 1935

.87 **N.H. Rubin**, New York to **Shakespeare and Company** and **James Joyce**
He has written a book called *Brick and Mortar: Index Studies in the Form and Development of Joyce's Ulysses, 2 letters*

RUBIN
24 February,
24 March
1932

.88 **John Louis Rushton**, 4 Ashdell Road, Broomhill, Yorks, England to **James Joyce**
Came across a poem on *The Liffey: a fable* (1726) in the Bodleian, hopes to hear directly from Joyce about *Work in Progress*

RUSHTON
30 May 1932

RUSSELL
[c. 1933]

.89   **Vera [Russell]** to **Paul Léon**
Tyrone Guthrie would like an introduction to James Joyce

SCHAUREK
12, 27
January 1932

.90   **Paul Léon** to **Eileen Schaurek**
Encloses copy of her late father's will, James Joyce wishes to
know what papers etc were left by his father in addition to
enclosed list of books and insurance policy, Mr James Joyce
wishes to inform her that there are no cemetery papers in Paris
with regard to the late John Joyce, *2 letters*

12 March
1935

Eileen Schaurek, London to **James Joyce**, rue Edmond
Valentin, Paris, *telegram*
HAVE LEFT MASCOT PLEASE SEND MONEY CARE MISS
WEAVER WRITING

c.20 March
1935

Eileen Schaurek to **James Joyce**
Received money, Lucia is enjoying Bray with Boshenska and
Nora, Eileen will leave them alone for a little, Lucia left two
hotels, the Gresham and Buswells in Kildare Street which
Eileen booked because Lucia wanted to be near the College of
Art, [part of letter missing], Lucia wants to go to Galway

21 December
1937

Paul Léon to **Eileen Schaurek**, 118 Pembroke Road, Dublin
Encloses £2 from Mr Joyce with best Xmas wishes, Mr Joyce
asked him to add that whenever letters come from his family in
Dublin it causes trouble here

14
September
1938

Eileen Schaurek, 32 Claude Rd, Drumcondra to **James Joyce**,
27 Rue Casimer[sic]-Périer VIIe, Paris
Thanks for remittances, would like a copy of *transition*, hopes
war not likely, Isobel Murray has married again

SHERIDAN
2 May 1939

.91   **Niall Sheridan**, 21 Herbert Place, Dublin to **James Joyce**
Thanks for suggesting to M. Jolas that he should send Sheridan
an article referring to Sterne, his friend Nolan is flattered at Mr
Joyce's interest in his book, he has informed Mr Curran of Mr
Joyce's new address, thanks for receiving him in Paris, *3p*

SKEFFING-
TON

.92   **Hanna Sheehy Skeffington** to **James Joyce**
Encloses petition about the dismissal of a teacher by his clerical

manager because of his political views, news of her family, *2p,* *with enclosed petition for signature and typescript 'Some facts about the Frank Edwards case'*

.93   **Philippe Soupault** to **James Joyce**, *picture postcard*
He has received nothing from M. Byrne

.94   **Theodore Spencer**, E.11 Eliot House, Cambridge, Mass. to **James Joyce**
The Harvard College Library has recently bought pp. 521-902 of the manuscript first draft of *Portrait of the Artist as a Young Man*, asks permission to write for publication a critical account of the manuscript comparing it with the published version, *3p, endorsed in hand of Paul Léon with pencilled draft reply*

Paul Léon to **Theodore Spencer**
The manuscript first draft of *Portrait of the Artist as a Young Man* has been sold in lots to different institutions in the United States, Mr Joyce did not foresee this when he made a presentation of it, he does not regard the publication of these varied lots in America with much enthusiasm

David Fleischman, Claverly 43, Cambridge, Mass. to **Paul Léon**
Writes on behalf of Theodore Spencer who wants to know can he quote from the manuscript in a critical essay he is writing, he does not want to publish the whole fragment

.95   **Paul Léon** to **James Stephens**, Eversleigh, Queen's Walk, Kingsbury, London
Mr Joyce has asked him to forward the enclosed letter from Albatross Editions and ask Stephen what he is to reply to Mr Wegner

.96   **B.F. Stevens & Brown Ltd**, New Ruskin House, 8-30 Little Russell Street, London to **James Joyce** and **Paul Léon**
They are seeking copies of all the press notices which have appeared in connection with the republication of *Ulysses* on behalf of Judge John M. Woolsey, *2 letters*

STUART
8 June 1939

.97 **Michael Stuart**, 1425 Taylor Street, San Francisco, California to **James Joyce**
Mr Joyce's letter made them happy and not a little sad, praises *Finnegans Wake*, invites Mr Joyce to San Francisco

SULLIVAN/
PUTNAM'S
6 March 1933

.98 **G.P. Putnam's Sons Ltd**, London, W.C.2 to **James Joyce**, Hotel Lord Byron, Champs Elysees, Paris
Asks for reply to letter of 20 January asking in what role Mr Joyce suggested having a picture of Sullivan for Kobbé's *Opera Book*

14 March
1933

J. Sullivan to **Paul Léon**
Encloses photograph, hopes to have better news of Mr Joyce's health

17 March
1933

Paul Léon to **G.P. Putnam's Sons Ltd**
Mr Joyce has been very indisposed, encloses photograph of Mr Sullivan furnished by Mrs Sullivan who says she has already furnished it twice

11 July 1933

G.P. Putnam's Sons Ltd to **Paul Léon**
Encloses portrait of Mr Sullivan as Eleazar, *with two photographs of Sullivan as Eleazar*

July 1934

Marguerite Sullivan to **Paul Léon**
Asks Léon to inform Madame Joyce of her new address

18 January
1935

[Maurice Lambert to **Monsieur Dadechkeliani]**
Mlle Sullivan's rent has not been paid, will he intervene to rectify the situation

SZILAGYI-
FISCHER
21 January
1933

.99 **Agatha Szilagyi-Fischer** to **James Joyce**
Why did Joyce choose a Hungarian Jew as hero of *Ulysses*, *with reply from Léon referring her to Stuart Gilbert's book, 2 letters*

THOMPSON
20 December
1934

.100 **John Hinsdale Thompson**, Grosse Pointe, Michigan to **James Joyce**
He has acquired the manuscript of Joyce's translation of Gerhart Hauptmann's play *Before Sunrise*, asks permission to publish it, *endorsed in hand of James Joyce 'this should be stopped at once. The translations I made of 2 of H's plays, this and Michael*

Kramer, were simply exercises to learn German. They have no value as translations at all. I made the translations because these plays were then untranslated and I wanted to read them. One of my family in Dublin must have sold the copybooks I left there in 1904. H. would have a fit if they were published too.'

Paul Léon to **John Hinsdale Thompson**
Mr Joyce's translation of two plays by Hauptman was done 30 years ago and has no literary value, Mr Joyce is absolutely opposed to any idea of publication, he wonders how this manuscript reached the market and suspects indiscretion

14 January 1935

John H. Thompson, *Signatures*, 3153 Union Guardian Building, Detroit, Michigan to **James Joyce**
Refers to his letter of two years ago about the translation by Joyce of *Before Sunrise* in his possession, he would now like to return it to Mr Joyce

21 October 1936

Paul Léon to **John Thompson**
Mr Joyce would be glad to receive back the translation done when he was beginning to study German, he will inscribe a copy of any available edition of his books which Mr Thompson might like in return

4 November 1936

John Thompson to **Paul Léon**
The Hauptmann translation represented an investment of several hundred dollars, encloses a list of Mr Joyce's works which he lacks

16 November 1936

.101   **Robert Valançay**, 34 Rue Lucien Jeannin, La Garenne to **James Joyce**
Following their telephone conversation he wishes to give Mr Joyce details of his meeting with John O'Sullivan who gave him Mr Joyce's address and said that Mr Joyce would autograph a copy of *Ulysses* for him, he did not realise that Mr Joyce did not give dedications as a matter of principle

VALANÇAY 5 May 1932

.102   **Dr D.G. van der Vat**, Corfstraat 5, Alkmaar, Holland to **James Joyce**
Thanks for advance copy of *Finnegans Wake*, hopes to publish an article on it in the near future

VAN DER VAT 29 April 1939

VITRAC
30 December
1932

.103　**Paul Léon** to **Roger Vitrac**, *French*
Mr Joyce heard from Mr Jolas that Vitrac was looking for a photograph of Mr Joyce to use in a review, at Mr Joyce's request Léon will lend a photograph in his possession, there is no question of a sequel to the translation of a passage of *A.L.P.* as the seven translators are dispersed, Mr Soupault who was the driving force behind the translation is in America, Vitrac may choose any article he likes to dedicate to Mr Joyce, probably one written by someone outside Mr Joyce's immediate circle would be best, Mr Joyce greatly admired an article on the interior monologue by Daniel Rops, something along those lines would be best

VOGT
9 March 1933

.104　**C. Vogt**, Zurich to **[James Joyce]**
Thanks for copy of *Pomes Penyeach*

WALKER
25 October
1935

.105　**William J. Walker**, 423 State Street, Albany, New York to **James Joyce**
It was a great pleasure for him to have had an interesting chat with Mr Joyce on the Le Havre-Paris train of the 2 October, the results of his investigation of the reasons for the extra fare and slower time of the special train of which they both complained, quotes a letter from *Time* magazine about the origin of the term 'G-Men', perhaps Mr Joyce will divulge where he found or how he evolved the term, hopes Mrs Joyce and himself are well, it was a delight to have visited them and when he sees Padraic Colum he will tell Joyce about their chat, *with card bearing photograph and legend 'William J. Walker Globe Trotter is now available for the following humourous travel talks illustrated by fine motion pictures: 'Everywhere in France'...'*

WILSON
21 November
1932, 6 April
1933, 18
December
1936

.106　**Charles Wilson**, Watling Villa, Willington, Co. Durham, England to **James Joyce**
Invites Joyce to Willington, thanks him for his offer to sign books but asks him instead to sign cards for insertion into books, asks for contribution to charity dinners, *3 letters, with signed photograph of Wilson and printed account of Treat Fund for Children of the Unemployed & Orphans of Willington*

.107 **Heinrich Zimmer**, Heidelberg, Bergstrasse 147 and 3 Bevington Road, Oxford to **[?James Joyce]**
Hopes the Celtic philology of his father who did the paper about Finn will compensate for the pidgin English of the son who did the commentary, thanks Mr Joyce for his intention of presenting him with a copy of his book

ZIMMER
5 September 1938, 16 April 1939

.108 **Stefan Zweig**, 11 Portland Place, London to **James Joyce**
Asks Mr Joyce to join a committee to prepare an open letter to Sigmund Freud to mark his eightieth birthday, praises Hermann Broch's essay on Mr Joyce

ZWEIG
25 February 1936

.109 **Paul Léon** to **[?]**
Answer to enquiry giving information about editions of Mr Joyce's poems, the next issue of *transition* and Mr Joyce's birthday

UNIDEN-TIFIED
3 March 1932

.110 **[?]**, 22 Avenue Mozart to **Paul Léon**
Thanks for [?] given on behalf of James Joyce, *illegible*

4 October 1933

.111 **[signature illegible]**, Salle des Professeurs, Université de Strasbourg to **Paul Léon**, *Russian*
No need for intervention with the Ministry of Culture, message for Lévy-Bruhl, *2p*

6 May 1937

4.

GENERAL CORRESPONDENCE: MISCELLANEOUS

Miscellaneous letters mainly from admirers, students, book collectors and autograph hunters arranged in chronological order, *100 letters with enclosures.*

1932–1937

5.

BUSINESS CORRESPONDENCE: JOYCE'S SOLICITORS, MONRO SAW & CO, AND HIS AGENTS, PINKERS

.1   MONRO SAW & CO IN CORRESPONDENCE WITH JAMES JOYCE AND PAUL LÉON, 562 letters with enclosures, 1928-40

2 January 1928,	**Monro Saw & Co** to **James Joyce** Arrangements for payment of dividends and fees
15, 19 January 1929	**Monro Saw & Co** to **James Joyce** Sale of stock
30 September 1931	**Monro Saw & Co** to **James Joyce** Encloses copies of firm's letters to Dr Rothschild and money draft for monthly payment less miscellaneous costs including costs for drawing up will
1 April 1932	**Monro Saw & Co** to **James Joyce** Encloses annual account
18, 26 April 1932	**James Joyce**, Hôtel Belmont, 30 rue Bassano, Paris to **Monro Saw & Co**, *carbon typescripts, unsigned* Asks that money from Pinker should be forwarded to Paris, his agent pays British income tax when it is due, he is domiciled in England though he doubts whether the condition of his daughter's health will allow him to continue that domicile, *2 letters*
27 April 1932	**Monro Saw & Co** to **James Joyce** Re British income tax, remittance
9 May 1932	**Paul Léon**, Paris to Messrs **Monro Saw & Co** At Mr Joyce's wish Léon sends a copy of a letter which he sent to Messrs Pinker re an English or Colonial edition of *Ulysses*, Mr Joyce finds his agent careless in the handling of his affairs for example the negotiations with Miss Beach were left to Mr Joyce

himself and his son, if Mr Joyce terminated his contract with Pinker would Pinker still be entitled to collect Mr Joyce's royalties and draw commission, the negotiations re *Work in Progress* with Faber and Faber and the Viking Press were conducted by Mr Joyce himself, the firm of Pinker have done practically nothing for him though he finds the young manager Ralph Pinker personally sympathetic

Monro Saw & Co to **Paul Léon**   11 May 1932
On what terms did Pinker & Sons make sales of Mr Joyce's works

Paul Léon to **Monro Saw & Co**   17 May 1932
Pinker & Son concluded contracts on the basis of royalties for Mr Joyce with Jonathan Cape, Random House, Faber & Faber and Viking Press, bills for London flat

Monro Saw & Co to **Paul Léon** and **James Joyce**   18, 25, 30 May 1932
Should Pinker's contract be determined they would still be entitled to commission on royalties, bills for London flat, *3 letters with enclosures*

Paul Léon to **Monro Saw & Co**   7, 14 July 1932
Mr Joyce's address in Zurich, encloses Mr Joyce's certificate of existence, Mr Joyce wants to know the exact amount of the war loan held by him, seeks reply to letter of 7th

Monro Saw & Co to **Paul Léon**   18 July, 25 October, 1 November 1932
Encloses copy of letter they sent to Mr Joyce on 11 July, urgent that Mr Joyce should communicate with the Public Trustee, sale of stock, encloses money draft, *4 letters*

Paul Léon to **Monro Saw & Co**   12 November 1932
Mr Joyce wishes to give up his London flat

Monro Saw & Co to **Paul Léon** and **James Joyce**   15, 18 November, 1 December 1932
Terms of the lease of Mr Joyce's London flat, sale of stock, monthly draft, asks for Mr Joyce's authorisation to take instructions from Paul Léon, *4 letters*

James Joyce, 42 rue Galilée, Paris XVI to **Monro Saw & Co**,   6 December 1932
carbon typescript unsigned
Acknowledges receipt of his monthly cheque and authorises

Monro Saw & Co to follow instructions and queries addressed to them by Paul Léon on Joyce's behalf

14, 16 December 1932

Monro Saw & Co to **James Joyce**
Encloses money drafts on instructions of Miss Weaver and contract note for sale of Johannesburg stock

27 December 1932

Paul Léon to **Monro Saw & Co**
Mr Joyce wishes to receive his monthly remittance by Friday the 30th instead of Monday the 2nd

28 December 1932, 2 January 1933

Monro Saw & Co to **Paul Léon** and **James Joyce**
Rent from new tenant of Mr Joyce's London flat at Camden Grove to be paid to them, Mrs Saks an unsatisfactory tenant

6 January - 2 October 1933

Monro Saw & Co in correspondence with **Paul Léon** and **James Joyce**
Routine correspondence re monthly payments, sale of stock, forwarding of money to Mr Joyce, *34 letters with enclosures*

19, 23 October 1933

Paul Léon to **Monro Saw & Co**
Mr Joyce has asked him to send enclosed opinions from four doctors re his daughter's health to be kept with the opinion of Dr Coudert and to have translations made of them, Mr Joyce wants the medical certificates to be collected and held in order to dispel any doubt as to why he abandoned his residence in England, Mr Joyce wants to sell a further £100, *3 letters*

21 October - 1 November 1933

Monro Saw & Co to **Paul Léon** and **James Joyce**
Routine acknowledgements and correspondence re sale of stock, *4 letters with enclosure*

3 - 14 November 1933

Monro Saw & Co in correspondence with **Paul Léon**
Mr Monro will see the persons who wrote to the Shakespeare Press about *Ulysses*, the Private Subscription Book Club, encloses copy of undertaking by Edward S. Hylems, Private Subscription Book Club, 2, Amen Corner, London not to print an edition of *Ulysses* without the written consent of James Joyce, *8 letters*

14 - 17 November 1933

Monro Saw & Co in correspondence with **Paul Léon** and **James Joyce**
Re sale of stock, *4 letters*

124

Paul Léon in correspondence with **Monro Saw & Co**
What is Mr Joyce's legal right to *Ulysses* in England, two
partners of Faber & Faber discussed the matter with Mr Joyce
for six hours but could not reach a conclusion; opinions of
Counsel the Hon. S.O. Henn Collins K.C. and copy letter from
T.S. Eliot of Faber & Faber about the copyright of *Ulysses* and
the legal basis for its seizure by customs, *6 letters, with enclosed
opinions and copy letter of T.S. Eliot*

19 November
- 5 December
1933

Paul Léon to **Monro Saw & Co**
Léon's interpretation of Collins's opinion, publishing history
of *Ulysses*, Mr Pinker does not seem to be sufficiently interested
in bringing out a British edition of *Ulysses*, criticises Faber's
method of procedure, Mr Joyce may issue a British edition
himself, *3p, 2 copies*

7 December
1933

Monro Saw & Co to **Paul Léon**
Léon's interpretation of Collins's opinion is correct, encloses
copy of letter sent to Faber, obliged for copy of Léon's letter to
Pinker, *2 letters with enclosure*

13, 14
December
1933

Paul Léon in correspondence with **Monro Saw & Co**
Re interest of Miss Beach and Shakespeare & Co in the
copyright of *Ulysses*, further opinion of Mr Henn Collins, sale of
stock, *8 letters*

18 - 22
December
1933

Monro Saw & Co to **Paul Léon**
Letter enclosing Mr Joyce's monthly income payment, *endorsed
with pencilled draft of letter by Paul Léon to Harriet Weaver of 9
January 1934, see p. 48*

1 January
1934

Paul Léon to **Monro Saw & Co**
Encloses John Lane's offer for a British edition of *Ulysses*,
acknowledges receipt of second opinion of Mr Henn Collins
and will try to obtain necessary document from Miss Beach

3 January
1934

Monro Saw & Co in correspondence with **Paul Léon**
Routine correspondence re sale of stock, payments, Mr Joyce's
accounts, includes references to negotiations with John Lane,
13 letters

5 - 27 January
1934

Paul Léon to **Monro Saw & Co**
Encloses contract between Mr Joyce and John Lane for the

28 January
1934

option and eventual publication of *Ulysses* in England, he has changed one of the clauses in order to prevent the publication of a cheap edition before three years elapse

29 January - 9 May 1934	**Monro Saw & Co** in correspondence with **Paul Léon** Routine correspondence re sale of stock, monthly payments, income tax, fees, *25 letters with enclosures*
15 May 1934	**Monro Saw & Co** to **James Joyce** Re implications of bringing Mr Joyce's contract with Pinkers to an end
21 May 1934	**Paul Léon** to **Monro Saw & Co** Mr Joyce is determined to sever his links with Pinker against Léon's advice, Léon has persuaded Mr Joyce to join the Society of Authors in England at Mr Lane's suggestion, *The Author*'s campaign for the publication of *Ulysses*
25 May - 1 August 1934	**Monro Saw & Co** to **Paul Léon** and **James Joyce** Routine acknowledgements, subscriptions, monthly payments, *5 letters*
6 August 1934	**Paul Léon** to **Monro Saw & Co** Mr Joyce has taken a new flat, Mr Joyce left a large box containing his books with Thos Cook when he was last in England, will Monro Saw & Co arrange to have them sent to Paris
13, 14, 16 August 1934	**Monro Saw & Co** to **Paul Léon** Instructions for Thos Cook, message given to Mr Pinker, *3 letters*
26 August 1934	**Paul Léon** to **Monro Saw & Co** Encloses copy of judgement against U.S. government and copies of letters to John Lane, Ralph Pinker and Harold Nicolson, *5 letters*
1 September - 31 December 1934	**Monro Saw & Co** in correspondence with **James Joyce** and **Paul Léon** Routine correspondence mainly re sale of stock and monthly payments, *5 letters with enclosures, letter dated 1 September 1934 endorsed in hand of James Joyce 'This came just now. Am too bewildered to write on any subject' and miscellaneous notes in hand of Paul Léon*

Monro Saw & Co in correspondence with **James Joyce** and **Paul Léon**
Routine correspondence mainly re sale of stock and monthly payments, *60 letters with enclosures, contract note dated 25 October 1935 endorsed with pencilled draft letter in French probably by Lucie Léon about a cheque that was not honoured*

1 January - 31 December 1935

Monro Saw & Co in correspondence with **James Joyce** and **Paul Léon**
Routine correspondence mainly re sale of stock and monthly payments, *6 letters with enclosure*

1 - 13 January 1936

Paul Léon to **Monro Saw & Co**
Re contract with Lane, does not wish delay in publication of *Ulysses*, Mr Joyce is apprehensive of coming reaction, Director of Public Prosecutions has published lecture on obscene literature

27 January 1936

Monro Saw & Co to **Paul Léon** and **James Joyce**
Sale of stock and remittance, *2 letters*

28 January, 1 February 1936

Paul Léon to **Monro Saw & Co**
Queries re implications of Mr Joyce signing copies of *Ulysses* and of Matisse's illustrations, best price to charge for *Ulysses*

5 February 1936

Monro Saw & Co to **Paul Léon**
Not advisable to sell stock, concern about position of Miss Weaver, answers queries raised by Léon in his letter of the 5th, *3 letters*

7, 11 February 1936

Paul Léon to **Monro Saw & Co**
Mr Joyce has not signed the transfer of stock to Miss Weaver as Léon had to explain to him that this would entail a sacrifice on her part

12 February 1936

Monro Saw & Co in correspondence with **James Joyce** and **Paul Léon**
Re sale and transfer of stock, *13 letters*

19 February - 26 March 1936

Paul Léon in correspondence with **Monro Saw & Co**
Re amendments to contract with John Lane The Bodley Head for the publication of *Ulysses*, opinion of Counsel on penalty clause *[enclosed]*, sale of stock, *14 letters*

27 March - 30 April 1936

30 April 1936   **Monro Saw & Co** to **Paul Léon**
Encloses copy letter from James Joyce to Mr Monro and copy of
Mr Monro's reply as well as copy letters from Allen Lane to
Pinker and from Monro Saw & Co to Pinker, *5 letters*

28 April 1936   **James Joyce**, Paris 7 to **Mr Monro**, *copy letter*
Dear Mr Monro,
I am interfering directly and exceptionally in the correspondence relative to the English publication of Ulysses to ask you
on receipt of the present letter to communicate directly with
Messrs. Allen (or whatever the publishers name is) and ask
them to let you have by Saturday morning next the contract
drawn up in accordance with the conditions in M. Leon's last
letter. If this contract is sent to you it can be forwarded here for
my signature and subsequently returned to my Agent. If,
however, the contract is not delivered to you I shall be obliged
if you will determine my contract with this publisher and also
with my agent.
    Furthermore, in case this contract is signed (after a three
years' exchange of inconclusive letters) I suggest that the
commission on the English edition be shared between my
Agent and M. Leon, the latter with your legal aid, having done
all the work. All the work in connection with the American
edition was also done by M. Leon together with my son here
and his brother-in-law in New York. This edition has already
brought in a large sum and will probably sell for the quarter of
a century. I think that my agent's commission on that edition
should satisfy him.
    In any case I should prefer to have the whole matter ended
one way or the other. Either they mean Yes or they mean No.
Let them try to make up their collusive minds before Saturday.
    Sincerely yours,
    James Joyce

30 April 1936   **F.R.D'O Monro** to **James Joyce,** *copy letter*
He has told the agents that unless the contract is sent by
Saturday it will be determined

1, 4 May 1936   **Monro Saw & Co** to **James Joyce** and **Paul Léon**
Encloses draft, Miss Weaver and sale of stock, *2 letters*

5 May 1936   **F.R.D'O Monro** to **Paul Léon**
He has heard through Mr Pinker that Mr Lane has agreed to

accept and sign the agreement, encloses copy of letter he has
written to Mr Joyce

James Joyce to **Mr Monro**, *draft autograph letter signed with*   6 May 1936
typescript copy
Dear Mr Monro,
Thanks for your letter. Mr Lane's promise and Mr Pinker's
assurance mean nothing to me. Please get the former to sign
the contract without further haggling and forward it direct to
Paris. I will sign it and when you receive it back you can pass it
on to my agent. If these two persons are given any more grace
they will change their wavering minds once more.
   Sincerely yours,
   James Joyce

Paul Léon to **Monro Saw & Co**, *carbon typescript unsigned*   7 May 1936
Dear Sirs,
Ulysses: I beg to thank you for your letters of the 30th of April
and the 5th of May with all the enclosures.
   Mr Joyce has written to you himself yesterday and I take it
that he will now sign the contract as corrected by you except for
the clause concerning the Matisse edition which it is best to
delete as you suggest making the necessary modifications in the
other clauses containing references to it. Will you please allow
them no delay in the matter as it must finally be brought to an
end.
   The letter from Mr Lane to Mr Pinker of the 30th of April
however shows such impudent bad faith in view of the fact that
he is raising objections not to your corrections but to clauses
drafted by himself leaves me disarmed as far as Mr Joyce's
attitude towards his agent is concerned. Though my
experience with the latter has led me to doubt his ability I am
afraid that the suspicions can go a little farther. As I know
however that in your opinion a determination of Mr Joyce's
contract with him cannot effect any economy for Mr Joyce a
reduction of his commission might be the best way to penalise
him for his conduct.
   One thing however I must make quite clear about Mr Joyce's
suggestion. Whatever form this reduction takes officially I
cannot for a moment entertain the idea of its being divisible
with me. My position as legal adviser does not permit me to
have any claim for any renumeration on a commission basis on
whatever case I handle. You will therefore please act according

to Mr Joyce's instruction in whatever manner you think best except for this particular thing.
  Sincerely yours,

7 May 1936	**Paul Léon** to **Monro Saw & Co**, *carbon typescript* Mr Joyce will need money soon, encloses bills from Dr Delmas of the Maison de Santé d'Ivry and from Dr Casalis, Maison de Santé de la Villa des Pages, Le Vésinet for Mr Joyce's daughter, also 5000Frs must be ready to forward to Mr J. Kahane, sale of £200 will be necessary
8, 12, 14, 15 May 1936	**Monro Saw & Co** to **Paul Léon** Sale of stock, Lane says it is impossible to get anyone to print *Ulysses*, encloses agreement for signature by Mr Joyce, *6 letters*
16 May 1936	**Paul Léon** to **Monro Saw & Co** He will try to get Mr Joyce's signature on the contract on Monday, the new difficulty with the printers seems to him a new excuse in order to avoid the liquidated damages clause, *2p*
19 May 1936	**Monro Saw & Co** to **Paul Léon** They do not entirely agree with all that Léon says, enclose copy letter from Pinker
22 May 1936	**Paul Léon** to **Monro Saw & Co** Encloses contract signed by Mr Joyce, has received a letter and telegram *[enclosed]* from Mr Pinker which proves that a printer has been found, would it be possible for the publisher to provoke a legal action after the first edition was sold and his expenses covered which he could leave undefended and thus free himself from any obligation arising under the contract, it would be essential to embody some legal material in the edition as was done in America, *2p + letter and telegram*
25, 29 May 1936	**Monro Saw & Co** to **Paul Léon** Answers points raised in Léon's letter, returns letter and telegram from Mr Pinker and encloses copy letter to Pinker *[enclosed]*, Mr Lane is away until after Whitsun, *2 letters*
2 June - 1 July 1936	**Monro Saw & Co** in correspondence with **Paul Léon** and **James Joyce** Letter from Pinker re *Ulysses*, transmission of money to Mr Joyce, *7 letters*

Paul Léon to **Monro Saw & Co** 6 July 1936
Encloses correspondence with Mr Lane and Mr Pinker, wants
to get a letter from Mr Lane which will enable him to insist on
Lane's defending *Ulysses*, an increase in the size of the edition
should be accompanied by an increased guarantee of the
defence of the case, *2 copies*

Monro Saw & Co to **Paul Léon** 8 July 1936
Acknowledges letter of 8th

Paul Léon to **Monro Saw & Co** 10 July 1936
Encloses correspondence with Mr Lane and Mr Pinker, will
Monro authorize them to increase number of unsigned first
edition from 400 to 900, he has no objection to raising price of
signed copies, Mr Lane's reply with regard to the defence of
Ulysses not as clear as he could have wished though Lane seems
to have realised that *Ulysses* is a commercial proposition

Monro Saw & Co in correspondence with **Paul Léon** 16 July - 1
Signature of supplemental agreement for *Ulysses*, opinion of Mr September
Monro on the publication of a selection of Mr Joyce's poetry 1936
and prose, transmission of money to Mr Joyce, *9 letters*

Paul Léon to **Monro Saw & Co** 3 September
Encloses letter from Mr Joyce by which Mr Joyce seems to need 1936
money, Léon is loth to transmit the letter, *see letter from James
Joyce to Paul Léon dated 2 September 1936*

Monro Saw & Co to **Paul Léon** 4 September
They have transferred the equivalent of £100 to Mr Joyce's 1936
account

Paul Léon to **Monro Saw & Co** 17, 18
Lane sent the proofs of the Appendices very late and has asked September
for a delay, Léon wishes to fix a definite date of publication, Mr 1936
Joyce has grown very nervous in case Lane might ruin the
publication after fourteen years preparation, Lane had six
months to set up the book whereas Albatross set up their
edition in six weeks, *2 letters*

Monro Saw & Co to **Paul Léon** 19
Agree that definite date of publication should be arranged September
1936

20
September
1936

Paul Léon to **Monro Saw & Co**
Encloses letter from Messrs John Lane, the paper problem is solved but the reason for their request for a delay is vague, there may be a spy in their office who wants to have the sheets seized before publication so the date of publication should be adhered to, *2 copies*

21
September
1936

Monro Saw & Co to **Paul Léon**
They approve of all possible pressure being put on publisher to publish on the due date

28, 29, 30
September
1936

Paul Léon to **Monro Saw & Co**
Publication date fixed for 3 October, encloses Lane's letter which says that signed copies will be oversubscribed, Lane's untruths, Lane wants to delay placing advertisements in the newspapers as specified in the contract, Léon wishes to insist that an advertisement be placed at least in the *Times Literary Supplement* rather than the *New Statesman* in order to show that the edition was not issued in a surreptitious way, *4 letters*

30
September -
17 October
1936

Monro Saw & Co in correspondence with **Paul Léon**
Instructions re advertisements, transfers of stock between Mr Monro, Miss Weaver and Mr Joyce, they have threatened Lane with proceedings if money is not paid, *6 letters*

19 October
1936

Paul Léon to **Monro Saw & Co**
Thanks for the help Mr Monro has given him in the publication of *Ulysses*, Mr Joyce will write personally to express his appreciation

21 October -
18 December
1936

Monro Saw & Co in correspondence with **Paul Léon**
Fees, sale of stock, transmission of money to Mr Joyce, Mr Joyce's position following the liquidation of John Lane The Bodley Head, *15 letters*

27 December
1936

Paul Léon to **Monro Saw & Co**
Did not mention Monro Saw's letter of the 15th about Mr Pinker to Mr Joyce as knowing his poor opinion of Mr Pinker it might have led to an outburst, from enclosed letter of Mr Pinker it seems they are free to deal with the Receiver as they think best, will Monro Saw instruct Pinker with regard to the earliest possible publication of a cheap edition of *Ulysses* which Mr Joyce is very anxious to see, suggests buying out unsold

copies of *Ulysses* and reselling them to Faber & Faber, Mr Joyce wishes Léon to add that he thinks the liquidation of Lane a month after the publication of *Ulysses* looks like an act of vengeance from certain quarters, *2p*

Monro Saw & Co to **Paul Léon**
Negotiations with Pinker, sale of stock, *3 letters*

29-30 December 1936

Monro Saw & Co to **Paul Léon**
Sale of stock, Mr Joyce's financial position

8 January 1937

Paul Léon to **Monro Saw & Co**
He tried to approach Mr Joyce about the sale of stock and reinvestment but the only answer he was able to obtain was "do as you please", agrees to Monro Saw's proposal for reinvestment, negotiations with Pinker and Lane's receiver

9 January 1937

Monro Saw & Co in correspondence with **Paul Léon**
Re sale of stock, negotiations re royalties and publication of a cheap edition of *Ulysses* with liquidator of John Lane The Bodley Head Ltd and with Mr Howe who is forming the new company to take it over, financial statement of Mr Joyce's income and expenditure from stocks, Miss Weaver wishes to continue a payment towards Mr Joyce's income, agreement for publication of *Ulysses*, *16 letters*

11 January - 19 February 1937

Paul Léon to **Monro Saw & Co**
Mr Joyce wishes to receive monthly payments of his income, approves draft agreement for *Ulysses* with new John Lane company, answers Monro's queries re price and other clauses, the publishers should use the Albatross edition as their text, the text of the limited Lane edition is full of misprints but it incorporates about a hundred corrections chiefly of punctuation, they should use the limited edition as their basis correcting words from the Albatross, the Appendix contains blunders, *2 letters*

22 February 1937

Monro Saw & Co in correspondence with **Paul Léon** and **James Joyce**
Money due from liquidators of John Lane, income payments for Mr Joyce, documentation proving Mr Joyce's intention of establishing an English domicile in 1931, Mr Joyce attaches great importance to the establishment of the points relating to

23 February 1937 - 3 April 1937

his daughter's breakdown and the consequent abandonment of his residence in England, John Lane The Bodley Head have sent a new draft agreement which will lead to more legal work and delays, *14 letters, letter dated 23 February 1937 endorsed with notes in Italian in hand of Paul Léon; letter dated 10 March 1937 endorsed with note in French*

[8] April 1937

James Joyce, Zurich to **F.R.D'O. Monro**, *carbon typescript unsigned*
He does not wish to follow Mr Léon's suggestion to postpone the severance of his connection with Messrs Pinker, Monro can inform his publishers that he has made a decision in principle not to sign any contract unless it tallies with the document Monro has drawn up

12-16 April 1937

Monro Saw & Co to **Paul Léon** and **James Joyce**
They have given six months notice to Messrs Pinker, sale of stock, enclose copy of letter from John Lane, *3 letters*

20, 22 April 1937

Paul Léon to **Monro Saw & Co**
Apologizes for delay in answering letters about *Ulysses* but was only able to discuss the matter with Mr Joyce yesterday, refers to points in draft agreement, Mr Joyce is prepared to sign only a document prepared by Monro Saw & Co, referring to an interview with Mr Howard adds as a general remark that he would prefer a printed text to a photographic edition, nothing Léon can say has any effect on Mr Joyce with regard to Pinker, Léon sets out all the information he can get from Mr Joyce about how little help Pinker was in order to answer Monro's query, Mr Joyce wishes Léon to add that he is so sure of Pinker's incompetence that he does not want him to have anything to do with future discussions lest he become a tool in the hands of the new publishers, *2 letters, 4p*

26 April - 26 May 1937

Monro Saw & Co in correspondence with **Paul Léon** and **James Joyce**
Re agreement for *Ulysses* and dealings with Pinker including requests for permission to publish various poems and stories of Mr Joyce, *8 letters*

2 May 1937

James Joyce, 7 rue Edmond Valentin, Paris to **F.R.D'O. Monro**, *autograph letter signed*
Dear Mr Monro
    Mr Léon has read to me over the telephone your letter about

Mr Pinker. If he claims commission in perpetuity for work he never did and if he is entitled legally to draw this commission he can have it. My sole object is to get rid of this agency. It never was worth a pinch of salt to me. At the present moment I foresee the usual programme of incompetence, pusillanimity and tergiversation with the three men in a boat who have taken over the derelict S.O.S. John Lane and, in spite of the proverb, I think that three sheeps heads are better than four. It takes me, it seems, from eight to fifteen years to write a book. I never write for any review for money and no correspondence will come to my ex-agent except an occasional from a village idiot who wants to set to music one of my meagre poems. The fee is a guinea, I think, and my ex-agent may keep the change.

What is important is that the new contract should be drawn up and signed after it has been passed by me here as satisfactory. Mr Pinker's intervention is quite useless and will probably even be positively harmful.

sincerely yours

James Joyce

Paul Léon to **Monro Saw & Co**   27 May 1937
Replies to queries re agreement with John Lane, does not think there should be any reduction in royalties, *2p*

Monro Saw & Co in correspondence with **Paul Léon**   8 June - 24
Negotiations re contract for *Ulysses*, Pinkers have asked for   August 1937
commission to be deducted by Lane and given directly to them
to which Mr Joyce agrees, requests for permissions to publish,
sale of stock, small commissions due to Pinker, U.S. income tax,
necessity of taking a firm line with Pinker, exchange of contracts
for *Ulysses*, transmission of money to Mr Joyce, *30 letters*

Paul Léon to **Monro Saw & Co**   15
Mr Joyce has not yet received his cheque for the American   September
royalties, as the date for the new publication of *Ulysses*   1937
approaches Mr Joyce is getting nervous, the publishers should
distribute as many copies as possible in case the authorities
start any trouble and announcements should appear in the
usual papers

Monro Saw & Co in correspondence with **Paul Léon** and **James**   16-30
Joyce   December
Acknowledges letter, parcels containing 6 copies of *Ulysses*   1937

received from Pinkers, copies to be sent to Mr Joyce, Léon thinks the fact that Pinkers sent *Ulysses* to Monro Saw instead of direct to Mr Joyce is a proof of ill will, cheque from Lane, Monro Saw & Co's account, Pinker's commission, monthly payments, sale of stock, *14 letters*

3 January-28 December 1938

Monro Saw & Co to **Paul Léon** and **James Joyce**
Monthly payments, dossier concerning Mr Joyce's daughter sent to Dr Thompson, sale of stock, royalties from Lane, papers sent to Dr Gibier-Rambaud, accounts, letters enclosed from Pinker, translation of documents concerning Miss Joyce's illness forwarded to Dr Patrick O'Brien, letters exchanged between B. Huebsch and Paul Léon about the modification of the contract for *Work in Progress, 38 letters, letter of 16 July endorsed with notes in French in hand of Paul Léon, letter of 1 September endorsed with note in hand of James Joyce 'money recd. yr letter opened by mistake', letter of 1 December annotated with name and address of Charles Joyce*

25 January-15 March 1939

Monro Saw & Co in correspondence with **Paul Léon**
Sale of stock, letters from Pinker, monthly income, price of *Work in Progress*, copies of Léon's letters of 11 March to Faber and Viking, *17 letters*

15 March 1939

Paul Léon to **Monro Saw & Co**
Encloses cutting from *New York Herald Tribune* about Pinker's brother, worried about American royalties, can a criminal prosecution be made against Pinker for detaining money he receives for Mr Joyce, should they take this opportunity of severing all connection with Pinker or at least of making all royalties payable to Monro Saw & Co

17, 22 March 1939

Monro Saw & Co to **Paul Léon**
Cheques received from Pinker, does Léon wish them to get rid of Pinker as Mr Joyce's agent, *2 letters*

22, 24 March 1939

Paul Léon to **Monro Saw & Co**
Cable received from Viking, Mr Joyce will now sign the sheets of the 300 copies for the American market, Monro Saw & Co should issue instructions that payments are to be made direct to them rather than to Pinker and should insist that Viking pay promptly, *2 letters*

Monro Saw & Co in correspondence with **Paul Léon** — 24 March-8 May 1939
Form of authority required from Mr Joyce for royalty payments to be made to Monro Saw & Co, royalty statements, monthly income, annual account, income tax, date of publication of *Finnegans Wake*, return by Léon to Monro Saw & Co of set of documents concerning Miss Lucia Joyce, refuses permission to *Irish Digest* to print extract from *Finnegans Wake*, forwards letters from Faber and Viking, *20 letters*

Paul Léon to **Monro Saw & Co** — 9 May 1939
Nothing to be done about high cost of author's corrections, Viking's letter a poor excuse, Faber's income tax deduction

Monro Saw & Co in correspondence with **Paul Léon** — 10 May-5 June 1939
German translation, possibility of getting rid of Pinkers' agency, payments from publishers, income tax deductions, *8 letters*

Paul Léon and **James Joyce** in correspondence with **Monro Saw & Co** — 20 June 1939-2 October 1939
Termination of Pinker's agency, request from B.B.C. for Mr Joyce to take part in a broadcast, the disk Mr Joyce recorded for the British Orthological Society which was sold first by Alfred Imhof and then by His Master's Voice, accounts from Viking Press, newscuttings about American Pinker, sale of stock, Spanish and Portugese rights of *Ulysses*, OUP wish to include *On the Beach at Fontana* in an anthology, Samuel Beckett would be willing to do the broadcast for the B.B.C., monthly payments and royalty payments, B.B.C. Northern Ireland have abandoned their plan for a broadcast by Mr Joyce, *38 letters, letter dated 30 June 1939 endorsed with draft telegram in hand of Paul Léon from James Joyce to 'Turner' postponing dinner engagement as weather too stormy*

F.R. D'O. Monro to **Paul Léon**, *handwritten letter* — 17 November 1939
Thanks for trouble Léon has taken, Monro's son will fly to London

Monro Saw & Co to **James Joyce** — 26 January 1940
Encloses letter and brochure from Mr Pinker and letter from Mr Alfred Derfan

Paul Léon to **Monro Saw & Co** — 1 February 1940
Saw Mr Joyce yesterday after a long time, he was back in Paris

on the eve of a new departure, he was very worried about money, Léon thinks Mr Joyce needs about £100, Mr Joyce's address is Hôtel de la Paix, St Gérand-le-Puy, Allier, Léon had Mr Monro's son to dinner in Paris, Joyce matter very urgent

n.d.

James Joyce to **Public Trustee**
Draft of suggested letter to the Public Trustee

n.d.

Paul Léon to **Monro Saw & Co**
Mr Joyce asks for £100

n.d.

Commission note for sale of stock

.2   JAMES B. PINKER & SONS IN CORRESPONDENCE WITH JAMES JOYCE AND PAUL LÉON, 393 letters with enclosures, 1922-40

1924-31

Royalty accounts of James Joyce in account with James B. Pinker & Son, 14p

2 May 1927,
26 March
1928

F.C. Wicken, Manager, James B. Pinker & Sons to **James Joyce**, 2 Square Robiac, 192 rue de Grenelle, Paris
Has written to Eric Pinker about Mr Joyce's two manuscripts, enquiry about German rights, *2 letters*

9 December
1929

J. Ralph Pinker to **James Joyce**, 2 Square Robiac, 192 rue de Grenelle, Paris
Viking Press want to publish a volume of collected poems by Joyce

2, 26 January
1932

J. Ralph Pinker to **Paul Léon** and **James Joyce**
Italian edition of *Ulysses*, Danish-Norwegian rights in *Portrait of the Artist*, sends contracts for the Shakespeare company, *2 letters*

9-24 February
1932

Paul Léon and **James Joyce** in correspondence with **James B. Pinker & Son**
Miss Beach's annulment of her contract with Mr Joyce, Mr

Joyce is owner of the world rights for *Ulysses* and is to receive a proposal for an American edition of *Ulysses*, Pinkers should seek other offers, Mr Joyce's conditions, Pinkers receive offer from William Morrow, *6 letters, letter dated 24 February endorsed in hand of Paul Léon with draft telegram from James Joyce to Padraic Colum, see p. 88 and notes for letter to Pinker*

Paul Léon to **James B. Pinker & Son**   25 February
Has discussed letter re Morrow's offer with Mr Joyce who is not   1932
well, Mr Joyce expects an offer from Bennet Cerf and possibly
from Padraic Colum, points to be considered re loaning of
plates made in France, advance payment, Mr Joyce's
conditions, American copyright

James Joyce to **James B. Pinker & Sons**, *carbon typescript of*   c. March
telegram   1932
Cerf's offer, obtain Brace counteroffer

J. Ralph Pinker to **Paul Léon** and **James Joyce**   4 March 1932
Re offers of Harcourt Brace and Morrow

Paul Léon to **James B. Pinker & Sons**   6 March 1932
Mr Joyce made error in his cable, Mr Joyce inclined to accept
Cerf's offer as he is a good friend of his daughter-in-law's
family, will Pinker prepare contract, points to be covered by
contract, there will be no preface but Mr Joyce will write a letter
confirming authenticity of Cerf's publication

J. Ralph Pinker to **Paul Léon**   7 March 1932
Re draft contract, *2 letters and telegram*

Paul Léon to **James B. Pinker & Sons**   9 March 1932
Contract, plates of the Roth edition have been seized probably
at the instance of the French ambassador M. Paul Claudel, the
French printer Baron Bernard d'Avout wrote to the French
consul in New York, Padraic Colum has received another offer

Paul Léon and **James Joyce** in correspondence with **J. Ralph   14 March-
Pinker**   3 May 1932
Mr Joyce has signed contract with Random House, address of
Mr Holroyd-Reece, accounting dates of various publishers,
contract between Mr Joyce and Pinker, British income tax,
payments by Pinkers, *12 letters*

7 May 1932

Paul Léon to **Ralph Pinker**
Payments from Imhof-Ogden for disc, Mr Joyce greatly annoyed by delay in transfer of money from Mr Cerf, his daughter's breakdown, English domicile and income tax, copy of *Ulysses* sent to Random House to begin legal battle in U.S., Faber have refused to publish *Ulysses*, Mr Joyce wants to know does Pinker propose to offer it to other publishers, why did Faber reach their decision, in the case of each of Mr Joyce's works printers and publishers have refused to produce them but have given way in the end as has the B.B.C. recently to Mr Harold Nicolson's insistence on discussing *Ulysses*, *Fortnightly Review's* treatment of Stuart Gilbert's article, further points re censorship of *Ulysses*, *3p*

11 May-2
June 1932

J. Ralph Pinker in correspondence with **Paul Léon**
Royalty payments and accounts, John Lane have expressed an interest in publishing *Ulysses*, *5 letters and royalty accounts*

14 July 1932

Paul Léon to **Ralph Pinker**, *2 copies one annotated 'for M Joyce'*
Mr Joyce under strain because of his daughter's health, Mr Joyce hopes to give her confidence by getting her to decorate books, a book decorated by her is being published, Mr Joyce would like her to get an offer for the decoration of another book without his apparent intervention, he would like her to do the twenty six letters of the alphabet, a reputed English poet should be approached and instructed to make verses for children beginning with each letter of the alphabet, Mr Joyce would like Pinker's opinion of this idea and his suggestion of a possible author and publisher, Mr Joyce is in Zurich, the news of his eyesight is not good, *2p*

18 July, 3
August-26
October 1932

Paul Léon in correspondence with **J. Ralph Pinker**
Possibility of producing a book by Lucia Joyce, James Stephens and Padraic Colum possible authors though they should be approached with caution, fees due from Miss Allgood for readings, Albatross Press want to use the story *The Boarding House* in an almanach, letter from Mr Rubin, what has happened to Gorman who was authorised to write a biography of Mr Joyce, royalties, reissue of *Chamber Music* by Viking Press, *10 letters, letter of 8 August endorsed with typed letter signed by James Joyce, see p. 4*

26 October
1932

Paul Léon to **Ralph Pinker**
Met Paris manager of Warner Brothers re their proposal to film

Ulysses, press notices published in United States about film, Mr Joyce says he is in principle opposed to the filming of *Ulysses* and would like the notices in the press to be denied, Cerf supports the idea of a film, Mr Joyce takes the literary point of view and opposes the filming as irrealisable, does Mr Joyce own the film rights, Mr Joyce has heard from Gorman

Paul Léon in correspondence with **J. Ralph Pinker**   28 October
Pomes Penyeach seized by customs on account of their silk case,   1932-
Mr Joyce owns world film rights of *Ulysses*, negotiations with   10 January
Faber for publication of *The Mookse and the Gripes* and *The Ondt*   1933
and the Gracehoper for the Christmas market, Mr Joyce wishes
their title to be *'Two Tales Told by Shem and Shaun'*, Léon will try
to make Mr Joyce change his mind about the filming of *Ulysses*,
offer from Czech publisher for *Dubliners*, contract for *Two Tales*,
Faber wish to publish under title *Two Tales of Shem and Shaun*,
Mr Joyce's right under his contract with Faber to publish
fragments from *Work in Progress* in expensive editions, Servire
propose to publish a fragment, legal position with regard to
film rights of *Ulysses*, in answer to enquiry from Mr Huebsch Mr
Joyce has not done much work for *Work in Progress*, Huebsch
should do something to protect copyright of *Work in Progress* in
the U.S., a new edition of *Pomes Penyeach*, in view of the fact that
Warner do not wish to film *Ulysses* a flat denial of the rumours
about it should be issued, Viking Press fear that the issue of
fragments of *Work in Progress* may spoil the sales of the
completed work, Italian rights of *Ulysses*, contract with Faber
for *Pomes Penyeach*, Cape's proposal to include *The Dead* in an
anthology of short stories, Faber are willing to bring out a
limited edition of new fragment from *Work in Progress*, *40 letters*

Paul Léon to **Ralph Pinker**   10 January
He will send a copy of *Ulysses* by diplomatic bag, agrees to   1933
proposal for Cape's anthology, thinks Cape has treated Mr
Joyce very badly, could Pinker transfer all Mr Joyce's works to
Faber, alternatively could he approach Cape about an English
edition of *Ulysses*, Léon has a plan for the eventual publication
of an English edition of *Ulysses*, Cape and Faber could approach
the Home Secretary and Director of Public Prosecutions, *2p*

J. Ralph Pinker in correspondence with **Paul Léon**   12 January-
Viking to issue *Pomes Penyeach*, contract with Cape, Italian offer   15 February
for translation rights of *Ulysses*, proposal for Dutch rights for   1933

Ulysses, correspondence with OUP re leaflets for *Pomes Penyeach*, Huebsch objects to publication of fragments, letter denying report of filming of *Ulysses* published in *Evening Standard*, *14 letters*

18 February 1933

Paul Léon to **Ralph B. Pinker**
Defends publication of fragments on ground that they help familiarise the public with the language and objects of Mr Joyce's book, Faber should publish fragment in association with Servire, thanks for letter to *Evening Standard*, notes conversation with Cape about British edition of *Ulysses*, *2p*

21 February 1933

J. Ralph Pinker to **Paul Léon**
Viking Press argument valid for American market

22 February 1933

Paul Léon to **Ralph Pinker**
Encloses letter which refers to Italian copyright of *Dubliners*, Pinker will receive copy of *Pomes Penyeach* with illuminated capitals by Mr Joyce's daughter, will Pinker see that it is placed in the British Museum Library, a copy has also been placed in the Bibliothèque Nationale, *2 letters*

23 February-16 March 1933

J. Ralph Pinker in correspondence with **Paul Léon**
Lapsing of Italian copyright of *Dubliners*, Léon does not insist on an American edition of the new fragment, Faber should publish the fragment in association with Servire, proposal for American production of *Exiles*, Italian translation of *Ulysses*, royalties, Faber have decided not to issue a limited edition of the latest fragment from *Work in Progress*, the Bibliothèque Nationale has requested copies of Mr Joyce's works, *13 letters, letter of 16 March endorsed with draft in Léon's hand of letter dated 20 March*

20, 27 March 1933

Paul Léon to **Ralph Pinker**
Will Pinkers inform Farrar and Rheinhard [sic] that the London publishers Messrs Greyson have commissioned Mr F. Budgen to write a book on the composition of *Ulysses* in Zurich, if Mr Gorman has not abandoned his biography of Mr Joyce he can communicate with Mr Budgen in London, agrees with Servire's terms for publication of fragment, money due for discs, Burns & Oates will publish Chaucer *ABC* with illustrations by Miss Joyce, *2 letters*

20-28 March 1933

J. Ralph Pinker to **Paul Léon**
Poems by Mr Joyce included in braille anthology, encloses letter

from Huebsch asking that no more fragments be published until after publication of the complete work, *4 letters*

Paul Léon to **J. Ralph Pinker**   3 April 1933
Encloses four illuminations for the Servire Press fragment, does not like type Servire Press have chosen, has not shown Huebsch's preposterous letter to Mr Joyce

J. Ralph Pinker in correspondence with **Paul Léon**   4 April-26
Permission to Mr J.P. Kaestlin to quote from *Pomes Penyeach* in   July 1933
an article in *Contemporaries and Makers*, Servire Press and the fragment, Huebsch's reply to Léon's points and Léon's rejoinder, royalties, difficulty with colours for Miss Joyce's illuminations, title of fragment is to be *The Mime of Mick, Nick and the Maggies*, send a recording of *Anna Livia Plurabelle* to Miss Philomena Byrne, contract for Tokyo edition of *Portrait of the Artist*, *18 letters*

J. Ralph Pinker in correspondence with **Paul Léon**   26 July-16
Confidential correspondence with Werner Laurie and   October 1933
Albatross re *Ulysses*, Servire Press and *The Mime*, *10 letters*

Paul Léon in correspondence with **J. Ralph Pinker**   21 October-3
Random House are confident of the result of the case in   November
America, they want permission to publish a plan in their   1933
edition of *Ulysses*, Mr Joyce is opposed to this, the plan was among the documents given to Mr Gorman, can Mr Gorman's authorisation be withdrawn, contract for Servire, Mr Joyce has nothing to say to his publishers about the date of completion of *Work in Progress*, proposal from Private Subscription Book Group of Amen Corner for publication of *Ulysses* which should be rejected, Léon has advised Mr Joyce to take out an injunction forbidding the Private Subscription Book Group to publish *Ulysses*, Private Subscription Book Group do not intend to sell *Ulysses*, *13 letters and 1 telegram*

Paul Léon to **J. Ralph Pinker**   3 November
Essential to protect rights to *Ulysses*, an injunction will serve to   1933
protect rights against anybody who threatens them, Pinker should find out who is behind the Private Subscription Book Group, as soon as the American edition is allowed the situation in England will change and publication of *Ulysses* will become necessary, Mr Joyce considers the Private Subscription Book

Group's letter a piece of tremendous impudence, owing to the carelessness of those who should have safeguarded Mr Joyce's rights pirated editions were published in Japan and America, a letter has been received from Faber which raises doubts about Mr Joyce's copyright and property rights in England, Mr Joyce's instructions are that he will institute legal proceedings against anyone who does not apply to him directly or through Pinker for the publication of *Ulysses*, *2p*

6 November-
6 December
1933

J. Ralph Pinker in correspondence with **Paul Léon**
Gorman is in London and says he will finish the book by January when he will show it to Mr Joyce, authorisation given to Gorman was verbal, date of publication of the fragment by Servire Press, Mr Joyce is sure that he gave a written authorisation to Mr Gorman and insists on its withdrawal, letter received from Private Subscription Book Group giving required assurance, offer for Italian rights of *Ulysses*, Pinker is unable to find out anything about the Subscription Book Group, Albatross would like a story by Mr Joyce for inclusion in an anthology apart from those published in *Dubliners*, *10 letters*

8 December
1933

Paul Léon to **Ralph Pinker**
Favourable decision given by the American court in the *Ulysses* case, Italian translation, Mr Joyce has not written any short stories apart from those in *Dubliners* any of which Albatross can include in an anthology, reasons Léon considers the wording of the Private Subscription Book Club's assurance to be reticent and guarded, cannot answer re Mr Gorman, copyright of *Ulysses* in Great Britain belongs to Mr Joyce, favourable outcome of American case will carry weight with the British authorities, the greatest obstacle to the publication of *Ulysses* is the absence of courage and inertia of British publishers, Albatross has right of first refusal so no offer should ever be communicated to them, important to obtain as many proposals as possible to stimulate a spirit of competition, Faber should be left out at the moment, if everything else fails Léon will recommend that Mr Joyce bring out an edition himself, need for stick-to-it-iveness and boldness, letter confidential, *3p*

12 December
1933-11 May
1934

J. Ralph Pinker in correspondence with **Paul Léon**
Allen Lane's proposal for *Ulysses*, cover for *The Mime of Mick, Nick and the Maggies*, negotiations with Lane and Albatross for publication of *Ulysses*, Faber also interested, terms of contract

with Lane, avoid provoking the authorities, necessity of being prepared for a court case, clause regarding cheap edition, Italian translation of *Ulysses* has fallen through, Mr Morley wants to know whether specimen page of *Work in Progress* is satisfactory, royalty payments, film offer for *Ulysses*, request by Miss Muriel Harris to set to music Mr Joyce's poem *Strings in the Earth and Air*, length of time taken to clear American cheques, documents relating to *Ulysses*, *31 letters*

Paul Léon to **Ralph Pinker**   14 May 1934
Mr Joyce has not received cheque from Random House, last letter from Pinker relayed a request from Faber, Pinker is Mr Joyce's agent not the agent of his publisher, no answer given to Mr Faber because the type set is the same as that of two or three years ago and it is probably to soon to start setting the book, remit money to Mr Joyce by return of post

J. Ralph Pinker to **Paul Léon**   15 May 1934
Surprised at Léon's letter, cheque not sent because not received

J. Ralph Pinker in correspondence with **Paul Léon**   25 June-
Will Mr Joyce modify his terms for the Italian translation of   31 December
Ulysses, sales of *Ulysses* in United States, Mr Joyce will not lecture   1934
in United States, permission to set Mr Joyce's poems *Strings in the Earth and Air* and *Lean out of the Window Goldenhair* to music by Margaret Meacham, Society of Authors has started a campaign for the publication of *Ulysses*, decision of American appellate court in favour of *Ulysses*, number of copies Mr Joyce will sign, price, permission for Mr Thaddeus Ramy Brenton to quote from *Work in Progress*, negotiations with Lane for royalties, Léon's niece Olga Poliakoff is going to marry a partner in a printing firm to whom Lane could make an approach about printing *Ulysses*, Léon hopes to obtain an appreciation of *Ulysses* by the greatest legal authority in England, will Pinker tactfully seek payment due from Random House who have been very good about making advance payments, Mr Vernon Barker has permission to use *Araby* in his Hungarian anthology, Lane unwilling to pay for Mr Joyce's signature, Mr Harold Triggs seeks permission to set *She Weeps over Rahoon* to music, money due from Lane, ask Servire Press to send a copy of *The Mime* to Mr George Goyert and others, royalties on cheap edition of *Portrait of the Artist*, payment for *The Mime*, no arrangements made for proof reading of *Ulysses*, neither Léon nor Mr Joyce

could do it, Lane should be able to find a specialist in England to do it, Faber wish to publish the forthcoming fragment of *Work in Progress*, Lane will give printers instructions to doublecheck the proofs themselves, Lane should follow the American edition and verify it with the Albatross as Gilbert made hundreds of corrections for the Albatross, *41 letters*

10 January-
13 December
1935

J. Ralph Pinker in correspondence with **Paul Léon**
Lane wants to have corrections before he sets up from American edition and suggests it would be better to set up from the Albatross/Odyssey edition, an American editor is interested in serial publication of fragments of *Work in Progress*, Mr Joyce unwilling to sign contract with Augener because of small amount involved, accounts due, Broadhursts seek permission to publish a musical setting of *Go Seek Her Out All Courteously*, queries re accounts of Random House, Léon has received a contract for a screenplay for *Ulysses* from New York which he cannot advise Mr Joyce to sign, Mr Joyce has given permission for Mrs Hazel Felman-Buchbinder's setting of *Anna Livia Plurabelle* though he has a poor opinion of it, account from Alfred Imhof, reference to *Ulysses* by Hugh Walpole in the *Star*, Lane plans to publish *Ulysses* in the autumn, royalties due from Servire, Jonathan Cape wish to reprint *Exiles* in their play series, neither Léon nor Mr Joyce authorised the publication of the musical arrangement of *Anna Livia Plurabelle* by the Argus Bookshop, *43 letters*

22-29 January
1936

J. Ralph Pinker to **Paul Léon**
Allen Lane's plan for the publication of a limited edition of 3,000 copies of *Ulysses* illustrated by Matisse, *2 letters and copy*

16 February
1936

Paul Léon to **Ralph Pinker**
Disagrees with Lane's and Pinker's proposal, suggests an unillustrated edition of 1,000 or 1,500 copies for subscription with 10% signed by author, does not want an expensive edition following the experience of the Oxford University Press Joyce book, *2p*

19, 25
February
1936

J. Ralph Pinker to **Paul Léon**
Allen Lane would like to meet Léon in Paris, *2 letters*

10 March
1936

Paul Léon to **Ralph Pinker**
Lane has delayed too long, will Pinker see him and ask him to

forfeit his contract or bring the book out soon as intended before the Matisse idea was thought of, is Pinker willing to act energetically in this matter, perhaps he would prefer to give up acting as agent for Mr Joyce, situation has its comic side in that *Ulysses* is available everywhere in England, what are the British and American sales of Mr Joyce's other books, Imhof, royalties for American *Ulysses, 2p*

J. Ralph Pinker in correspondence with **Paul Léon**   11-25 March,
Royalties, Cape will sell off their original editions of *Dubliners*   8 May 1936
and *Portrait of the Artist as a Young Man* at 2/6d, Lane has accepted Léon's conditions, copy letter from Monro Saw & Co re contract with Lane for *Ulysses, 5 letters*

Paul Léon in correspondence with **J. Ralph Pinker**   25 May-24
Printers should follow Albatross edition correcting caption on   June 1936
page 143, Lane suggests asking a prominent literary figure such as E.M. Forster to work up the material on the history of *Ulysses* into an introduction, Léon would prefer such material to be made into an appendix, proposed edition of collected poems of Mr Joyce by Mrs Crosby of the Black Sun Press, *7 letters*

J.R. Pinker to **Paul Léon**   2 July 1936
Queries from Lane re five misprints in slip proofs of *Ulysses*, *annotated with answers*

Paul Léon in correspondence with **J. Ralph Pinker**   6 July-13
Variation in contract for *Ulysses* agreed, business with Mrs   August 1936
Crosby and Mr Huebsch about their editions of the collected poems, negotiations with *Sur* of Buenos Aires for Spanish translations of *Exiles* and *Ulysses, 10 letters*

Paul Léon in correspondence with **J. Ralph Pinker**   8 September-
Royalties due to Mr Joyce, the queries for the corrections to   29 December
Ulysses have reached only p 620, Lane has not sent Léon the   1936
proofs of the Appendix and Léon has not reminded him of them as he does not wish to cause any delay in publication, publication date of *Ulysses* set for 3 October, one copy to be given to Miss Harriet Weaver and two to Mr Joyce, Léon would like extra author's copies, *Ulysses* looks extremely well, advertisements appeared, cheque from Lane for *Ulysses* overdue, Léon had to give the *de luxe* copy of *Ulysses* which John Lane brought over for him to Mr Joyce and would like to

purchase a copy at trade price through Pinker as a replacement, negotiations for Danish edition of *Ulysses* with Martins Forlag, negotiations with *Sur*, Thomas Pitfield has permission to broadcast his manuscript song settings of two of Mr Joyce's poems, John Lane The Bodley Head put into the hands of a receiver, negotiations with receiver, *26 letters*

6-19 January 1937

Paul Léon in correspondence with **J. Ralph Pinker**
Presentation copies due from Mrs Crosby of the Black Sun edition of Mr Joyce's collected poems, negotiations with receiver of John Lane, as there is a difference of opinion between Monro Saw and Pinker about the interpretation of Mr Joyce's contract with Messrs Lane Léon asks Pinker to withdraw from negotiations, Léon questions Pinker's unbeneficial attitude to Mr Joyce, it has been difficult for Léon to prevent Mr Joyce from terminating his agency, Pinker is not aware of any difference of opinion with Monro Saw and is always most anxious to help Mr Joyce who is a personal friend, *6 letters*

24 February-29 November 1937

J. Ralph Pinker in correspondence with **Paul Léon**
Contracts with Viking Press for collected poems, royalties, request from B.B.C. to record extract from *Work in Progress* refused, musical setting by Samuel Barber for *Rain Has Fallen All Day, Sleep Now, O Sleep Now, I Hear an Army*, *10 letters*

3 February-2 December 1938

J. Ralph Pinker to **Paul Léon**
Request to set poems from *Chamber Music* and *Pomes Penyeach* to music, Mr Kilham Roberts would like to include *Strings in the Earth* and Cassells would like to include *Simples* in anthologies, letters from Imhof, B.B.C. wish to broadcast poems, Doubleday Doran wish to include short story in an anthology, Penguin want to use *Two Gallants*, will Mr Joyce authorise an increase in the number of copies of *Work in Progress* to be printed by Faber, *15 letters*

4 January 1939-25 January 1940

J. Ralph Pinker to **Paul Léon**
Dents want to include *Clay* in an anthology, enquiry from Faber re published price of *Work in Progress*, requests from B.B.C. to use poems by Mr Joyce and extract from *Finnegans Wake*, Torch Theatre wish to produce *Exiles*, B.B.C. would like Mr Joyce to give a reading from his work, are Spanish rights of *Dubliners* still available, Longmans would like Mr Joyce to write an introduction to the volume on Freud in their 'Living Thoughts' library, *13 letters*

6.
BUSINESS CORRESPONDENCE: PUBLISHERS, BROADCASTERS ETC

.1   J. HOLROYD-REECE AND M.C. WEGNER OF THE ALBATROSS PRESS, 37 RUE BOULARD, PARIS IN CORRESPONDENCE WITH JAMES JOYCE AND PAUL LÉON, 115 letters with enclosures, 1932-39

ALBATROSS

J. Holroyd-Reece, Leipzig to **James Joyce**, Hotel Ecu, Geneva, *telegram*
Asks to call on Joyce re Albatross proposal to publish *Ulysses*

17 September 1932

S. Hambourg, Secretary, **M.C. Wegner** to **Paul Léon**, *French and English*
Encloses copies of letters to Sylvia Beach and copy of American contract, *2 letters*

28 September, 7 October 1932

R.H. Boothroyd, Albergo Torcolo, Verona to **James Joyce**, Hôtel Métropole, Nice
He is preparing the composition of *Ulysses* for Albatross, Albatross have requested him to adhere to the 1930 Shakespeare edition and to eliminate only the 'literals' therein, he will send a list of corrections for Joyce's approval, wants to substitute the English custom of quotation marks for the French one of dashes

10 October 1932

M.C. Wegner and **Paul Léon** to **Miss Sylvia Beach**
Financial terms of agreement for continental edition of *Ulysses* as they affect Miss Beach

12 October 1932

M.C. Wegner to **James Joyce**, *French*
Terms of the contract for the publication of the continental edition of *Ulysses, 3p, with 2 copies on Hôtel Métropole, Nice writing paper, 1 carbon and 2 drafts*

12 October 1932

Paul Léon to **J. Holroyd-Reece**
Encloses extracts from memorandum about eventual publication of *Ulysses*, he will report their conversation to Mr Joyce who would be pleased to have an English publication of *Ulysses*

14 October 1932

14 October 1932	**Paul Léon** to **M.C. Wegner**, *German* Acknowledges receipt of advance for *Ulysses*, Léon has received a letter from Mr Joyce about Mr Boothroyd's proposal to change the dashes for quotation marks but Mr Joyce wants to keep the dashes, Miss Beach has been in touch about the contract
15 October 1932	**S. Hambourg**, Secretary pp **J. Holroyd-Reece** to **Paul Léon** Returns memorandum
after 12 October 1932	**James Joyce**, Hôtel Métropole, Nice to **The Albatross**, *French* Acknowledges receipt of letter confirming contract for continental edition of *Ulysses* and sets out its terms, *2p*
[c. November 1932]	Page from *L'Avvisatore Librario Settimanale* announcing the publication of *Ulysses* by the Odyssey Press
3 November 1932	**J. Holroyd-Reece** to **Paul Léon** enclosing letter signed by Reece and M.C. Wegner to James Joyce Confirms that *Ulysses* will appear with the specially created imprint 'Odyssey Press' for which Holroyd-Reece and M.C. Wegner will be responsible, *3 letters*
7, 11 November 1932	**Paul Léon** to **M.C. Wegner**, *German and English* Mr Joyce agrees with the contents of the letter of 3rd, period for which Albatross's right of 'first refusal' should be valid, *2 letters*
15, 22 November 1932	**M.C. Wegner** to **James Joyce**, Hôtel Lord Byron, 14 rue Lord Byron, Paris Confirms agreement with letter of 11th, they will print special copies of *Ulysses* on hand made paper for Joyce, Stuart Gilbert, Sylvia Beach, Giorgio Joyce, Harriet Weaver and Paul Léon, the copies for Joyce and Stuart Gilbert to have a special binding, *2 letters*
23 November 1932	**M.C. Wegner** to **Paul Léon** Asks for letter from Mr Joyce granting right of first refusal for publication of *Ulysses* in England to expire within five years
28 November 1932	**James Joyce**, 42 rue Galilée, Paris to **M.C. Wegner**, *carbon typescript unsigned* Agrees that Albatross's right of first refusal for a British edition

of *Ulysses* will expire only if they have failed to take steps to obtain permission for such publication

M.C. Wegner to **Paul Léon**
Encloses colophons for *Ulysses* for signature by Mr Joyce

28 November 1932

M.C. Wegner, The Odyssey Press, Paris to **Paul Léon**
Encloses special edition of *Ulysses* printed with Léon's name as a sign of his appreciation

22 December 1932

Paul Léon to **J. Holroyd-Reece**
Mr Joyce wants to know if Reece has had any reply from Burns and Oates about the publication of the Chaucer ode with initials by Miss Joyce

28 December 1932

J. Holroyd-Reece, Casa Beata, Via Monte Allegro, Rapallo to **Paul Léon**
He is doing all he can in the matter of the Chaucer verses

31 December 1932

S. Hambourg, Secretary, The Odyssey Press to **James Joyce**
Encloses letter from Editorial Zeus of Madrid asking about Spanish translation rights, *with translation, 3 items*

2 January 1933

M.C. Wegner to **Paul Léon**
Requests press excerpts about *Ulysses, endorsed with pencilled notes in Léon's hand: '-telephoned - & cabled - as no reply came I telephoned first to her to my niece to [ ] - [illegible] First published July MCMXXVII by Shakespeare and Co. Paris'*

24 January 1933

M.C. Wegner to **Paul Léon**
Wants address of Susmann Tabakow

9 February 1933

Paul Léon to **J. Holroyd-Reece**
Mr Joyce wants the return of the Miss Joyce's alphabet

10 February 1933

J. Holroyd-Reece to **Paul Léon**
His continued efforts to have Miss Joyce's alphabet published

14 February 1935

Paul Léon to **J. Holroyd-Reece**
Mr Joyce wants the return of Miss Joyce's alphabet, Reece has probably received the *Hull Daily Mail* report of the resolution passed by the Literary Club of Hull University in favour of

20 March 1933

lifting the ban on *Ulysses*, Professor Richards of Cambridge devoted two of his lectures on the modern novel to *Ulysses*

24 March 1933

[E. Tommamaul], Secretary to **Paul Léon**
Mr J. Holroyd-Reece will report developments resulting from action in connection with article in *Daily Mail*

28 March 1933

M.C. Wegner to **Paul Léon**
Encloses royalty accounts for *Ulysses* for 1932

3 April 1933

Paul Léon to **J. Holroyd-Reece**, Connaught Club, 75 Seymour Street, London
Mr Joyce wants to draw Reece's attention to article in *Saturday Review* referring to Mr Caradock Evans whom he has recommended together with *Etched in Moonlight* for the Albatross Collection

7 April 1933

J. Holroyd-Reece to **Paul Léon**
Albatross is interested in Caradoc Evans and James Stephens, Burns and Oates will publish the *Alphabet* on commission, they have asked Reece to look after the production

18 April 1933

M.C. Wegner to **Paul Léon**
Re error in royalty accounts

3 May 1933

Paul Léon to **J. Holroyd-Reece**
Mr Louis Gillet will write a preface to the Chaucer Alphabet

3, 6 May 1933

J. Holroyd-Reece, Casa Beata, Monte Allegro, Rapallo to **Paul Léon**
Confirms that Burns and Oates will publish the Chaucer *Alphabet*, he is willing to undertake the production unless Mr Joyce wishes someone else to do it, as the initials will be done by *pochoir* in Paris it will be best to have printing done in France, terms offered by Burns and Oates, needs to know length of Gillet's preface in order to prepare the layout of the book

12 May 1933

Paul Léon to **J. Holroyd-Reece**
Mr Joyce wants to know what would be a fair remuneration for Mr Gillet whose preface will be 700 words, Gillet should not be told that the book is being brought out on a commission basis

J. Holroyd-Reece in correspondence with **Paul Léon**   17 May 1933
Difficult to decide what fee would be appropriate for Gillet, arrangements for Gillet to see the *lettrines*

Paul Léon to **J. Holroyd-Reece**   20 June 1933
Mr Gillet has written the preface without seeing the *lettrines*, if Reece were to show them to Gillet now he might be able to modify his text, Mr Joyce asks Reece to offer Gillet twelve guineas without letting Gillet know that it is Mr Joyce who is paying

J. Holroyd-Reece, The Pegasus Press in correspondence with   11-21 July
Paul Léon   1933
Correspondence with Louis Gillet, arrangement for his payment, *7 letters*

M.C. Wegner to **Paul Léon**   20 September 1933
Encloses royalty report for *Ulysses* to 30 June and cheque

Paul Léon to **J. Holroyd-Reece**   27 October 1933
Mr Joyce wishes Léon to communicate with Reece about the publication of *Ulysses*, various firms have approached Mr Joyce with proposals but none have matured, danger of plagiator bringing out an edition which will rob Mr Joyce and his publishers of earnings, Léon will do his best to prevent this happening but may not succeed therefore some British publisher should be courageous enough to publish *Ulysses*, *2 carbon copies*

J. Holroyd-Reece, The Connaught Club, London to **Paul Léon**   1 November 1933
Sympathises with Mr Joyce's position, no chance of publishing a trade edition in England which would not be suppressed immediately, against Mr Joyce's interests to have the book officially suppressed

M.C. Wegner to **Paul Léon**   8 December 1933
Encloses royalty report for *Ulysses* to 30 September and cheque, *endorsed with pencilled names and addresses in hand of Paul Léon*

Paul Léon to **J. Holroyd-Reece**   10 December 1933
Mr Joyce asks for the return of the *lettrines* and of Mr Gillet's preface from Messrs Burns and Oates and thanks Reece for what he has done

11 December 1933	**J. Holroyd-Reece**, London to **James Joyce**, *telegram* CONGRATULATIONS ON RELEASE OF *ULYSSES* IN AMERICA
12 December 1933	**Paul Léon** to **M.C. Wegner** Refers to conversation that morning with Wegner, astounded that Mr Reece could think of using the absence of copyright to circulate any edition other than that of Random House in the United States, to do so would be in violation both of Mr Joyce's agreement with Random House and of his agreement with Albatross, Léon will not tell Mr Joyce of his conversation with Wegner, if Mr Reece wants to increase the sale of *Ulysses* he should publish it in England, *2 carbon copies*
14 December 1933	**J. Holroyd-Reece** to **Paul Léon** Will spare Léon the repetition of what he told him on the telephone, would like Léon to write confirming that he had misunderstood the situation and regards his letter of the 12th as withdrawn, Reece and Wegner will forget the incident with no hurt feelings, encloses copy of his letter to Bennet Cerf *[not enclosed]* sorry for delay of Miss Joyce's book
18 December 1933	**S. Hambourg**, Secretary to **Paul Léon** Mr J. Holroyd-Reece has had no reply to his letter of the 14th
18 December 1933	**Paul Léon** to **J. Holroyd-Reece** Glad that since Reece does not want to import his edition of *Ulysses* into the U.S.A. but on the contrary to prevent such importation Léon's protest does not serve any purpose, in order to prevent future misunderstandings suggests that all future communications of importance should be in writing, does not know what policy Cerf intends to follow, *2 copies*
3 January 1934	**Paul Léon** to **The Albatross** He has received a formal offer from a British firm for the publication of *Ulysses*, does Albatross wish to avail of its right of first refusal, no reply by the 8 January will be interpreted as a refusal to publish a British edition of *Ulysses* and an abandonment of the right of first refusal
4 January 1934	**M.C. Wegner** to **Paul Léon** Cannot reply by the 8th as they cannot get in touch with J. Holroyd-Reece who is travelling in Italy, *with carbon copy*

Paul Léon to **The Albatross**
5, 6 January 1933
Cannot extend time limit beyond midday on the 11 January, has received another offer from another British firm, *2 letters*

P.E. Macdonell, Secretary, Mas Saint Gabriel, Saint Mathieu, Grasse to **Paul Léon**
8 January 1934
Mr J. Holroyd-Reece acknowledged receipt of Léon's letter of the 18 December to which he will reply on his return, encloses preface by M. Gillet with 2 photographs of Miss Joyce *[enclosed]* and copies of English translation, payment for translation, *2 letters*

M.C. Wegner to **Paul Léon**
12 January 1934
Confirms telephone conversation in which Wegner agreed Léon should accept offer made by English publishers, if they fail to publish right of first refusal reverts to Odyssey, Odyssey will facilitate English edition by delivering sheets of their edition

Paul Léon to **J. Holroyd-Reece**
22 January 1933[4]
Acknowledges letter of 8th and enclosures, Mr Joyce would appreciate if he could use his influence with Burns and Oates to have the *lettrines* returned to him

Paul Léon to **M.C. Wegner**
22 January 1934
The firm which acquired the option for the publication of *Ulysses* in England is John Lane The Bodley Head, their first success is recorded in *The Sunday Dispatch*, does not agree that the right of first refusal will revert to Albatross if John Lane fails

J. Holroyd-Reece to **Paul Léon**
23 January, 10 February 1934
Acknowledges letter of 22nd, apologizes for delay in returning *lettrines*, *2 letters*

Paul Léon to **J. Holroyd-Reece**
11 February 1934
Needs Miss Joyce's *lettrines* as he has a proposal for the publication of the Chaucer poem

J. Holroyd-Reece to **Paul Léon**
15 February 1934
The *lettrines* are probably in Reece's safe in Grasse, apologises for delay in returning them

M.C. Wegner to **Paul Léon**
2 March 1934
Encloses royalty account for *Ulysses* for 1933, *endorsed with pencilled notes in hand of Paul Léon*

16 April 1934

J. Holroyd-Reece to **Paul Léon**
Thanks for Léon's letter of the 13th, apologises for delay in return of *lettrines*

2 June 1934

Paul Léon to **J. Holroyd-Reece**
The return of Miss Joyce's *lettrines* is absolutely necessary as the publisher will not be able to publish them for the Xmas holiday unless he gets them now

12 June 1934

J. Holroyd-Reece to **Paul Léon**
Apologizes for delay in returning *lettrines*, they are not in his safe at Grasse, he has written to England for them

18 June 1934

Paul Léon to **J. Holroyd-Reece**
Asks for return of *lettrines* without further delay as publisher is menacing that he will hold Léon responsible for the delay if he does not get them in time for the Christmas market, if Léon does not get the *lettrines* he will have to transfer the responsibility to Reece

20 June 1934

J. Holroyd-Reece to **Paul Léon**
The *lettrines* were apparently sent to Paris, he is doing everything he can to have them traced, he feels very guilty in these unpleasant circumstances, *with carbon copy extract*

4 July 1934

Paul Léon to **J. Holroyd-Reece**
Mr Joyce has not yet received the *lettrines* and cannot wait any longer, a Dutch editor has made an offer to publish them and if he does not receive them on the specified date Léon's client will be involved in a pecuniary loss and Léon will be reluctantly compelled to claim damages from Reece, *with manuscript draft*

11 July 1934

P.E. Macdonell, Secretary to **Paul Léon**, *postcard*
Mr J. Holroyd-Reece will answer Léon's letter of the 4th direct to Mr Joyce

12 July 1934

J. Holroyd-Reece, Connaught Club, London to **James Joyce**
He is unwilling to deal any longer with Paul Léon whose manner and methods he dislikes, he feels mortified with regard to the *lettrines*, objects to the vulgarity of Léon's semi-commercial, semi-threatening attitude, nevertheless he is doing everything he can to find the *lettrines*, at the moment the

matter is in the hands of the Paris Postmaster General, *2p,
annotated in hand of James Joyce: 'What should I do about replying to
this?', with three carbon typescript copies*

M.C. Wegner to **Paul Léon**   13 July 1934
Encloses royalty account for *Ulysses* to 30 June 1934

James Joyce, Grand Hôtel Britannique, Spa (Belgique) to   4 August
J. Holroyd-Reece, *3 typescript copy letters one initialled 'J.J.'*   1934
Dear Mr Reece,
   I received your letter of the 12th July just before I left Paris. I
am sure that you meant to be of service to me as far as you could
in the matter of my daughter's lettrines and I thought that
everything was satisfactorily concluded when I got Mr Louis
Gillet to write the preface and paid for it and its translation into
English and was prepared to agree to pay Messrs Burns and Oats
[*sic*] the £225 to bring out the Chaucer book on commission,
provided it was included in their next catalogue. You said this
would be done but nothing at all happened. Then warned by my
thirty years experience of English publishers and their ways, I
accepted a Dutch firm's offer to bring out the book without any
payment from me and it appears that Messrs Burns and Oats
[*sic*] to whom you entrusted the lettrines are unable to restore
them to you.
   I have a very high opinion of these lettrines and an opinion
which so eminent an art critic as Mr Gillet endorses, but apart
from that they are also a family document of great value to me
and I regard their eventual loss in the same light as I should
regard the loss of one of my own MSS which had cost me
months of labour.
   Could you send me a copy of the letter sent by Messrs Burns
and Oats [*sic*], or their art adviser, to you in reply to your
request for the restitution of the lettrines?
   As for Mr Léon, he has always had my interests at heart but I
cannot imagine that, though he is more practical than I in his
outlook, he had any intention of offending you when he wrote
as you say. I hope the wording of this letter is correct. I never
write letters of business and it seems that this is one, and that
the shorter and clearer I make it the better. But indeed I
looked forward to the publication of the Chaucer book with my
daughter's illustrations before Christmas and now, it appears,
that is impossible even if the lettrines are found now. I do not
know whose fault it is but it is somebody's fault surely.
   sincerely yours.
   J.J.

16 August
1934

James Joyce, Hôtel Brasseur, Luxembourg to **J. Holroyd-Reece**, *carbon typescript unsigned*
Dear Mr Reece,
   I have had no reply from you since I wrote to you last and as you will see from the enclosed letter of my Dutch publisher he insists on the matter.
   I think that you must by now have had ample time to ascertain from your Paris office where the lettrines are as it is essential for me to have them as quickly as possible.
   I think it would be advisable to ask Mr Verhulst to see Messrs Burns and Oates and Mr Morrison during his stay in London. It will I hope help matters along and save the incomprehensible delays in the return of the lettrines.
   As I am not staying long at the above address you would oblige me by replying care of Mr Paul Léon at his usual address in Paris.
   sincerely yours.

1 September
1934

J. Holroyd-Reece, Hotel Fürstenhof, Leipzig to **James Joyce**
M. Gillet is not in Paris now, the search continues

11-13
December
1934, 29
March 1935-3
August 1936

M.C. Wegner in correspondence with **Paul Léon**
Royalty cheque, error in calculation, royalty accounts, German income tax, delays due to German authorities, enquiry from Martins Forlag, Copenhagen about terms for a Danish edition of *Ulysses, 13 letters*

15 February
1937

J. Holroyd-Reece, Bernard Tauchnitz, 16, Place Vendôme, Paris to **James Joyce**
Asks Joyce to contribute to a booklet containing extracts from letters by prominent authors in praise of the Tauchnitz Edition, *with enclosed booklet 'Tauchnitz Edition: collection of British and American authors' and typescript article 'The Work of Messrs. Bernard Tauchnitz 1837-1937'*

7 April 1937

J. Holroyd-Reece to **Paul Léon**, *French*
Léon wrote to him asking for Mr Joyce's half yearly account, M Wegner has instucted them to make up the accounts on a yearly basis rather than half yearly, the accounts for 1936 are enclosed and will be paid as soon as the German authorities give authorisation

Paul Léon to **J. Holroyd-Reece**, *French*
Has no objection to yearly accounts, has not yet received anything for 1936 or 1937

6 December 1937

J. Holroyd-Reece to **Paul Léon**, *French*
Delays in payment inevitable as accounts have to be submitted to the German authorities, *annotated in Léon's hand 'written on May 24 1938 asking for payment for 1936 and accounts for 1937'*

9 December 1937

[Sonia] Hambourg and **J. Holroyd-Reece**, Albatross & Tauchnitz in correspondence with **Paul Léon**
Royalty payments, new impression of *Ulysses*, payments due to Miss Beach, complaints that edition of *Ulysses* is sold out, receipt for corrected copy of proofs of *Finnegans Wake*, *15 letters*

25 May 1938-
23 August
1939

.2 THE ARGUS BOOKSHOP, CHICAGO AND HAZEL FELMAN (MRS J.R. BUCHBINDER) IN CORRESPONDENCE WITH PAUL LÉON AND ERIC S. PINKER
Negotiations for the publication of a fragment of *Anna Livia Plurabelle* with a musical setting by Hazel Felman, *8 letters*

ARGUS
20
September
1934-13
January 1936

.3 HENRY BABOU, ÉDITEUR, 1 RUE VERNIQUET, PARIS IN CORRESPONDENCE WITH PAUL LÉON, *French*
Authorisation for Faber & Faber to advance the publication of *"Haveth Childers Everywhere"* to 15 March 1931 and proposed publication of Mr Joyce's poems with *lettrines* by Lucia Joyce, *4 letters*

BABOU
9 March
1931, 29
January, 4
February
1932

.4 SYLVIA BEACH, "SHAKESPEARE AND COMPANY", 12 RUE DE L'ODÉON, PARIS IN CORRESPONDENCE WITH JAMES JOYCE AND PAUL LÉON, 41 letters with enclosures, c.1931-39

BEACH

List of German, Swiss and English articles about James Joyce in the possession of Sylvia Beach and Supplementary lists of books, *4p*

c.1931-39

[Paul Léon] to **Sylvia Beach,** *typescript draft unsigned*
Acknowledges her letter of 4 February which he has transmitted to Mr Joyce, need for a contract for the future publication of

[?8 February
1932]

159

Ulysses, glad that she admits the prejudicial character of Mr R[osenfeldt]'s letter to Mr L[evy], *with manuscript draft endorsed with pencilled drafts of letters re death of Joyce's father*

8 February 1932

Paul Léon to **Sylvia Beach**
Thanks for her letter annulling the contract existing between her and Mr Joyce and recognising his ownership of the rights of *Ulysses*, Léon wishes to draw up a contract regarding the Continental rights to *Ulysses*

9 February 1932

Sylvia Beach to **Paul Léon** enclosing letter to **Mr Rosenfeldt**
Will Léon show enclosed letter to Mr Rosenfeldt to Mr Joyce and if Mr Joyce approves send it to Rosenfeldt, *with 2 copies of Sylvia Beach's letter to Rosenfeldt and copy extracts from Rosenfeldt's letter to Louis Levy dated 2 November 1931 and from Rosenfeldt's covering note to Sylvia Beach dated 9 January 1932, endorsed with pencilled notes in hand of Paul Léon*

11 February 1932

Paul Léon to **Sylvia Beach**
Mr Joyce has not yet given instructions about her letter of the 9th, he encloses a letter from Cape to Mr Joyce with a copy of the reply

9 March 1932

Paul Léon to **Sylvia Beach**
Mr Joyce has shown him the cable which she received from America about the seizure of Roth's plagiarized edition, he would like to meet her in order to make a decision about the future continental edition of *Ulysses*, *with manuscript draft*

15 April 1932

Sylvia Beach to **James Joyce**
Royalty account for *Ulysses*

14 July 1932

Paul Léon to **Sylvia Beach**
Mr Joyce told him that Miss Beach said the number of copies of *Ulysses* left for sale was ninety, will she let him know of her decision about a new edition

8 August 1932

Jean Henley pp **Sylvia Beach** to **James Joyce**
Miss Beach asked her to send enclosed letter from Warner Brothers, National Films asking the price of the film rights of *Ulysses*, the address he wanted was under the pen name 'W.K. Magie' [*sic*], *with enclosed letter from Warner Bros. annotated in hand of James Joyce 'Est ce une plaisanterie? Qui sont ces gens-là?'*

BEACH

Sylvia Beach to **James Joyce**
Royalty account for *Ulysses*

M.C. Wegner, The Albatross to **Sylvia Beach**, *copy letter*
With reference to their recent conversation he thinks that her idea that *Ulysses* should be published in the Albatross Library is excellent, will she forward proposals to Mr Joyce

6 September 1932

Paul Léon to **Sylvia Beach**, *copy letter*
Encloses letter for Mr Joyce, Albatross would be willing to pay her an extra fee of 10%

6 September 1932

Paul Léon to **Sylvia Beach**
Mr Joyce has telephoned from Nice to ask him to ask Miss Beach to send the royalties of the 11th edition of *Ulysses* as quickly as possible as he is in need of money

27 September 1932

Sylvia Beach to **Paul Léon**
She has wired money to Mr Joyce

28 September 1932

Paul Léon and **M.C. Wegner** to **Sylvia Beach**
They have come to an agreement about a continental edition of *Ulysses*, at the particular request of Mr Joyce she is to receive 25% [*sic, recte 2.5%?*] of the sum received by him at signature of the contract and then 25% [*sic, recte 2.5%?*] of the royalties for five years, *2 copies*

12 October 1932

Sylvia Beach to **James Joyce**
Sends complete Chaucer, letter and articles from Mr Okakura and letter asking permission to quote one of Joyce's poems, perhaps Léon could reply to these now that he has taken charge of Mr Joyce's affairs, she is sorry she no longer has the time or energy to do so, thanks Mr Joyce for the sacrifice to her of part of his royalties in the contract with Albatross, she will not accept it for an indefinite period, *2p*

24 October 1932

Paul Léon to **Sylvia Beach**
Wishes to discuss a new edition of *Pomes Penyeach* which is running out of print, Mr Joyce will be hurt if she does not agree to the arrangement he made for her share of the royalties of *Ulysses*

31 October 1932

2 November 1932	**Sylvia Beach** to **James Joyce** She found his *pneu* when she got back last night, she will wait for him in the shop tomorrow
7 November 1932	**Paul Léon** to **Sylvia Beach** Does she consider making a new edition of *Pomes Penyeach*
8 November 1932	**Sylvia Beach** to **Paul Léon** Only fifty copies of *Pomes Penyeach* left, as they are first editions she has raised their price to 20 francs, Mr Joyce need not feel that his contract with her binds him if he wishes to go to an English or American publisher, she could accept twenty thousand francs under the arrangement with Albatross as an equivalent of the value of the plates of *Ulysses*, and more later if Mr Joyce becomes rich
14 November 1932	**Paul Léon** to **Sylvia Beach** Mr Joyce strongly wishes her to accept the arrangement he has made with Albatross, he is opposed to the sale of what he calls a book of inoffensive verse for as much as 20 frs and would like to buy the remaining copies, he will accept proposals for a new edition from another publisher
15 November 1932	**Sylvia Beach** to **Paul Léon** She will accept Mr Joyce's arrangement with Albatross though she thinks he has been too generous, she is sending Mr Joyce twenty five copies of *Pomes Penyeach* and will give away the other twenty five to friends, she hopes Mr Joyce has found his manuscript
24 November 1932	**Paul Léon** to **Sylvia Beach** Mr Joyce wants to know whether she wishes to continue the administration of his accounts with his German and other publishers, if not Léon will do it, Léon is glad to read that she accepted the arrangement with Albatross
28 November 1932	**Sylvia Beach** to **Paul Léon** She will be glad for Léon to take over Mr Joyce's affairs with his continental publishers and will hand over the papers to him, it is interesting to hear about the limited edition of *Ulysses* that will soon appear
1 March 1933	**Paul Léon** to **Sylvia Beach** Mr Joyce wants to know how many copies are left of *Our*

Exagmination and at what price she would be willing to remainder them, he supposes the price she mentioned in 1931 will now be lowered

Sylvia Beach to **Paul Léon**   3 March 1933
The price quoted to Mr Eliot in 1931 was not exorbitant but what it cost her, when Mr Joyce's new book comes out she may have a chance to sell the copies she has left so it would be stupid to let some publisher have them for a song, however she will listen to any reasonable offer, with regard to *Ulysses* she asked for what she thought it was worth

Paul Léon to **Sylvia Beach**   17 March 1933
On behalf of Mr Joyce asks for a copy of *Our Exagmination*, 10 copies of the announcement of the OUP Joyce book, the Japanese cheque, and manuscript copies of *Chamber Music* and *Pomes Penyeach* bound in leather

Sylvia Beach to **Paul Léon**   20 March 1933
Encloses 200 yen cheque, she will send *Our Exagmination* to Léon and the prospectuses for *The Joyce Book* to Mr Joyce, she will look up the books Mr Joyce mentions but thinks that he may have them somewhere himself

Sylvia Beach to **Paul Léon**   31 March 1933
Asks for acknowledgement of Japanese 200 yen cheque

Paul Léon to **Sylvia Beach**   3 April 1933
Acknowledges Japanese cheque

Sylvia Beach to **James Joyce**, *postcard detached from accompanying*   14 April 1933
letter
She has replied that she has handed their letter to him

Sylvia Beach to **Paul Léon**   8 May 1933
A copy of Chaucer's poems including the A.B.C. hymn to the Virgin was sent to Mr Reece, Mr Joyce's account, *with invoice*

Sylvia Beach to **Paul Léon**,   22 June, 1
Encloses letters from Tibor Lutter and cheque from Whitman   July 1933
Publishing Company, where should she forward letters to Mr Joyce, *with enclosures*

6 July 1933

Paul Léon to **Sylvia Beach**
Acknowledges cheque, Mr Joyce's address in Evian is the Grand Hôtel

16 March
1935

Sylvia Beach to **James Joyce**
Kahane has given his consent so she sends Miss Dorothy Pantling's two books for his signature

13
September
[193?5]

Sylvia Beach to **Paul Léon**, *picture postcard*
Asks him to forward letter to Herbert Gorman.

31 July 1936

Paul Léon to **Sylvia Beach**
Encloses her share of the royalties due on *Ulysses* from Albatross for 1936

3 August
1936

Margaret H. Newitt pp **Sylvia Beach** to **Paul Léon**
Miss Beach sailed for America last week, receipt for royalties

3 March 1939

Paul Léon to **Sylvia Beach**
Encloses her share of the additional royalties due on *Ulysses* from Albatross for 1936

6 March 1939

Sylvia Beach to **Paul Léon**, *postcard*
Acknowledges royalties

BLACK SUN
PRESS

.5 CARESSE CROSBY, EDITOR, THE BLACK SUN PRESS, RUE CARDINALE, PARIS AND 36 WEST 59TH STREET, NEW YORK IN CORRESPONDENCE WITH JAMES JOYCE AND PAUL LÉON, 32 letters, 1932, 1935-36

11, 17
November
1932

Paul Léon in correspondence with **Caresse Crosby**
As Mrs Crosby is first publisher of *Tales Told of Shem and Shaun* Léon informs her that two of the tales will be published in a popular edition by Faber, *2 letters, draft and carbon*

5 December
1935

Caresse Crosby to **James Joyce**
She would like to bring out an edition of his collected poems with an unpublished portrait of him

12 January
1936

Paul Léon to **Caresse Crosby**
Agrees in principle to her proposal, what would be the circulation, permission required from New York and English

publishers, *Ecce Puer* is the only additional poem he can think of, suggests the portrait by Augustus John would be suitable, there is also a portrait by Jacques Emile Blanche

Caresse Crosby to **Paul Léon**   30 January, 2
She would like to bring out an edition of 1,000 to 2,000 copies,   March 1936
she has reached an agreement for a limited edition by Black
Sun Press and a trade edition by Viking Press, she would like to
publish 50 copies on Japan paper signed by Mr Joyce, Eugene
Jolas suggested using limericks that Mr Joyce has written for his
friends and other poems from *Ulysses* and from *Work in Progress*,
2 letters

Paul Léon to **Caresse Crosby**   10 March
Mr Joyce's royalty, payment for his signature, her edition   1936
cannot be sold in England unless she makes agreements with
Cape and Faber, she could deal with Miss Beach or Brentano or
Galignani on the continent, Mr Joyce will not agree to have any
extracts from *Ulysses* or *Work in Progress* included in a collection
of his poetry

Caresse Crosby to **Paul Léon**   20 March
Disappointed that she cannot use poems from *Work in Progress*,   1936
Eugene Jolas says there are several limericks of Mr Joyce's that
he once expressed a wish to have published, her payment for
Mr Joyce, she has had no answer from Augustus John

Paul Léon to **Caresse Crosby**   6 April, 12
Terms for her edition of poems, no reply received, 3 letters and   May, 23, [?]
2 typescript telegrams   1936

Caresse Crosby, Ermenonville to **James Joyce**   [24] June
Terms of agreement reached with Mr Léon, encloses cheque   1932 [*recte*
                                                      1936],

Paul Léon to **Caresse Crosby**   29 June 1936
Her letter and cheque reached Mr Joyce too late so matter
abandoned

Caresse Crosby, Ermenonville to **Paul Léon**   1 July 1936
Reasons for delay, breakdown of her costs

Paul Léon to **Caresse Crosby**   6 July 1936
He is empowered to resume negotiations, objects to the tenure

[*sic*] of her letter, the only point which interests him is the royalties, he wonders whether they are having a business discussion or merely making a tea appointment which can easily be broken

7 July 1936

Caresse Crosby, Paris to **Paul Léon**
Hopes to make a satisfactory arrangement before returning to America

10 July 1936

Paul Léon to **Caresse Crosby**
Terms agreed with Mr Huebsch

10, 16, 18 July 1936

Caresse Crosby, Paris to **Paul Léon**
Arrangements for payment, encloses letter from Michael Sevire *(enclosed)* seeking return of drawing of Joyce by Augustus John which she will bring back with her to London, *4 letters*

21 July 1936

Paul Léon to **Caresse Crosby**
Terms of agreement

22 August 1936

Caresse Crosby to **Paul Léon**, *telegram*
Terms agreed

3 September 1936

Paul Léon to **Caresse Crosby**
Returns her cheque, signed photos of Augustus John's portrait sent some time ago

8, 21 October 1936

Caresse Crosby to **Paul Léon**
Acknowledges cheque, surprised to receive from Pinker Léon's letter of 21 July

15 October– 21 December 1936

Eric S. Pinker in correspondence with **Caresse Crosby**
Terms of agreement, extra copies, *5 copy letters*

BBC

.6   B.B.C. (BRITISH BROADCASTING CORPORATION) IN CORRESPONDENCE WITH JAMES JOYCE AND PAUL LÉON, 4 letters, 1933-39

21 August 1933

British Broadcasting Corporation, London to **James Joyce**, c/o Messrs. Shakespeare & Co, 12, rue de l'Odéon, Paris
Seeks reply to letter regarding broadcast of Mr Joyce's poem *On the beach at Fontana*

British Broadcasting Corporation/Lawrence Gillian and **R.G. Walford**, London in correspondence with **Paul Léon**
Confusion re proposals for broadcast in connection with *Finnegans Wake*, Mr Joyce feels his eyesight would prevent him taking part in a broadcast, he recommends Madam Rachel Berendt who would be willing to give a reading from *Finnegans Wake*, proposed broadcast for 11 July abandoned, *3 letters*

15 June-7 July 1939

.7   JONATHAN CAPE, 30 BEDFORD SQUARE, LONDON IN CORRESPONDENCE WITH JAMES JOYCE AND PAUL LÉON, 6 letters and royalty reports, 1927-30, 1932-37

JONATHAN CAPE

Hamish Miles, Hotel Lutetia, 43 Boulevard Raspail, Paris to **James Joyce**
Messrs Jonathan Cape would like to publish a truncated version of *Ulysses* which would have a general circulation in England, he would like to call on Joyce to discuss this

9 February 1932

James Joyce, 2 avenue St Philibert, Paris, XVI to **Hamish Miles**, *carbon typescript unsigned*
Dear Mr Miles,
   Messrs. Cape had an opportunity of publishing such a book as you allude to some years ago when they were offered Stuart Gilbert's *Ulysses* (a commentary with extracts). They refused it stating that the subject had no interest for the British public. The book was at once accepted by Messrs Faber & Faber who are bringing out a cheaper edition this year, I am told. It has since been published in America and Germany and a French edition will also be arranged.
   My agent in London, Mr Ralph Pinker is at present negotiating for an American edition of *Ulysses* and possibly also an English one. I have given him my instructions. My text is to be published as I wrote it, unabridged and unaltered. I do not discuss this matter with publishers.
   Sincerely yours,

9 February 1932

Jonathan Cape to **James Joyce**
He did not manage to see Joyce when he was in Paris, he was amused that Joyce's son and daughter-in-law thought they met him in Nice

16 January 1933

6 April 1934   **Rupert Hart-Davis**, Director, Jonathan Cape Ltd. to **James Joyce**
Has sent copies of *Portrait of the Artist as a Young Man* and of *Dubliners* in the new 'Flexibles' edition

20 December 1937   **G. Wren Howard**, Director, Jonathan Cape Ltd to **Paul Léon**
Thanks for Léon's letter of December 18th re permission for Doubleday Doran to publish Mr Joyce's story

[? September 193?]   **N. Templeton [Durcan]**, Jonathan Cape Ltd to ?
Acknowledges letter of 21st September, wants to know exact length of quotations from James Joyce's work in order to reply to letter regarding acknowledgements

1927-30   Royalty reports for *Dubliners, Exiles, Chamber Music* and *Portrait of the Artist as a Young Man, 24p*

1932-36   J. Curwen & Sons Ltd in account with James Joyce/Jonathan Cape for royalties, *4p*

CONNER   .8   BENJAMIN H. CONNER OF CHADBOURNE, STANCHFIELD & LEVY, NEW YORK AND PARIS IN CORRESPONDENCE WITH JAMES JOYCE AND SYLVIA BEACH, 12 letters with enclosures, 1926-27, 1930-32, 1935, 1939

23 November, 9, 14 December 1926, 1 February 1927   **Benjamin H. Conner** to **Sylvia Beach**
Arranges meetings, encloses cable correspondence with New York office, refers to correspondence re claim for piracy of *Ulysses, 4 letters, in envelope marked in hand of Sylvia Beach 'Business with Conner'*

June 1929   Injunction against Samuel Roth and Two Worlds Publishing Company Inc prohibiting them from publishing any work of James Joyce. Reprinted from *transition*, June 1929, *in envelope marked in hand of Sylvia Beach 'certificate of copyright registration, injunction'*

21 January, 1 May 1930   **Benjamin H. Conner** to **James Joyce**
Encloses copies of interim deposit and final registration of Part XV of *Work in Progress* in the Library of Congress, encloses copy of his letter of 12 February and statement of account from Messrs. Chadbourne, Stanchfield & Levy, New York, *8p*

James Joyce to **Mr. Conner**, *typed draft letter unsigned*
Asks Conner to forward his previous letter to Conner's partners in New York, not surprised Conner has separated from them if his experience of them has been as disastrous as Joyce's has been, on all previous occasions Joyce paid Conner's account promptly, the brochure brought out by Conner's ex-partners useless for protecting his rights, he believed he was the owner of the rights to *Ulysses* when he attempted to defend them against Roth but has recently discovered that he does not possess them, copy of contract with Miss Beach was never sent to Conner, *with carbon copy*

18 December 1931

James Joyce to **Mr Conner**, *manuscript draft letter in hand of Paul Léon*
Had he known he was not the owner of the American rights of *Ulysses* he would not have sued Roth or paid Conner's bill, he feels no obligation for the rest of Conner's fees, he did not express his opinion before of the way the case was conducted because he believed the injunction gave him some protection

[? January 1932]

Benjamin H. Conner to **James Joyce**
Letters seeking payment and summons, *3 letters, 8p*

23 December 1932, 19 December 1935, 27 July, 24 August 1939

.9 VISCOUNT CARLOW OF THE CORVINUS PRESS, 34 CHESHAM PLACE, LONDON AND 12-14 RED LION COURT, FLEET STREET, LONDON IN CORRESPONDENCE WITH JAMES JOYCE AND PAUL LÉON, 14 letters, 6 August 1936-[?April 1939]

CORVINUS PRESS

Paul Léon to **Lord Carlow**
Encloses two *lettrines* intended to illuminate the first letter of the text and the first letter of the notes of Mr Joyce's fragment, Mr Joyce attaches great importance to the *lettrines*, he would not have considered publication of the fragment if it had not been for them, typographical difficulties in printing of fragment

6 August 1936

Lord Carlow to **Paul Léon** and **James Joyce**
Acknowledges receipt of initials and corrected copy of *transition*, encloses pages of different types assembled to see what effect they produce, *2 letters*

29 August [193?6], [? 1936-37]

169

4 January
1936[?=7], 14
July 1937

R.M. Kelly and **D.A. Culmore** pp **Lord Carlow** to **Paul Léon**
Lord Carlow will bring the proofs to Paris on 7 January,
comments on typography, he is anxious to pull final proofs, *2
letters*

17 July 1937

Paul Léon to **Lord Carlow**
Corrected proofs and *transition* returned a month ago

22 November
1937, 25
January, 23
February, 2,
28 March, 8
April 1938

D.A. Culmore, Secretary, Corvinus Press to **Paul Léon**
Despatch of proofs and finished copies of *Storiella* to Mr Joyce
and others, *6 letters*

31 January
1939

Lord Carlow to **James Joyce**, *telegram*
SAW DELAWARE YESTERDAY YOUR BOOK ALREADY
DESPATCHED FROM GLASGOW BY AIR

[?April 1939]

Lord Carlow to **James Joyce**
Thanks for poem on Ibsen, he missed Mr Joyce's son who had
left for Paris, thanks for inscription in book, does not
understand it all though Mr Joyce's explanation made it a little
clearer

DENT

.10   BRIAN AND ERNEST RHYS OF J.M. DENT & SON IN
CORRESPONDENCE WITH JAMES JOYCE AND PAUL LÉON,
14 letters, 1936-38

29 July 1936

Brian Rhys to **James Joyce**
His father has asked him to write to Joyce about publishing a
selection of Joyce's writings in the Everyman's Library, suggests
a meeting

30 July, 3
August 1936

Paul Léon to **Brian Rhys**
Thinks the idea of publishing a one volume selection of Mr
Joyce's work a good one, Rhys will have to get in touch with Mr
Joyce's London publishers, asks who will write the intro-
duction, arrangements for meeting with Mr Joyce, he will write
to Mr Lane, *2 letters*

5 August
1936

Brian Rhys to **Paul Léon**, *postcard*
Dent will have talks with other publishers

W.G. Taylor, Director, J.M. Dent & Sons to **Paul Léon**
Has Léon heard anything from Mr. Lane

21 August
1936

Paul Léon to **W.G. Taylor**
Lane would consider the idea of an Everyman's Library selection of Joyce favourably

3 September
1936

Ernest Rhys, Hotel Corneille, Paris, Grand Hôtel Continental, Beauvais and J.M. Dent, London to **James Joyce**
Would like to meet Joyce while he is in Paris, selection of work to appear in Everyman, Léon should point out to Cape and Lane that publication in the Everyman Library would lead to increased sales of his other work so they would gain rather than lose, *3 letters, 5p, with Everyman catalogue*

28, 29 April,
24 May 1938

Paul Léon to **E. Rhys**
Knows too little about Rhys's plans to be able to negotiate with the different publishers

30 May 1938

Ernest Rhys to **Paul Léon**
He hopes to have a revised list of contents ready in a few days, he is sure Léon will have a better chance of getting permission from Cape and Lane than Messrs Dent would

9 June 1938

Paul Léon to **E.Rhys**
Suggestions for contents of Everyman selection

10 June 1938

Ernest Rhys to **Paul Léon**
Agrees with selection proposed by Léon, other items selected by Rhys's son Brian, *2 letters*

15, 20 June
1938

.11   T.S. ELIOT, RICHARD DE LA MARE AND OTHERS OF FABER & FABER, 24 RUSSELL SQUARE, LONDON IN CORRESPONDENCE WITH JAMES JOYCE AND PAUL LÉON, 174 letters with enclosures, 1930-40

FABER

Richard de la Mare, Faber & Faber to **James Joyce**
Sorry that Mr Eliot's own copy of *Anna Livia Plurabelle* was sent to Joyce with the proofs by mistake, will he return it

3 January
1930

26
September,
14, 17
November
1930

C.W. Stewart and **Richard de la Mare**, Faber & Faber to **James Joyce**
Thanks for signed agreement for *Haveth Childers Everywhere*, they are forwarding proofs, what colour would Mr Joyce like the cover to be, *3 letters*

24 November
1930

T.S. Eliot, London to **Sylvia Beach**, Paris, *telegram*
IS JOYCE PARIS OR ZURICH PLEASE WIRE ADDRESS WRITING

[25
November
1930]

Sylvia Beach to **T.S. Eliot**, *carbon typescript copy of telegram*
JOYCE ZURICH HOTEL ELITE CARLTON PROBABLY RETURNING PARIS THURSDAY

[4 December
1930?]

James Joyce to **Faber**, London, *carbon typescript of telegram*
YOUR PUBLICATION FRAGMENT MUST BE POSTPONED TILL APRIL LETTER EXPLAINS

4 December
1930

Paul Léon to **T.S. Eliot**
Mr Joyce has asked him to explain all the details concerning the publication of a cheap edition of *Haveth Childers Everywhere*, conditions of contract with Messrs Babou and Kahane, Kahane's objection to cheap edition, *2p*

15 December
1930

T.S. Eliot to **Paul Léon**
Position very vexing, nothing to be done but to wait for Mr Kahane's permission to produce pamphlet by 1st May 1931

4 February
1931

Paul Léon to **T.S. Eliot**
Mr Joyce tired on account of failure of various persons to keep their promises to engage Mr Sullivan, he did not intend to write a libretto for Mr Antheil but merely introduced him to Mr Sullivan and suggested that Antheil should set Byron's *Caïn* to music for Sullivan to sing, Mr Babou says he will consent to publication of *Haveth Childers Everywhere* sooner than date Eliot mentioned, the French translation of *Anna Livia Plurabelle* is progressing well

4 March 1931

T.S. Eliot to **Paul Léon**
He has not heard from Mr Joyce, he would be obliged if Léon would write to Mr Babou to get permission to publish Faber's shilling edition of *Haveth Childers Everywhere* as soon as possible

Paul Léon to **T.S. Eliot**
9 February 1932

Miss Beach has annulled the contract which existed between her and Mr Joyce so that Mr Joyce is now the owner of the world rights for *Ulysses*, Mr Joyce is to receive a proposal for an American edition of *Ulysses*, it is urgent to obtain any other offers so as to have a basis for discussion, there are four preliminary conditions - no preface, text to be unabridged and unaltered, publication as soon as possible, text of the 11th Paris edition to be read by an expert proof reader

James Joyce to **T.S. Eliot**, *carbon typescript, unsigned*
9 March 1932

Dear Elliot [sic],

Here is book No. 8 about me etc. I think it should appear in America not England or France, but I suppose it will not interest you in which case please send the letter back by return.

Colum cables me about a sixth American offer for the American Ulysses asking me to hold over to the 16-th inst. My daughter in law's brother Mr Robert Kastor in whom I have complete confidence sailed for new York this morning. I gave him full power of attorney to deal with Cerf, Morrow, Colum or anybody else on the basis of a draft agreement I got Pinker to send over by air-mail.

Sincerely yours.

Paul Léon to **T.S. Eliot**
12 March 1932

Mr Joyce acknowledges receipt of his letter and thanks him for the addresses of Lady Morel [sic] and M. Schiff which he wanted in connection with the publication of a limited edition of a reproduction of his manuscript of *Pomes Penyeach* with capitals illuminated by Lucia Joyce, Eliot will receive under separate cover a proof copy of *James Joyce and the plain reader* by Mr Duff which he should read and send on to Miss Weaver

P. Wilberforce, Secretary, Faber & Faber to **Paul Léon**
15 March 1932

Mr Eliot acknowledges letter of 12 March

Paul Léon to **T.S. Eliot**
14 July 1932

Encloses extract from letter containing doctor's opinion on Mr Joyce's eyesight and copy of letter to Mr Joyce's literary agent in London, Mr Joyce would like Eliot's opinion about the projected book of his daughter

19 July 1932

T.S. Eliot to **Paul Léon**
Had already had a letter from Mr Joyce and was expecting a detailed report from Léon, he will write to Mr Joyce and will have a word with the literary agents about the work of Mr Joyce's daughter

9 November 1932

F.V. Morley, Faber & Faber to **James Joyce**
Saw the copy of *Pomes Penyeach* with Miss Joyce's initials, what else does she plan to do, he was told that Mr Joyce was again laid up, regrets delay in publishing *Two Tales of Shem and Shaun*, has arranged to have proofs collated with Black Sun edition, plans to publish Eliot's fragments of *Sweeney Agonistes* simultaneously, *2p*

17 November 1932

Paul Léon to **F.V. Morley**, Faber & Faber
Re applications from Servire Press to publish a *de luxe* edition of the new fragment of *Work in Progress*

22 November 1932

F.V. Morley, Faber & Faber to **Paul Léon**
Under the contract for *Work in Progress* Faber has the exclusive licence for publishing the work in volume form in the British Empire so they should be consulted about publishing *de luxe* limited editions of any fragments, if they do not want to publish such editions themselves they would not stand in anyone else's way, *2p*

23 November 1932

Paul Léon to **F.V. Morley**, Faber & Faber
Legally Mr Joyce is free to publish fragments as Faber's contract is only for the British Empire, Léon is glad to hear Faber would be interested in bringing out a limited edition of a fragment, text of fragment in question exists only in proofs and *transition* will not be ready for a month or so, Servire Press are anxious for an early reply because they have the text set and are anxious to make use of it, Faber might also be able to use it, it would be easier to get Mr Joyce to consent to publication if some work of his daughter could be incorporated

9 December 1932

F.V. Morley, Faber & Faber to **Paul Léon**
Does not agree with Léon's interpretation of the contract, nevertheless would be glad to see text of new fragment, unlikely that Faber would be able to use the type set by Servire, has been doing his best to find an opening for Lucia Joyce's work about which Mr Joyce wrote to him, would consider

incorporating her work in the limited edition of the fragment, will send copies of the next *Criterion* to Mr Joyce's sister and to his father's executor, *2p*

M. Evans, Secretary, Faber & Faber to **Paul Léon**
Copies of *The Criterion* have been sent to Mr Joyce's sister and his father's executor

22 December 1932

Paul Léon to **Faber & Faber**
Encloses copy of proofs of new fragment to be published shortly in *transition*, corrected text is in Mr Pinker's hands

3 January 1933

T.S. Eliot to **Harriet Weaver**
Enquires about the early publishing history of *Ulysses* with a view to discussing the matter with a high official, can she confirm his version, the legal position is obscure

5 January 1933

F.V. Morley to **Paul Léon**
Thanks for text of fragment, has discussed it with Mr Pinker who will communicate with Léon after he has been in touch with the American publishers

10 January 1933

Paul Léon to **F.V. Morley**
Faber should announce the publication of the OUP edition of *Pomes Penyeach* in their edition and vice versa

23 January 1933

F.V. Morley to **Paul Léon**
They will cooperate if the OUP gives them a leaflet for insertion in their edition

27 January 1933

F.V. Morley to **Harriet Weaver**
Receipt made out to Harriet Weaver on behalf of James Joyce for the first eight episodes of *Work in Progress*, being Part 1 of the whole

10 March 1933

Paul Léon to **F.V. Morley**
Forwards on behalf of Mr Joyce a sample of an edition of Mr Rémy de Gourmont, Mr Joyce would be pleased if Faber could obtain some similar character, any decision about new fragment of *Work in Progress*, pleased with first copies of *Pomes Penyeach*; Mr A. Bergan says no copy of December's *Criterion* reached him, will Morley send a copy of Stuart Gilbert's book on *Ulysses* to Mr F. Budgen, has Morley a copy of the cheap or large paper edition of

12, 14 March 1933

Our Exagmination, Miss Beach will remainder some, will Morley send a copy of *Haveth Childers Everywhere* for the Bibliothèque Nationale, Mr Joyce is very pleased with the edition of *Pomes Penyeach* especially with the corrections in the list of his works and the *'justification du tirage'*, he would like such *'justification'* to be introduced in the fragments of his *Work in Progress* as it is the only means to do justice to his first publishers, *2 letters, 3p*

16 March 1933

F.V. Morley to **Paul Léon**
The December *Criterions* were sent out, if Miss Beach will send a copy of the cheap edition of *Our Exagmination* they will consider the question again, sends complimentary copy of *Haveth Childers Everywhere* for the Bibliothèque Nationale, notes what Mr Joyce says about *'justifications'*, Faber has decided against bringing out a limited edition of the new fragment of *Work in Progress* as the Viking Press refuse to take part and a canvass of the bookshops had disappointing results, Faber would however like to bring out a cheap edition, *3p*

27 March 1933

Paul Léon to **F.V. Morley**
Sends a copy of *Our Exagmination*, what would be the best price to dispose of the remaindered copies on the British market

7 April 1933

F.V. Morley to **Paul Léon**
Faber is unable to do an edition of *Our Exagmination*, recommends a bookseller in Cambridge to take over Miss Beach's remaindered stock

19 July 1933

M. Evans, Secretary, Faber & Faber to **Paul Léon**
Acknowledges Léon's letter of the 15th, has sent copy of *Two Tales of Shem and Shaun* to Georg Goyert

25 September 1933

T.S. Eliot to **James Joyce**
Asks for news of Joyce, may visit Paris before the end of the year

4 October 1933

F.V. Morley to **James Joyce**
Asks Mr Joyce's permission to lend pages 28 and 29 of the corrected text of *Work in Progress* to the Sunday Times Book Exhibition, hopes Mr Eliot will write to Joyce soon, *2p*

13 October 1933

F.V. Morley to **Paul Léon**
Thanks for his letter of the 12th, he will get in touch with Miss

Weaver about the manuscript pages and will give Mr Joyce's message to Mr Eliot

Paul Léon to **F.V. Morley**   27 October 1933
Enclosure is evidence of another attempt to publish a plagiarised edition of *Ulysses* in England, while publishers are waiting to see the weather change some plagiator will bring out an edition which will deprive Mr Joyce and his publishers of their legitimate earnings, Léon will stop at nothing to prevent this happening, it is time for a British publisher to take the risk of publishing *Ulysses, 2 carbon typescripts*

F.V. Morley to **Paul Léon**   2 November 1933
Situation with Amen Corner Pirates infuriating but if *Ulysses* is copyright in England there should be no difficulty in securing an injunction against piracy, question of the copyright of *Ulysses*, Mr Eliot may be in Paris in November, *2p*

Paul Léon to **F.V. Morley**   19 November 1933
Encloses notes on the circulation of *Ulysses* in Great Britain, it is time to do something about bringing out *Ulysses* in England, the Home Office might hint that they would not start a case against it, there is a constant stream of copies going to England which take away the readers of the eventual British edition, Mr Joyce is strongly advised to undertake the publication of *Ulysses* in Great Britain himself

F.V. Morley to **Paul Léon**   21 November 1933
Thanks to Léon and Mr Joyce for their hospitality

T.S. Eliot to **James Joyce**   28 December 1933
Thanks for his letter of the 18th, sorry Mr Joyce's solicitors misunderstood his query, Eliot accepts that *Ulysses* is copyright in England in Joyce's name, he would merely like to have a lawyer at hand who was completely conversant with the publishing history of *Ulysses*

Paul Léon to **Messrs Faber & Faber**   3 January 1934
He has received an offer in writing for the publication of an edition of *Ulysses* in Great Britain with a six months option to allow negotiation with the British authorities, will Faber & Faber make a counter offer

177

9 January
1934

F.V. Morley to **Paul Léon**
Legal preparations and the interest of people in power vital for the successful publication of *Ulysses* which can be damaged by a customs ban, a magistrate's decision or a Home Office action, private opinions of people in power in the Home Office are not encouraging therefore Faber consider there is little possibility of publishing *Ulysses* without a court action and little possibility of winning that action, Faber would like to publish *Ulysses* as well as *Work in Progress* so if their rival's option lapses they would like to be able to cut in, encloses original page specimen for *Work in Progress* for Mr Joyce's approval, *3p*

9 January
1934

T.S. Eliot, *The Criterion* to **James Joyce**
Faber & Faber are prepared to publish *Ulysses* as soon as publication feasible, history of the banning of *Ulysses* difficult to establish, impossible to get a definite statement from the Home Office but it would be possible to take the official temperature, it is not vital that *Ulysses* should be available before *Work in Progress*, public opinion is changing and will be more favourable in a year's time, to provoke a court case would be premature, *3p*

3 February
1936

T.S. Eliot to **James Joyce**
Received the manuscript of Part III from Mrs Jolas last week, the printers are capable of handling it, Mrs Jolas thought Part II would be finished in four or five months, Eliot had a pleasant time in Dublin, *2p*

16 February
1936

Paul Léon to **T.S. Eliot**
Encloses correspondence and insertions for Part III delayed owing to Mr Joyce's attacks of episcleritis over the past seven weeks, Mr Joyce thinks Eliot is over optimistic about the capacities of British printers, *2 carbon typescripts one shorter than the other*

21 February
1936

T.S. Eliot to **Paul Léon**
Acknowledges letter of 16th

17 April 1936

T.S. Eliot to **James Joyce**
Cost of setting up text by printers outrageous, better if it could be clearly typed first as suggested by Mrs Jolas, this would be done under Léon's supervision in Paris, it would save trouble if Joyce could correct the typescript, he will bring the manuscript of which no copy exists to Paris himself in a month's time when he plans to give a reading in Sylvia Beach's shop, *2p*

T.S. Eliot to **James Joyce,** *telegram* — 7 May 1936
REFERRING MY LETTER SEVENTEENTH APRIL AM COM-
ING PARIS JUNE SIXTH SHALL I BRING MANUSCRIPT, *anno-
tated in hand of Paul Léon 'Stated my opinion five months ago'*

Paul Léon to **T.S. Eliot** — 3 July 1936
Progress and cost of typing, Mrs Léon will bring Parts I and III
to London, wants Eliot to send over copies of *Anna Livia
Plurabelle* and of *Tales told*, there are only three corrections in
Haveth Childers but the corrections in *Anna Livia* are much
more numerous

T.S. Eliot to **Paul Léon** — 7 July 1936
Has sent a cheque for the typing to Joyce, he may be away when
Madame Léon comes

Paul Léon to **T.S. Eliot** — 12 July 1936
They have just finished Parts I and III in time for Mrs Léon to
bring them to London, wants more money for typing of Part I,
Mr Joyce is working on Part II so the book may be out within a
year

T.S. Eliot to **James Joyce** — 24 July 1936
Encloses cheque for typing of Part I which is more than was
originally agreed to

F.V. Morley to **James Joyce** — 10 September 1936
Thanks for Joyce's letter of the 5th to Eliot, has been unable to
find the copy of *Mesures* in his room, he will get hold of another
copy and study it for a specimen page as Joyce suggests

Paul Léon to **T.S. Eliot** — 7 December 1936
Mr Joyce asked Léon to return the three types of printing
marking the one he prefers with a red pencil, the work is
progressing well and could be out within a year from July last

Brigid O'Donovan, Secretary, Faber & Faber to **Paul Léon** — 10 December 1936
Mr Eliot acknowledges Léon's letter of the 7th

M.E., Faber & Faber to **Paul Léon** — 29 January 1937
Miss Weaver asked for a duplicate of page 182 of *Work in
Progress* which they enclose

23 April 1937   **Dorothy Groling, Secretary,** Faber & Faber to **Paul Léon**
Sending galley proofs of pp126-209 of *Work in Progress*

27 April 1937   **Anne Bradley, Secretary,** Faber & Faber to **Paul Léon**
Acknowledges his letter and list of misprints

3 June 1937   **T.S. Eliot,** *The Criterion* to **Paul Léon**
Apologies for delay in answering Léon's letter of 24th, Lord Carlow will bring the parts of Part II which he is to print privately, they do not dare to assemble the parts of Part II published in *transition*

14 December 1937   **T.S. Eliot,** *The Criterion* to **Paul Léon**
Thanks for letter of 11 December and enclosures, another section of Part II printed by Lord Carlow also arrived, how much more matter will there be, is Lord Carlow going to publish another section, if so he must obtain a licence from Faber, *2p*

18 December 1937   **Paul Léon** to **T.S. Eliot**
Distressed that his covering letter with the manuscript was lost, details of the four sections of Part II of *Work in Progress*, Parts I and III have all been corrected, an epilogue will complete the whole work, better to compose Part II section by section, pages of *The Mime of Mick and the Maggies* are being translated into French for *La Nouvelle Revue Française* who are bringing out an issue in homage to Mr Joyce, *2p*

21 December 1937   **Anne Bradley, Secretary,** *The Criterion* to **Paul Léon**
Mr Eliot acknowledges Léon's letter of the 18th and enclosures

1 January 1938   **Paul Léon** to **T.S. Eliot**
Mr Joyce has received enclosed letter from Mr Huebsch from New York and is upset at the idea that his book should appear in the autumn rather than the spring, will Eliot get in touch with the Viking Press about bringing the book out in the spring and about the other points Huebsch raises, when will the proofs of the first sections of Part II be back in Paris for correction

6 January 1938   **T.S. Eliot** to **Paul Léon**
Very surprised at how near book is to completion, impossible for either Faber or the Viking Press to bring it out in

February but they would need to have the complete text in their hands by February in order to bring it out in the autumn, the production department ask that Mr Joyce should make his divisions very clear on the galleys, they had not allowed for side notes in arranging the format of the page, it would be a help if they could know the title of the book in confidence, *4p*

T.S. Eliot, *The Criterion* to **Paul Léon** — 18 January 1938
Encloses specimen pages for Mr Joyce, Lord Carlow gave him the dummy for the page arrangement of the book, Lord Carlow also said Mr Joyce would like to have the book published on July 4th which would not be possible

[**Paul Léon** to **T.S. Eliot**], *draft letter in hand of James Joyce* — 23 January 1938
I spoke with Mr J this morning over the telephone when I rang him up to inform him that I had received 15 short galleys of "Lord Carlow's [private version] corrected". He asked me to point out for the third time that Lord Carlow never had anything whatever to do with the version in question which was printed in The Hague and distributed by Faber & Faber in England and to add that, so far from expediting the work of printing, the English printer has apparently taken 6 weeks to do what a French printer would do in a couple of days.

He also asked me to transmit unto you the following:

After my receipt of yours of the – he cabled to his son (at present visiting N.Y.) to telephone Mr Huebsch on this subject. His son replied by cable to say Mr H considered publication in July unreasonable but would await the arrival in New York early in February of Mr Morley of your firm in order to confer with him before deciding. Mr Joyce wishes me to remind you, in view of this proposed conference, that Mr Huebsch is the person who always believed that a publication of *Ulysses* in the United States was impracticable and that Mr Morley is the person who believed, even after Mr Huebsch had been proved by events to be wrong that a publication of *Ulysses* in England was also impracticable. Mr Joyce is perfectly well aware that the 4th July is the American National holiday (five members of his family owe their Christian names to this fact, including his son) and it is precisely for this reason, among others, that he wishes his book to be published in England on that day and in the U.S.A on the eve of that day, his fathers *[sic]* birthday. If no intelligent effort will be made to comply with his wishes he sees no use in continuing to work night and day as he has done and plans to leave for Switzerland after his own birthday (2 February) for a holiday of several months, resuming work on his book in the autumn, *annotated in hand of Paul Léon 'Reply to Mr Eliot sent on January the 23rd 1938'*

26 January 1938

Geoffrey Faber to **Paul Léon**
Mr Eliot handed him Léon's letter of the 23rd and previous correspondence, he has replied direct to Mr Joyce, copy enclosed

26 January 1938

Geoffrey Faber to **James Joyce,** *carbon typescript*
Mr Eliot felt Léon's letter of the 23rd needed to be answered by the head of the firm, Faber could publish on July 4 provided they received the rest of the manuscript in the next two or three weeks and provided they could be sure the correction of the proofs would not take too long, it would be very difficult for the Viking Press to publish on July 3, Joyce should recognise his publisher's difficulties and reconcile himself to publication in early September if July proves impracticable rather than instructing Léon to write in such extraordinary terms, *2p*

21 February 1938

Geoffrey Faber to **Paul Léon**
Thanks for letter of 17th, sorry to hear Mr Joyce's eyesight has been suffering

11 March 1938

T.S. Eliot to **James Joyce**
Encloses specimen page, the only possible alteration would be for the notes on the right hand side to be set out in italics instead of capitals, they did not know that one section of the book would present these features, how much more fresh matter is to come, *2p*

18 March 1938

T.S. Eliot, *The Criterion* to **Paul Léon**
Will pass Léon's letter of the 16th to Mr de la Mare, sorry to hear of the cause of the interruption to Mr Joyce's work

23 May 1938

T.S. Eliot to **Paul Léon**
Mr de la Mare needs information about the proofs, what do the red pencilled lines mean, does Mr Joyce wish to see revised galley proofs, can they assume there will not be any additions or omissions, *2p*

Richard de la Mare to **Paul Léon**
Further points on which he needs instruction, progress of the printing of *Work in Progress*, when may they expect to receive the final part of Mr Joyce's manuscript, *15 letters and postcards, 17p*

24, 27 May, 1, 14, 16, 27, 30 June, 11, 25 July, 22, 24 August, 5, 27 September, 13 October 1938

Paul Léon to **Richard de la Mare**
Thanks for his letters, repaging of episode with marginal notes in Part II, Mr Joyce has made corrections to the last pages of his book as a result of a dinner given in his honour on Thanksgiving Day when his daughter-in-law read aloud those pages, he would also like to introduce an alteration on page 1

6 November 1938

Richard de la Mare to **Paul Léon**
Details of printing and proof corrections of *Work in Progress*, cannot give a definite date of publication at this stage, would like to know the title of the book, *3 letters, 5p*

18, 21, 22 November 1938

Paul Léon to **Richard de la Mare**
Sends new version of last pages of book and corrected revise of the sixty four first pages, there won't be any dedication or preface, corrections and additions to galleys of Part III will be more or less equal to those on Part I but Part II will have much less except a little more on episode IV

26 November 1938

Richard de la Mare to **Paul Léon**
Details of printing and proof corrections of *Work in Progress*, they should be able to send Mr Joyce an advance copy of his book by 2 February though the actual date of publication will be later than that in order to allow for simultaneous publication in London and New York, can he tell Mr Huebsch about the title, the covers, the limited edition, the Canadian rights, spoke to Mr Eliot about the unpublished poem of Byron, why does Mr Joyce wish to keep the title a secret, *8 letters and 1 postcard, 15p, letter dated 29 November endorsed in Léon's hand: 'And all because, loosed in her pond reflexes, she seem she seen Ericoricori Coricome huntsome with his three poach dogs aleashing him. But you came safe through Unless? Away!'; letter dated 20 December endorsed in Léon's hand with draft of his letter to De la Mare dated 22 December*

28, 29 November, 2, 6, 8, 15, 20, 27 December 1938

22 December 1938

Paul Léon to **Richard de la Mare**
Mr Joyce wishes to keep the title a secret because he is afraid of attack by American Irish elements who used their influence against *Ulysses*, the title is a form of a song of a comic Irish musichall type and would give opportunity for advance attack, the Canadian rights

23, 28, 30 December 1938, 2, 3, 9, 10 January 1939

Richard de la Mare to **Paul Léon**
Details of printing and proof corrections of *Work in Progress*, 4 letters, *2 postcards and 1 telegram, 8p*

12 January 1939

Paul Léon to **Richard de la Mare**
Encloses corrections, strongly objects to indentation of text on page 307 as it spoils the idea of a text-book annotated by studying children

12, 13 January 1939

Richard de la Mare to **Paul Léon**
Details of printing and proof corrections of *Work in Progress*, 2 letters, *3p*

14, 16 January 1939

Paul Léon to **Richard de la Mare**
Encloses corrections, hopes advance copy will be ready for 2 February, what will be the price of the ordinary edition, wants to know approximate date of publication in view of impending international crisis, Mr Joyce says he wrote to Mr Eliot many months ago about the 'Lessons' episode and Lord Carlow showed him a '*maquette*' of it but Léon does not wish to start a controversy about it at this stage, *2 letters*

17, 20, 24, 25, 26, 27 January 1939

Richard de la Mare to **Paul Léon**
The printers are reaching the end of their tether, price for ordinary edition will be 25/-, publication date will probably be April, they did not see Lord Carlow's expensive production till long after they had begun setting up the earlier parts of the book, has no explanation for enquiries Léon has been getting for the words of Tim Finnegan's Wake, progress of printing and corrections, he should be able to get an advance copy to Mr Joyce in time, he is not happy about the style of the binding, *7 letters and 1 telegram, 13p, letter dated 20 January endorsed with notes of corrections in Léon's hand*

Paul Léon to **Richard de la Mare**   29 January
Glad that de la Mare intends sending copy on Monday,   1939
alternatively Lord Carlow could bring it over on Wednesday,
final corrections for pages 614 and 526

Richard de la Mare to **Paul Léon**   30 January
Léon's letter of the 29th came too late, could still make 1939
correction on page 614 but he understands it depends on
correction on page 526, advance copy will be sent off today by
airmail, faults in the binding, *2p*

Paul Léon to **Richard de la Mare**   30 January
The book arrived, thanks for the trouble de la Mare took, Mr 1939
Joyce will write himself, final corrections

Richard de la Mare to **Paul Léon**   31 January, 1,
Re jacket for *Finnegans Wake*, Mr Joyce's name should be 6, 7 February
printed as big as possible, he is glad that Mr Joyce was pleased 1939
with the appearance of the book, what does he think of the
binding, glad Mr Joyce is leaving dust jacket to them, encloses
revised proofs of title page of *Finnegans Wake*, *4 letters*, *5p*, *letter
dated 7 February endorsed with addresses of Arthur Power and James
Stephens in Léon's hand*

Paul Léon to **Richard de la Mare**   8 February
Encloses copy of letter sent to Huebsch, Huebsch's slackness, 1939
will show proofs of title page to Mr Joyce tomorrow, hopes he
can have the sheets for signature before Mr Joyce goes away to
rest, agrees to Pinker's wire for proposed prices of 25/- and
£5.5 for ordinary and limited editions of *Finnegans Wake*

Faber & Faber to **Paul Léon**
Invoice for cost of airmail postage of advance copy of Joyce's
new book from Glasgow

Richard de la Mare to **Paul Léon**   10 February
Where to make the break for the second volume of the limited 1939
edition of *Finnegans Wake*, *2p*

Paul Léon to **Richard de la Mare**, *signed letter*   12 February
Encloses title page with indication of changes, referring to 1939
telephone conversation thinks it should be possible for
Huebsch to have the book out in forty five days rather than

sixty five, Mr Joyce would prefer *Finnegans Wake* to be printed in one volume, Louis Gillet is preparing an article for his *Revue des Deux Mondes* for the date of publication, could de la Mare send him an advance copy, *2p*

13, 16, 17, 23
February, 2,
10 March
1939

Richard de la Mare, A.B.V. Drew to **Paul Léon**
Unsure of date of publication, has abandoned idea of publishing in two volumes, will send an advance copy to Louis Gillet and to Edmond Jaloux, title page, hopes to bring book out on 4 May, sends alternative binding case, wants gold lettering but Mr Joyce's plan for the contrasting yellow can be used on the top edges of the book, *4 letters and 1 telegram, 7p*

15 March
1939

Geoffrey Faber to **Paul Léon**
De la Mare is ill, Léon has misinterpreted preliminary announcement in the catalogue of Viking Press, to advise Mr Joyce not to sign the sheets of the limited edition would place Faber in an impossible position and would hold up the ordinary edition

17 March
1939

Paul Léon to **Geoffrey Faber**
Returns specimen cover, sheets will be signed after receipt of satisfactory reply from America, publication has been postponed three times, he is taking steps for the early publication of a cheap European edition, *2 copies*

17, 23, 28
March 1939

Richard de la Mare to **Paul Léon**
Re signature sheets, assumes Mr Joyce approves of binding, Huebsch says he can publish three weeks after shipment is cleared, hopes to publish on 4 May, a cheap European edition would spoil sales in England, acknowledges receipt of all the signed sheets, *3 letters, 6p*

28 March
1939

Paul Léon to **Richard de la Mare**
Has submitted to Mr Joyce de la Mare's remarks about a cheap European edition, will let him know when Mr Joyce makes a decision, has heard a rumour that Huebsch says he 'hopes' to bring the book out on 8 May, advance copies have not yet been received by the French critics

29 March
1939

James Joyce to **Messrs Faber & Faber**, *carbon typescript, unsigned*
Letter revoking his authorization to James B Pinker & Sons to act as his agents and receive payments on his behalf

A.B.V. Drew, David Bland to **Paul Léon**

29, 30 March 1939

Mr de la Mare is ill, Mr Eliot has sent advance copies of *Finnegans Wake* to Gillet and Jaloux, will try to persuade Mr Huebsch to keep to the 4th of May publication date, sends finished copy of dust jacket, *2 letters, letter of 30 March endorsed with draft letter in Léon's hand*

Paul Léon to **Richard de la Mare**

2 April 1939

Mr Joyce does not approve of the jacket, the title and name of the author make a sentence which will be a standing joke, the back in equal characters does not look good, the unbound pages sent to Louis Gillet are not what Mr Joyce and Léon understand by advance copies which are always papercovered and look like books

David Bland to **Paul Léon**

3 April 1939

Agrees that addition of word 'by' to the jacket will be an improvement, they were anxious to forward advance copies as soon as possible, they are almost certain to publish on 4th May depending on date by which limited edition can be cleared in the American customs

Paul Léon to **R. de la Mare**

12 April 1939

What will Faber do with the English edition if Huebsch abandons the idea of publication, list of persons on the continent to whom review copies should be sent, what will be the price and time of publication of the second edition, he needs this information for his meeting with the continental editors

Richard de la Mare, A.B.V. Drew to **Paul Léon**

18, 24, 26, 27 April, 4 May 1939

He is confident the American publishers will publish, the price for the second edition will be the same as for the first, cannot give a time of publication, review copies sent out, publicity department want a photograph of Mr Joyce, *5 letters, 6p*

Paul Léon to **Richard de la Mare**

8 May 1939

Has obtained from Mrs Joyce two photographs taken in Zurich last year, wonders what Faber needs them for as there does not seem to be much advertising of the book, *Irish Times* contained a notice for *Finnegans Wake* by Sean O'Casey, Faber deducted the extra 80% of the author's corrections from amount due to him, Léon cannot therefore understand how the corrections contribute to the exorbitant price of the book, it looks like a book of about 15/-, press copy should be sent to Frank Budgen

10, 16 May 1939

A.B.V. Drew, Richard de la Mare to **Paul Léon**
Error on page 34, photographs wanted for review purposes, they wrote to *Irish Times* about mistake, book has been extensively advertised, price not unreasonable, he did not mention heavy cost of proof corrections as a contributory factor to the price but the heavy cost of setting the book up, they have sent many review copies, *2 letters*

16 May 1939

Paul Léon to **Richard de la Mare**
Confirms error on page 34

30 May, 14, 15, 20, 26 June 1939

Richard de la Mare, A.B.V. Drew, Morley Kennerley to **Paul Léon**
They have written to *Irish Times* about their mistake in attributing the authorship of *Finnegans Wake* to Sean O'Casey, their failure to print a correction has nothing to do with Faber's not advertising in the *Irish Times*, they do not find advertising in the *Irish Times* much good but have reconsidered the matter as Mr Joyce feels so strongly about it, the book is selling well, *5 letters, 6p*

c. June-July 1939

Paul Léon to **Faber & Faber**, *draft letter in hand of Paul Léon*
Complains re refusal of publicity manager to put advertisement for *Finnegans Wake* in the *Irish Times* and re meagre advertisement in the *Sunday Times* which was inserted only after repeated requests, the lack of advertising and the book's prohibitive price will reduce its chances of circulation

3 July 1939

Paul Léon to **M. Kennerley**
Encloses advertisement approved by Mr Joyce, the editor of the *Irish Times* wrote Mr Joyce a personal letter of apology though Mr Joyce laughed at the comical side of their error, Mr Joyce has special reasons for wanting an advertisement in the *Irish Times*, he also wanted an advertisement in the *Sunday Times*, the good sales are in spite of limited advertisement and exorbitant price, broadcast by Mr A. Péron on the radio station Paris P.T.T. about *Finnegans Wake*, the B.B.C. plan something similar, *2p*

6 July 1939

Richard de la Mare to **Paul Léon**
Acknowledges letter to Mr Kennerley

Paul Léon to **Richard de la Mare**   22 July 1939
Every time Mr Joyce looks at *Finnegans Wake* he finds misprints, he would like to start making corrections for the second edition on the sewn sheets sent to Monsieur Gillet, the advertisement in the *Irish Times* pleased him

C.W. Stewart, A.B.V. Drew to **Paul Léon**   28 July, 24, 30 August 1939
Acknowledging and passing on letters, *3 letters*

Corrections for Finnegan's Wake:

Additions to the first revise pages (end of Part II), pp. 386-99, *carbon typescript page*

Copy of corrections made on first revise pages 497 to 512

Galley 43, *carbon typescript page*
Galley 46, *carbon typescript page*
Galley 47, *carbon typescript page endorsed with notes in Léon's hand*

> Muta   So that when we shall have acquired unification We shall pass on to diversity and when we shall have passed on to diversity we shall have acquired the instinct to combat and when we shall have acquired the instinct of combat we shall pass back to the spirit of appeasement?
>
> Juva   By the light of the bright reason which daysends to us from the high.
>
> Muta   May I borrow that hordwanderbaffle from you, old rubberskin?
>
> Juva   Here it is and I hope it's your worming pen, Erinmouker!

Koot

There'll be others but non so for me. I read in that to be continued tale that while blubles blows there'll still be sealskers.

Sketches for title page and cover of Finnegan's Wake in hands of James Joyce and of Paul Léon, *2 items*, [1939]

Faber & Faber's prospectus and order form for Finnegan's Wake 'Ready in April or May', and Faber & Faber compliment slip, *3 items*, [1939]

GALLIMARD

6 December
1937

.12   PAUL LÉON TO LA LIBRARIE GALLIMARD, Paris
Publication by Gallimard of *Ulysses* without any preliminary agreement

HARMS-
WORTH

.13   DESMOND HARMSWORTH, 13 HYDE PARK GARDENS, LONDON IN CORRESPONDENCE WITH PAUL LÉON, 6 letters, 1932-33

12, 15 March
1932

Paul Léon to Desmond Harmsworth
Mr Joyce does not wish to comment on Mr Duff's book with prefatory letter by Herbert Read as he thinks it improper for an author to give an opinion on a book about himself, Philippe Soupault's name was omitted from the list of translators of the fragment from *Anna Livia Plurabelle*, *2 letters*

30 November
1932, [?]
December
1933

Paul Léon to Desmond Harmsworth
Mr Joyce and his daughter are surprised that they have not heard from Harmsworth since *Pomes Penyeach* came out, which of the subscribers have paid, Mr Joyce had to hand over 1.000 frs to Mr Kahane who paid that amount to his daughter; request for an account of copies sold and for a statement of account, *2 letters*

13 December
1933

Desmond Harmsworth, 15 Quai Bourbon Paris IV to **Paul Léon**
Ten copies of *Pomes Penyeach* have been sold and 7000 frs received, further orders and cancellations, cost of production was approximately 10.000 frs, *3p*

18 December
1933

Paul Léon to Desmond Harmsworth
Acknowledges letter of 13th

LANE

.14   ALLEN LANE, JOHN LANE, THE BODLEY HEAD, VIGO STREET, LONDON IN CORRESPONDENCE WITH PAUL LÉON, 73 letters with enclosures, 1934-39

2 January
1934

Allen Lane, S.A.G.A., T.S. "Côte d'Azur" to **Paul Léon**
Arranging a meeting, *2p*

3 January
1934

Allen Lane, 27, Rue Casimir-Périer, Paris VII
Letter confirming his offer for the publication of *Ulysses*, *2p*, *with 2 carbon typescript copies*

Paul Léon to **Allen Lane**   28 January
The history of the publication of *Ulysses* in England from the   1934
point of view of its suppression on the grounds of alleged
obscenity, sources for information about its author, the
American story of the publication of *Ulysses*, hopes to collect
opinions of *Ulysses* published in French reviews, an article in
the *Law Journal* 16 March 1929 shows the heads under which
Ulysses could be attacked, *2p*

Allen Lane to **Paul Léon**   5, 28
Collection of evidence in favour of *Ulysses*, *2 letters*   February
                                                                   1934

Paul Léon to **Allen Lane**   14 March
Encloses documents and articles favourable to *Ulysses*, Mr   1934
Harold Nicolson would help

Allen Lane to **Paul Léon**   20, 25 March
Thanks for material received, would like to arrange a meeting   1934
with Mr Joyce in Paris, *2 letters*

Allen Lane to **J. Ralph Pinker,** *copy letter*   21 July 1934
In reply to letter of 20th John Lane have decided to print
Ulysses but have had difficulty in finding a printer

Paul Léon to **Allen Lane**   11, 21 August
Desirable to give the decision of the U.S. Appellate Court   1934
regarding *Ulysses* wide publicity in England, campaign started
by Society of Authors gratifying, he met a Mr Cork who wishes
to write about the censorship story of *Ulysses*, approves of plan
to publish edition in Britain, encloses copy extract of letter
from Mr Verhulst of The Servire Press to Mr Joyce about review
copies of his last fragment which Faber seem unwilling to send
out, *2 letters, 4p*

Allen Lane to **Paul Léon**   24 August
Impossible to get a definite opinion from anyone in authority   1934
as to whether or not proceedings would be taken against
Ulysses, because they were unable to find printers to undertake
its printing they have registered a separate company to do it,
will Mr Joyce sign 250 copies

Allen Lane to **J. Ralph Pinker,** *copy letter*   29 August
Present position with regard to *Ulysses*, size of the edition, legal   1934

191

expenses and costs of publication, they cannot afford to let the present royalty stand, *2p*

27 November 1934

Paul Léon to **Allen Lane**
Professor Laski has offered to obtain a letter in support of *Ulysses*, the U.S. government has abandoned the idea of lodging a new appeal against *Ulysses*

27 November 1934

Paul Léon to **Professor H.J. Laski**
Thanks for his letter, John Lane will reply to him

4 December 1934, 10 January 1935 *with enclosure 9 January 1935*

Allen Lane to **Paul Léon**
Thanks for letter of 27th November, they will wait to see what space they have for literary and other opinions before taking up Professor Laski's offer; encloses copy letter from Francis Meynell who is in charge of the typography of *Ulysses* suggesting descriptive running page headlines on all the recto pages possibly following the Random House divisions.

23 January 1935

Paul Léon to **Allen Lane**
Mr Joyce is opposed to headlines at the top of the pages, Léon had thought the American edition followed the Albatross one, as this is not the case Lane should follow the Albatross edition which has been corrected by Mr Gilbert, mistake on p141 of the first issue

29 January 1935

Allen Lane to **Paul Léon**
He has told typographer to follow Albatross version

24 October 1935

Allen Lane to **J. Ralph Pinker,** *copy letter*
He has not been pushing on with the publication of *Ulysses* as the Public Prosecutor has been particularly vigilant of late, Laurence Meynell has however designed a layout for the book, *endorsed with notes in Léon's hand*

20 February 1936

Paul Léon to **Allen Lane**
His letter to Pinker in reply to Lane's plan of producing an illustrated edition of *Ulysses*, objects to price of such an edition, failure of *The Joyce book* issued by the Oxford University Press at two guineas, the profit from it was intended to go to Mr Joyce but he never received anything, Lane should check with Hughes who was the moving spirit of the book

Allen Lane to **Paul Léon**, *telegram*
WOULD APPRECIATE YOUR TELEGRAPHING MOST CON-
VENIENT TIME TO SEE ME ON FRIDAY OR SATURDAY

18 March
1936

Paul Léon to **Allen Lane**
He managed to see Mr Joyce for a few minutes on Saturday,
Mr Joyce was very sceptical about what Léon told him of
Lane's progress with the publication of *Ulysses*, Léon would
now like a definite undertaking from Lane and sets out the
conditions for the publication of the first edition of *Ulysses*
and for a subsequent edition with illustrations by Matisse
along the lines of what Lane himself suggested; thanks Lane
for his letter of the 24th accepting the conditions, will accept
Lane's modification so far as price and number of copies are
concerned, cannot accept delay in bringing out trade edition,
2 letters, 3p

22, 25 March
1936

Paul Léon to **Allen Lane**
Thanks for letter of 30 June re progress in printing and fixing
of tentative date of publication for 25 September, points about
increase of first edition to 1,000 copies, answers queries about
misprints in letter to Mr Pinker; thanks for letter of 8th July,
agrees to edition of 1000 copies, important to be prepared for
interference from authorities, wants to know what material
Lane proposes to put in an appendix, *2 letters, 3p*

6, 10 July
1936

Edward Young, Production Department, John Lane The
Bodley Head Ltd to **Paul Léon**
Encloses batch of queries, *not enclosed*

14 July 1936

Paul Léon to **Messrs John Lane**
Encloses reply to first batch of queries, glad about meticulous
way they establish the text, he takes up every individual query
with Mr Joyce himself

16 July 1936

Allen Lane to **Paul Léon**
Thanks for letter of 10 July, will send proofs of material for
appendix and 100 sheets for Mr Joyce's signature

16 July 1936

Edward Young to **Paul Léon**
Encloses batches of queries, *not enclosed*, pages for Joyce's
signature, design by Eric Gill for binding, *2 letters, 3p*

20, 30 July
1936

30 July 1936	**Paul Léon** to **Allen Lane**, *signed letter annotated 'copy'* Has reached with Mr Young page 350 of the Albatross text, it will be difficult to reach Mr Joyce after 10 August about the rest and about the signatures as he will be far from Paris, proposal from Everyman's Library to publish a selection of Mr Joyce's work including a selection from *Ulysses*
6, 10, 13, 15, 21 August 1936	**F. Baker,** John Lane The Bodley Head to **Paul Léon** Encloses pages for signature by Joyce and lists of queries, *not enclosed, 5 letters*
24 August 1936	**Edward Young** to **Paul Léon** Encloses batch of queries, *not enclosed, annotated in hand of James Joyce: 'Unanswered questions, Cead mile failte, I think 'mile' is correct Irish for 1000 with one 'l', See my Irish-English or English-Irish dictionary in flat, Can't place last question, Perhaps wrongly indicated, To be repeated in next batch'.*
26 August 1936	**Allen Lane** to **Paul Léon** Printer says he will have final batch of slip proofs by 10 September, would welcome extracts from *Ulysses* being included in Everyman Library
1 September 1936	**Edward Young** to **Paul Léon** Encloses further queries, *not enclosed*, including repetition of last query for which he gave wrong line on page
3 September 1936	**Paul Léon** to **Allen Lane** Has written to Dent's but reserves for Mr Joyce final right to approve choice for Everyman Library, worried about the printing of *Ulysses*, Mr Joyce is away so queries cannot be attended to swiftly as Mr Joyce must verify every reply, does not want any delay so corrections which are mostly punctuation marks could be attended to by the reader who must be conversant with Mr Joyce's orthography by now, hopes the book will be out by 1 October
7 September 1936	**Allen Lane** to **Paul Léon** Has had trouble keeping printer up to date with proofs, wants their edition of *Ulysses* to be as perfect as possible hence referring of smallest matters to Mr Joyce, has employed a man especially to supervise the work, it would be a pity to risk any imperfections and Léon must see the Appendix material

Edward Young to **Paul Léon**
Confirms at Mr Joyce's request that he has received answers to all queries, complete text has now been composed, they are waiting to hear from Mr Joyce about the Appendix material which was sent to Hamburg

12
September
1936

Paul Léon to **Allen Lane**
On receipt of the Appendix in Liège Mr Joyce interrupted his holiday and returned to Paris, suggests the inclusion of the international protest against the unauthorised and mutilated edition of *Ulysses* and the decision of the Appellate Court, also the bibliography needs correction, *annotated 'copy for Messrs Monro P.L.'*

12
September
1936

Allen Lane to **Paul Léon**
Agrees to the inclusion of the additional Appendix material, present time contract should be extended to within 14 days of the complete material being returned to the printer

14
September
1936

Paul Léon to **Allen Lane**
Delay is due to no fault of Léon, if the book is out by the 3rd of October Léon could persuade Mr Joyce not to claim any damages, advertisements, Mr Joyce objects to his being referred to without the 'Mr' so Lane should insert it if it has been omitted in the Appendices, agrees to price of signed copies

17
September
1936

Edward Young to **Paul Léon**
In reply to Léon's letter of the 14th, agrees with Léon's rearrangement of Appendix material and has sent new material to printer, point re bibliography, owing to the additional appendix material there may be a shortage of paper for the signed edition, should they publish the unsigned edition before the signed or wait, *2p, with proof of bibliography*

17
September
1936

Paul Léon to **Allen Lane**, *carbon typescript of telegram*
Cannot possibly agree to delay therefore rush unsigned edition for schedule date stop for signed copies unless you find similar paper suggest printing appendices in smaller type as originally planned

[18
September
1936]

Paul Léon to **Allen Lane**
Very disappointed at Mr Young's letter, unsigned edition

18 September
1936

should be rushed for scheduled date, bibliography, small type solution for Appendices should work

18 September 1936

Paul Léon to **Messrs Monro Saw & Co**
Encloses letter received from John Lane and copies of telegraphic and mail reply, Mr Joyce very nervous, Léon blames John Lane, they had six months to set up the book whereas Albatross did it in six weeks

18 September 1936

Edward Young to **Paul Léon**
They have solved the paper problem, cannot meet the October 1 publication date, will Léon want to see revised proofs of Appendices

20 September 1936

Paul Léon to **Allen Lane**
Glad paper problem solved, Young cannot have heard about Léon's reply to Lane's request for a delay in publication, Léon does not need to look through the proofs of the Appendices, *annotated in Léon's hand 'Copy for Messrs Monro Saw & Co'*

4 October 1936

Paul Léon to **Lindsay Drummond,** John Lane The Bodley Head
Copies of *Ulysses* arrived and look very fine, some mistakes in the Appendix, announcements to be made in Sunday papers, hopes Drummond has made copyright deposits because if anything happens he might be prevented from doing so later, *with delivery docket for 2 copies of Ulysses to James Joyce and one to Harriet Weaver*

7 October 1936

Lindsay Drummond to **Paul Léon**
Glad Léon and Mr Joyce were pleased, progress of sales and advertisements, Mr Harold Nicolson praised the edition

20 October 1936

Paul Léon to **John Lane**
Thanks for bringing over *de luxe* copy of *Ulysses* which would be a splendid production were it not for the misprints, he had to give it to Mr Joyce who did not have a copy, suggests it should be exhibited at Sunday Times Book Exhibition

22, 23 October 1936

Allen Lane to **Paul Léon**
Misprints, advertisements, *Ulysses* will be their principle exhibit at the Sunday Times Book Exhibition, his reader found 2 misprints in a hundred pages, should Léon find any further mistakes he should let Lane know in time for the trade edition, *2 letters, 3p, with 'pull' of advertisement*

Paul Léon to **Allen Lane**   27 October
Silence of authorities is tantamount to approval, importation of   1936
cheap copies of the Albatross edition may damage future sales
of Lane's cheap edition, could its publication date be
advanced, eight or nine misprints on pp 368-73, Mr Joyce
found one misprint on pp 600-10

Allen Lane to **Paul Léon**   28 October
Purchasers of 3 guinea edition would have serious grounds for   1936
complaint if cheap edition was produced soon after they had
made their purchase, six guinea edition is out of print but sale
of 3 guinea edition is slow because Lane's four largest cus-
tomers have refused to stock it, advertisements

K.A. Layton-Bennett, Receiver to **[James Joyce]**   9 January
Form letter to authors re the liquidation and sale of John Lane   1937
The Bodley Head

G. Wren Howard, John Lane The Bodley Head to **Messrs**   15 April 1937
Monro Saw & Co, *copy letter*
Re James Joyce's contract with John Lane The Bodley Head, *3p*

G. Wren Howard to **Paul Léon**   26 April, 5
Preparations for cheap edition of *Ulysses* in the early autumn,   May 1937
has arranged for a reader to compare the Albatross edition
with the John Lane 3 guinea one, encloses lists of queries, *not
enclosed*

G. Wren Howard, Director, Jonathan Cape Ltd to **Paul Léon**   5 May 1937
Hopes his interview with Mr Monro will result in a speedy
conclusion of the agreement between James Joyce and John
Lane The Bodley Head, he does not know of any photographic
edition of Lawrence's *Seven Pillars of Wisdom* mentioned by
Léon to Mr Monro, he does not know of any plates of *Ulysses*
already in existence and even if there were any the corrections
which Léon and Joyce want would be difficult to make on
stereotype plates, a book printed by offset lithography is just as
much a book as one printed by letterpress

G. Wren Howard to **Paul Léon**   14 May 1937
Reader has finished comparing the Odyssey Press and John
Lane editions, sends further list of queries, *not enclosed*

16 May 1937   **Paul Léon** to **G. Wren Howard**
Is going through batches of queries with Mr Joyce, will go through the appendix himself, the edition he saw of T.S. [*sic*] Lawrence's book was the Doubleday one which seemed of poorer quality than Howard's one

18 May 1937   **G. Wren Howard** to **Paul Léon**
American edition of *Seven Pillars of Wisdom* printed poorly from type set up in the United States

27 May 1937   **Paul Léon** to **G. Wren Howard**
Encloses corrections, *not enclosed*, mystery of date of December 37th on injunction

2, 3 June 1937   **G. Wren Howard** to **Paul Léon**
Acknowledges letter of 27 May, Mr Fifield has collated all corrections for new edition of *Ulysses*, queries re bibliography

12 June 1937   **Paul Léon** to **G. Wren Howard**
Answers queries

25 September 1937   **P.P. Howe,** Director, John Lane The Bodley Head to **Messrs. Monro Saw & Co**
Acknowledges letter of 24 September, encloses copies of advertisements, too prominent advertising might force the hands of the police, please tell Mr Joyce that they must retain complete liberty of action, *with 3 'pulls' of advertisements*

31 August 1938   **P.P. Howe** to **Paul Léon**
Sales of *Ulysses* are maintained at a steady fifty a month, a single letter from a member of the public expressing ignorance of the 25/- edition should not be given too much importance

16 March 1939   **John Lane The Bodley Head** to **James Joyce**
Royalty account, 1 July 1938 to 31 December 1938

4 April 1939   **P.P. Howe** to **Paul Léon**
There is no Colonial edition of *Ulysses*, they have posted two free of royalty copies at half price to Mr Joyce, *with invoice*

28 June 1939   **F. Baker**, John Lane The Bodley Head to **Messrs. Monro Saw & Co,** *copy letters*
Encloses letter re Spanish translation rights of *Ulysses*

.15   T. WERNER LAURIE LTD, PUBLISHERS, COBHAM HOUSE, BLACKFRIARS, LONDON IN CORRESPONDENCE WITH JAMES JOYCE, PAUL LÉON AND MESSRS J.B. PINKER & SON, 7 letters with enclosures, July - September 1933.

LAURIE

T. Werner Laurie Ltd to **James Joyce**
Offers to publish *Ulysses* in England, *with printed list and copy*

19 July 1933

J.R. Pinker and **Paul Léon** in correspondence with **T. Werner Laurie**, *copy letters*
What figures does Laurie have in mind, Laurie is not in a position to make a definite proposal, *5 letters*

26 July-15 August 1933

Paul Léon to **T. Werner Laurie**, *unsigned with carbon copy*
What is the nature of the difficulty, if it is of a literary or commercial nature Léon may be able to overcome it

4 September 1933

.16   GEORGE MACY, THE LIMITED EDITIONS CLUB, 551 FIFTH AVENUE, NEW YORK AND DENYSE CLAIROUIN, LITERARY AGENT, 90, RUE DE GRENELLE, PARIS IN CORRESPONDENCE WITH JAMES JOYCE AND PAUL LÉON, 31 letters, 1934-36

LIMITED EDITIONS CLUB

Paul Léon to **George Macy**, *draft and carbon typescript*
In reply to Macy's proposal to bring out an *édition de luxe* of *Ulysses* with illustrations by Matisse, terms Mr Joyce will accept

19 March 1934

George Macy to **Paul Léon**
Bennett Cerf has advised him to offer Mr Joyce more money for his permission and signature

4 April 1934

D. Clairouin to **James Joyce**
Mr Macy has been unable to get a reply to his proposal from M Léon

1 May 1934

Paul Léon to **George Macy**
He has not replied because Mr Joyce has been away and he wanted to see Mr Cerf, Mr Joyce cannot be brought to sign 1500 copies, he is however very interested in the artistic value of Matisse's illustrations, Léon could probably obtain his consent for the edition for 10000 francs

6 May 1934

7 May 1934	**Paul Léon** to **D. Clairouin,** *French* Encloses reply for Mr Macy
26 June 1934	**George Macy** to **Paul Léon** Offers combination payment for Mr Joyce's signature and Mr Joyce's permission, if more of their subscribers want signed copies they will award the signed books by lottery
17 July 1934	**Paul Léon** to **D. Clairouin**, *French* Encloses copy of letter to M. Macy, M. Joyce has agreed to sign 250 copies, asks her to draw up a contract for signature, M. Joyce is going away but when he comes back it will be necessary for him to meet M Matisse
17 July 1934	**Paul Léon** to **George Macy** Accepts his terms, colophons for signature by Mr Joyce should be sent in September when Mr Joyce will be back in Paris, reminds him of his promise to send a copy of the *Saturday Literary Review* containing the chart on *Ulysses*
26 July 1934	**George Macy** to **Paul Léon** He will draw up an agreement and will ask M. Matisse to arrange a meeting with Mr Joyce in October, thought Bennett Cerf would have given him a copy of the *Saturday Review*
1 August 1934	**D. Clairouin** to **Paul Léon**, *French* Acknowledges Léon's letter of the 17 July
16 August 1934	**Paul Léon** to **George Macy** He had a meeting with M. Matisse who had a telephone conversation with Mr Joyce, as a result Mr Joyce has asked Léon to inform Mr Macy that he has full confidence in Matisse's plan for the illustrations
20 August 1934	**George Macy** to **James Joyce** Terms of contract for signature
28 August 1934	**George Macy** to **Paul Léon** Thinks Matisse's plan to illustrate *Ulysses* on the basis of the coincident episodes in Homer's *Odyssey* a good idea but hopes Matisse will also relate the illustrations to *Ulysses* itself

D. Clairouin to **Paul Léon**, *French*
Encloses contracts for signature

6 September 1934

Paul Léon to **D. Clairouin,** *French*
Encloses Mr Macy's letter of agreement

17 September 1934

D Clairouin to **Paul Léon**, *French*
Cheque for Mr Joyce, has received colophons for signature, *3 letters*

5, 31 December 1934, 4 April 1935

Paul Léon to **George Macy**
Requests payment for signatures

3 July 1935

George Macy to **Paul Léon**
Encloses cheque for Mr Joyce, has Mr Joyce seen M. Matisse's illustrations and what are his comments on them, *endorsed with notes by Paul Léon*

17 July 1935

D. Clairouin in correspondence with **Paul Léon**, *French*
Re her commission, *5 letters*

27 August, 4, 9, 23, 25 October 1935

George Macy to **Paul Léon**
Encloses copy of his edition of *Ulysses* for Mr Joyce, does Mr Joyce find any pleasure in the edition

6 December 1935

Paul Léon in correspondence with **George Macy**
Purchases by Mr Joyce of copies of *Ulysses*, the fact that Mr Joyce wants them is proof that he likes the edition, Macy is distressed that Mr Joyce has to pay for copies of his own book, *6 letters*

12 January-29 September 1936

.17 ADRIENNE MONNIER, LA MAISON DES AMIS DES LIVRES, 7 RUE DE L'ODÉON, PARIS IN CORRESPONDENCE WITH JAMES JOYCE AND PAUL LÉON, *7 letters, c.1931-37*

MONNIER

[Paul Léon] to **[Adrienne Monnier]**, *manuscript draft, French*
Thanks for her letter of the 12th, he is sorry to learn that the state of Miss Beach's health prevents the regularisation of the situation caused by the absence of a contract between herself and Mr Joyce with regard to the publication of *Ulysses* on the continent, he hopes this delay will not be to the prejudice of the sale of the book

[c.1931-32]

11 March
1932

Paul Léon to [**Adrienne Monnier**], *French*
Thanks for her letter of the 10 March, asks her to arrange to meet him and to pass on to Miss Beach an invitation which Mr Joyce received from the Irish legation which he has refused, the American colony in Paris has organised a dinner in honour of Mr Joyce for St Patrick's Day which he has accepted on condition that he does not have to make a speech, the Irish ambassador in Paris wants to attend which surprises Mr Joyce as Count O'Kelly never carried out his promise with regard to Sullivan, Mr Joyce is still more surprised to hear that the President of Ireland intends to send him a telegram of congratulations at the dinner, a M. Dottin has published a book on modern English literature in which he describes Mr Joyce as a defrocked priest, as Mr Joyce's publisher Miss Monnier should demand a correction, *2 copies*

7 February
1933

Paul Léon to **Adrienne Monnier**, *French*
Asks for accounts of the sales of the French edition of *Ulysses* and for a meeting

7 February
1933

Adrienne Monnier to **Paul Léon**, *French*
Encloses accounts and explains certain points in relation to them, arranges meeting

4 January
1934

Adrienne Monnier to **James Joyce**, *French*
Encloses her cheque for Mr Joyce's royalties from the sale of 91 copies of the French edition of *Ulysses* in 1933

15 March
1935

Adrienne Monnier to **James Joyce**, *French*
Sylvia Beach intends to sell her collection of Joyce manuscripts, Miss Monnier encloses an article in the *New Yorker* about the sale, necessity has forced Miss Beach to this extremity, a group of writers are making a petition to the Ministry for External Affairs to get her a grant, she and Miss Beach will price each item separately, Miss Monnier is preparing a catalogue and needs information as per enclosed typed note, *2p*

16 January
1937

Adrienne Monnier to **James Joyce**
Encloses cheque for Mr Joyce's royalties from the sale of 50 copies of *Ulysses* during 1936, she has not yet got any information on André Germain

.18   JACK KAHANE, LITERARY DIRECTOR, THE OBELISK PRESS, 338 RUE SAINT-HONORÉ, PARIS IN CORRESPONDENCE WITH JAMES JOYCE AND PAUL LÉON, 24 letters with invoices etc, 1932-38

'Pulchritudo Antiqua Etam Nova': les Lettrines de Lucia Joyce: description of the *lettrines* illuminating *Pomes Penyeach* written by Vanderpyl, *1p, typescript*

[1932]

Jack Kahane in correspondence with **Paul Léon**, *French and English*
Re signature of contract by himself, Mr Joyce, Lucia Joyce and Mr Harmsworth, *3 letters*

7-12 April 1932

Jack Kahane to **James Joyce**
Copy of letter from Mr Hubert Foss, Musical Editor, Oxford University Press thanking him for copy of Mr Joyce's *Pomes Penyeach* with illuminated capitals by Mr Joyce's daughter

13 December 1932

Paul Léon to **Jack Kahane**
Seeks payment for *Pomes Penyeach*, Mr Joyce proposes to buy the copies whose subscribers cancelled and present them to the British Museum Library, the Bibliothèque Nationale and to the daughter of Professor Vogt, an error in receipting, the Bibliothèque Nationale does not have the Obelisk Press edition of *Haveth Childers*, will the British purchasers ever pay for their copies of *Pomes Penyeach*, *4 letters*

10, 19, 24 February, 14 March 1933

Jack Kahane to **Paul Léon**
He cannot say what Mr Babou did about *Haveth Childers Everywhere*, Mr Babou is in liquidation, payments for *Pomes Penyeach* come in very slowly

16 March 1933

Paul Léon in correspondence with **Jack Kahane**
Re statement of copies sold of *Pomes Penyeach* and costs of publication, *4 letters*

27 June-20 October 1933

Jack Kahane in correspondence with **Paul Léon**
Account for *Pomes Penyeach*, efforts to find a publisher for the Chaucer *A.B.C.*, agreement for Obelisk to publish it drawn up, *with bill for advertising costs, 7 letters*

19 July 1935-11 August 1936

[1 January],
15 June 1938

Jack Kahane to **Paul Léon**
Notice of move of Obelisk Press to new premises under sole direction of Jack Kahane, request from Melbourne for the Chaucer *ABC, 2 letters*

n.d.

Pencilled note on Obelisk Press notepaper

n.d.

Jack Kahane's card annotated 'Received 1000 francs (contra account) J Kahane'

1932-39

Éditions Vendôme/ Imprimerie Vendôme Lecram-Servant/ Imprimerie Lecram-Servant, The Vendôme Press/Obelisk Press invoices and receipts for copies of *Pomes Penyeach*, the Chaucer *A.B.C.* and other items, *16 items, invoice dated 25 September 1936 endorsed with annotations in hand of Paul Léon including 'Colum care Macmillan Publishers N.Y. Finished tonight Joyce', 'Miss Harriet Weaver, 101 Gloucester Place Finished Work in Progress Many Thanks James Joyce'*

1936

Bundle of 8 order forms for *A Chaucer ABC* with illuminated initials by Lucia Joyce, names of subscribers filled in

RADIO
EIREANN

.19   [RADIO ÉIREANN], DR T.J. KIERNAN, DIRECTOR OF BROADCASTING, BROADCASTING STATION, GENERAL POST OFFICE, DUBLIN IN CORRESPONDENCE WITH JAMES JOYCE AND PAUL LÉON, 3 letters with newsclipping and scripts of broadcast, 1937-1938

8 October
1937

Dr. T.J. Kiernan, Director of Broadcasting, Dublin to **James Joyce**
Seeks permission for James Joyce programmme, asks for suggestion for someone to do the biographical note and personal sketch

20 October
1937

Dr T.J. Kiernan, Director of Broadcasting, Dublin to **Paul Léon**
Thanks for letter of 13th and for Mr Joyce's permission, will await biographical note from Mr Gorman

February
1938

Newspaper clipping *'Banned but broadcast'*

'Biographical sketch for James Joyce 56th Birthday Broadcast from Dublin, Feb 2, 1938', signed by Herbert Gorman, *typescript, 2p*

'Critical appreciation by Professor Jeremiah Hogan of the National University of Eire (formerly NUI)', signed by J.J. Hogan, *typescript, 4p, annotated in hand of James Joyce 'or in my time Royal University of Ireland (RUI)'*

Dr T.J. Kiernan, Director of Broadcasting, Broadcasting Station, General Post Office, Dublin to **James Joyce**
Thanks for Joyce's letter, he has conveyed Joyce's message to Professor Hogan, Mr Duff, Mr O'Higgins and Con Curran, good that Joyce heard some of the broadcast, Mr Moeran will play some of the accompaniments of *Chamber Music* at a symphony concert, calamity about Herbert Hughes

9 February 1938

.20   BENNETT A. CERF, RANDOM HOUSE, 20 E. 57, NEW YORK IN CORRESPONDENCE WITH JAMES JOYCE AND PAUL LÉON, 68 letters with enclosures and publicity material for *Ulysses*, 1932-40

RANDOM HOUSE

Draft power of attorney from James Joyce to [not filled in] to act as his agent for the securing of a contract for the publication of *Ulysses* in the United States of America

James Joyce, 2 Avenue Saint Philibert, Passy, Paris to **Bennett Cerf**, *typescript drafts, with manuscript annotations in hand of Paul Léon, 4p*
Published in the prefatory matter of James Joyce, Ulysses (Random House, Modern Library, New York, 1961), pp xiii-xv; also printed in Letters of James Joyce, Volume III, edited by Richard Ellmann

2 April 1932

Donald S. Klopfer, Random House to **Paul Léon**
Sends check to Mr Ralph Pinker binding the agreement with Mr Joyce

13 April 1932

Bennett A. Cerf to **Paul Léon**
Wants to begin the legal fight for *Ulysses*, instructs Léon to paste favourable opinions of *Ulysses* into a copy of the book and then to post it to Random House so that it can be caught by the Customs, *2p*

19 April 1932

Paul Léon to **Bennett A. Cerf**
Mr Joyce wishes him to forward two letters for perusal; *Ulysses* has been posted by registered mail, supplementary documents

20, 2?, 27 April, 3 May 1932

to help the defence, list of opinions pasted into copy of *Ulysses*, *3 letters and draft telegram, 5p*

6 May 1932

Bennett A. Cerf to **Paul Léon**
Thanks for two enclosed letters, does not think that another book on *Ulysses* would have a great chance of success but Miss Beach must decide

7 July 1932

Paul Léon to **Bennett A. Cerf**
Mr Joyce is anxious for news

18 July 1932

Bennett A. Cerf to **Paul Léon**
The Customs authorities seized *Ulysses*, the case should come to trial in the Fall, they have retained Mr Ernst as attorney

4 August 1932

Bennett A. Cerf to **Mrs Robert Kastor**, Ferme de May, St Jean Cap Ferrat, Alpes Maritimes, France
Has received letter from Bob saying James Joyce is anxious for news about *Ulysses*, gives details of progress, *top half of letter only*

27 September 1932

Paul Léon to **Bennett A. Cerf**
Mr Joyce has been approached by Warner Bros about filming *Ulysses*, Cerf should be on his guard in case there is some pirating idea behind this proposal

11 October 1932

Bennett A. Cerf to **Paul Léon**
No pirating idea in Warner Bros proposal, a film would help sales and Mr Joyce would be paid a large sum for the film rights

9 February 1933

Paul Léon to **Bennett A. Cerf**
Has received message and seen circular note on publication of *Ulysses* in USA, would like copy of material Cerf has gathered for possible future use in courts in England, Mr Joyce's letter should not be called an introduction, encloses announcement of new edition of *Pomes Penyeach* by Oxford University Press

17 February 1933

Bennett A. Cerf to **Paul Léon**
Still waiting for favorable and liberal judge to sit on Federal Bench in New York, agrees to points in Léon's letter

15, 22 March 1933

Paul Léon in correspondence with **Bennett A. Cerf**
Léon forwards resolution reported in clipping from *Hull Daily Mail*, *2 letters*

Bennett A. Cerf to **Paul Léon**   26 July, 30 August, 5 September, 13 October 1933
Request by Professor Huse to quote from *Ulysses*, trial of *Ulysses* postponed three times, now scheduled for 22 August before Judge Woolsey, progress of case, would like to reproduce chart on *Ulysses* prepared by Mr Joyce for Herbert Gorman in the Random House edition, rumours of a pirated edition by a German firm, *4 letters, 6p*

Paul Léon to **Bennett A. Cerf**, *carbon typescript telegram and letter*   21 October 1933
Mr Joyce opposed to inclusion of chart in American edition of *Ulysses*, Léon's reasons for agreeing with Mr Joyce's view

Bennett A. Cerf to **Paul Léon**   30 October 1933
Begs Mr Joyce and Léon to reconsider the inclusion of the chart

Paul Léon to **Bennett A. Cerf**   14 November 1933
Mr Joyce's decision is definite, his introductory letter will authenticate the Random House edition, T.S. Eliot shares his opinion

Bennett A. Cerf to **Paul Léon**   22 November, 1 December 1933
Very disappointed at Mr Joyce's decision about the chart, wonders at his lack of faith in their judgement; encloses newspaper clippings about *Ulysses* hearing, *letter of 1 December endorsed with pencilled notes in hand of Paul Léon*

Paul Léon to **Bennett A. Cerf**   5 December 1933
Reasons for non-inclusion of chart purely literary but the more absolute for that, in order to prove that there is no question of distrust Mr Joyce would be willing for the chart to be included in any publication about *Ulysses*, but not in the text itself

Bennett A. Cerf to **Paul Léon**, *telegram*   6 December 1933
ULYSSES CLEARED TODAY WILL PUBLISH IN JANUARY

Paul Léon to **Bennett A. Cerf**   7 December 1933
Thanks for cable, sends Mr Joyce's thanks and congratulations *2 copies*

Bennett A. Cerf to **Paul Léon**   7 December 1933
Encloses copy of the decision, hopes to have copies of *Ulysses* on sale by 25 January, *with copy of Judge Woolsey's decision*

12 December
1933

Bennett A. Cerf to **James Joyce**
Delighted with Joyce's cable of congratulations, publication date for *Ulysses* is 25 January 1934, they would like to publish *Work in Progress*

12 December
1933

Bennett A. Cerf to **Paul Léon**
Surprised to receive a letter from Herbert Gorman saying Léon had accused him of turning over to Cerf the *Ulysses* chart, Gorman had no knowledge that the chart had been given to Cerf

12, 16, 20
December
1933

Paul Léon to **Bennett A. Cerf**
Asks for details of legal proceedings, Holroyd-Reece's proposal to import copies of *Ulysses* into the U.S., *4 letters*

27, 29
December
1933

Bennett A. Cerf to **Paul Léon**
Impossible to send Léon preliminary memorandum referred to in *Ulysses* brief as it contains hundreds of items, the brief contains every important fact, encloses sample poster, asks for pictures of Mr Joyce for publicity purposes, encloses copy of answer to Mr Holroyd-Reece, *3 letters, 4p*

11, 17, 19
January 1934

Bennett A. Cerf to **Paul Léon**
They are certain to bring out *Ulysses* on the 25th and Mr Joyce will have copies by the 2nd February, tremendous publicity attends the publication, advance sales very good, asks Mr Joyce to inscribe copies of *Ulysses* for himself and his partner, would like a list from Mr Joyce of some books he has enjoyed reading in the last few months for publication in the *New York Herald Tribune, 3 letters*

30 January
1934

Paul Léon to **Bennett A. Cerf**
Thanks for letters and 6 copies of *Ulysses*, Mr Joyce would like to autograph copies for Mr Ernst and for Mr Kastor in addition to those for Mr Cerf and Mr Klopfer, Mr Joyce will not give a list of books he prefers reading and keeps postponing a visit to a photographer, gratifying to read of subscriptions for *Ulysses*

7 February
1934

Donald S. Klopfer to **Paul Léon**
Sending six copies of *Ulysses* under separate cover, *Ulysses* is selling well, *2p*

RANDOM HOUSE

Paul Léon to **Bennett A. Cerf**, *carbon typescript of telegram*
PLEASE CABLE WHETHER APPEAL AGAINST *ULYSSES*
LODGED

[? March 1934]

Southwest Literary Clipping Service, PO Box 1270, San
Antonio, Texas to **James Joyce**, Random House, New York City
They have 30 items in their file for James Joyce

13 March 1934

Bennett A. Cerf to **James Joyce**, *telegram*
WE HAVE NO OBJECTION TO LIMITED EDITIONS CLUB
DOING FIFTEEN HUNDRED COPIES OF *ULYSSES* IF
MROJECT [*sic*] MEETS WITH YOUR APPROVAL

14 March 1934

Bennett A Cerf to **Paul Léon**
He will arrive in Paris for one day on 20 April, hopes to meet
Léon and Mr Joyce

15 March 1934

Paul Léon to **Bennett A. Cerf**
Arrangements for meeting, would like Cerf's opinion on Mr
Macy's proposed *de luxe* edition of *Ulysses* and on the possible
results of the appeal against Judge Woolsey's decision, did he
receive copies of book for himself and Mr Klopfer

24 March 1934

Donald S. Klopfer to **Paul Léon**
Mr Cerf's copy of *Ulysses* came through Customs but his own is
held up awaiting the outcome of the appeal, sends Pinker an
additional advance payment against the *Ulysses* royalties to send
to Mr Joyce

3 April, 2 May 1934

Bennett A. Cerf to **Paul Léon**
He will be in London at least until 5 July, fragment that Léon
sent; encloses copy of advertisement for *Ulysses,* wishes they
were going to be publishers of *Work in Progress,* they have won
Ulysses appeal, *2 letters and telegram*

25 June (from Savoy Hotel, London), 2, 8 August 1934

Bennett A. Cerf to **James Joyce**
Thanks for cable of congratulations, upholding of Judge
Woolsey's decision was a narrow squeeze, he will forward copies
of opinions

10 August 1934

Paul Léon to **Bennett A. Cerf**
Thanks for his letter and telegram, comments on the report in
the *New York Herald Tribune* of the judges' opinions, the

21, 26 August, ? September 1934

dissenting judge's opinion does more to attract public attention to the "obscene" parts of the book than any publisher could do, Mr Joyce would not object to Cerf's publishing *Work in Progress* if he could come to some agreement with Huebsch, asks Cerf to fetch photographs taken for *Ulysses* publicity from George Joyce, *2 letters and carbon typescript telegram*

18 September, 13 November, 3 December 1934

Bennett A. Cerf to **Paul Léon**
Has received pictures for *Ulysses* publicity from George Joyce, there will be no appeal against *Ulysses* to the Supreme Court in the United States, would Mr Joyce write a foreword for an edition of Homer, *3 letters, 4p*

April 1936

P. Kreiswirth, Random House to **Paul Léon**
Notification of change of cable address

2 July 1937

Emanuel E. Harper, Random House to **Paul Léon**
Re royalty account and tax witheld, *annotated by Léon 'Please return after perusal PL'*

10 February 1939

Paul Léon to **Bennett A. Cerf**
Gave Cerf's letter to Mr Joyce who says he understands the situation and appreciates the efforts made by Cerf, having helped about a dozen refugees to go to various countries Mr Joyce finds his own credit on the wane, Mr Joyce adds that Mr Brauchbar is a man of the highest integrity

11 February 1939

Bennett A. Cerf to **Paul Léon**, *telegram*
APPARENTLY VIKING MAKING ACTIVE PREPARATIONS TO PUBLISH

17 February 1939

Bennett A. Cerf to **Paul Léon**
After he heard from Léon he got in touch with Viking Press, any delay in publishing *Finnegans Wake* was not the fault of Mr Huebsch, he appreciates their having thought of Random House in connection with this book but no other publisher could do better than Mr Huebsch

1 February 1940

Paul Léon to **Bennett A. Cerf**
Writes to confirm a letter of Mr Joyce asking that the royalties on *Ulysses* and his other publications be sent direct to him during the period of hostilities, *annotated in Léon's hand: 'Address Hotel de la Paix Saint Gerand le Puy Allier/ The same mutatis mutandis to Huebsch'*

Publicity material for Random House edition of *Ulysses* including

> Random House Advance Announcements, 1 February 1933 and Spring 1933
>
> Order form for Random House Books, Late Spring 1934
>
> 'How to enjoy James Joyce's *Ulysses* presented with the compliments of Random House and your bookseller', *1p folded. 2 copies*
>
> Poster bearing legend 'Now you can read one of the great novels of our time - James Joyce's *Ulysses* complete and unabridged - $3.50

.21   DR D. BRODY, RHEIN-VERLAG, MUNICH IN CORRESPONDENCE WITH JAMES JOYCE, SYLVIA BEACH AND PAUL LÉON, 26 letters with enclosures, 1930-39

[Dr D.] Brody, Rhein-Verlag, Munich to **Sylvia Beach**
Thanks to Mr Joyce for giving his consent, he wrote to Dr Goyert who is undertaking the work, will not abuse Mr Joyce's generosity in autographing *Ulysses*, advises Mr Joyce to accept Tauchnitz's proposal for *Portrait of the Artist*

21 March 1930

Dr D. Brody, Rhein-Verlag, Munich to **James Joyce**
Thanks for Mr Joyce's letter of the 26th, Edward Jaime Liebig's capacity as a translator, Mr Joyce could give Paul Winkler an option for a Hungarian translation

27 August 1932

Dr D. Brody to **James Joyce**, *German*
He has been unable to find out anything about the result of Mr Joyce's consultation with Professor Vogt, Dr C.G. Jung has enquired about Mr Joyce's welfare which will amuse Mr Joyce, refers to Jung's article and letter, he sends the literary supplement of the *Frankfurter Zeitung* which includes reports that a Hollywood film is to be made of *Ulysses* and that Mr Joyce has become a member of the Irish Academy, enquires after Miss Joyce, he has not yet received a reply from the German wallpaper factory, can he keep her designs till Christmas

31 October 1932

Paul Léon to **Dr D. Brody**, *German*
Miss Beach has probably told him that Léon has taken over Mr

28 January 1933

211

Joyce's business affairs, asks for an account of the sales of Mr Joyce's books and for any money outstanding, will Brody send a copy of the German *Ulysses* to Stefan Alter on Mr Joyce's account

1, 22 February 1933

Dr D. Brody to **Paul Léon**, *French and German*
They send accounts, *2 letters, 5p*

14 June 1933

Dr D. Brody to **James Joyce**, *German*
Writes to mark the occasion of Bloomsday, although he does not think it is opportune for *Anna Livia* to appear in German at this present time he hopes it will be so in the foreseeable future, he sends Mr Joyce a treatise on his work written by Hermann Broch which he may publish along with *Anna Livia Plurabelle*, he hopes everything is in order with Mr Joyce, he thinks the translation of *Anna Livia* is excellent and his random sample of the reactions of friends has been favourable

27 June-6 July 1933

Paul Léon in correspondence with **Rhein-Verlag**, *German*
Re balance due to Mr Joyce, *3 letters*

28 June 1934-29 January 1935

Rhein-Verlag in correspondence with **Paul Léon**, *German*
Re proposal by *Nova* for the Hungarian translation rights of *Ulysses*, a request for a contribution by Mr Joyce to a Hungarian edition of modern English prose, who owns the English language rights of Mr Joyce on the Continent, negotiations with the *Berliner Tageblatt* to bring out the translation of *Anna Livia Plurabelle*, payments for Mr Joyce, Herr Brody should visit Mr Joyce at the Carlton Elite in Zurich, invoice for copy of *Ulysses* sent to Dr. Paul von Monakow on Mr Joyce's account, *12 letters*

27 November 1935

Dr D. Brody to **James Joyce**
Encloses cutting from *Sunday Times* of November 24th of a review of Valdemar Langlet's *On Horseback through Hungary* which mentions Szombathely the home of the grandfather of Leopold Bloom

7 March 1939

Dr D. Brody, Den Haag to **James Joyce**, *postcard*
He will order *Finnegans Wake* again on the leaflet sent by Mr Joyce, encloses addresses of Prof. Dr R.W. Zandvoort and of Dr D.G. van der Vat

Dr D. Brody, Den Haag to **Paul Léon**   21 April,
He is astonished to hear that Albatross have got the option on   23 May 1939
the German rights of *Finnegans Wake* which should belong to
Rhein-Verlag by the terms of their contract, wants to meet
Léon in Paris, *2 letters*

.22   CAROLUS VERHULST, SERVIRE PRESS, RIETZANG-   SERVIRE
ERLAAN 15, THE HAGUE, HOLLAND IN CORRESPON-   PRESS
DENCE WITH JAMES JOYCE AND PAUL LÉON, 18 letters
and a publicity leaflet, 1932-35

Paul Léon to **Carolus Verhulst**   17 November
Acknowledges letter re fragment Mr Joyce is publishing in   1932
coming number of *transition*, Léon does not know the terms of
Mr Joyce's contract with the future publishers of *Work in Progress*
and has therefore forwarded Verhulst's letter to Mr Pinker

Carolus Verhulst to **James Joyce**   28 December
His proposal to publish a fragment of *Work in Progress*, suggests   1932
that Mr Joyce's daughter should have 10% and Mr Joyce 30%
of the profits

Paul Léon to **Carolus Verhulst**   12 February
Asks him to send two copies of *transition* to Mr Joyce to use to   1933
establish American copyright and an offprint of Mr Joyce's
fragment for Mr Joyce himself, cannot yet give an answer about
the separate publication of the fragment

Carolus Verhulst to **James Joyce**   17 February
Sends copies of *transition* and offprint of fragment   1933

Paul Léon to **Carolus Verhulst**   14 March
Mr Joyce is still waiting for a separate print of Mr Vander Peel's   1933
[*sic*] article, Verhulst should apply to Mr Pinker or to Faber
about the *de luxe* edition of the fragment of *Work in Progress*

Carolus Verhulst to **Paul Léon**   16 March
Copies of *transition* sent to Mr Joyce   1933

Paul Léon to **Carolus Verhulst**   26
How do things stand with regard to the publication of Mr   September
Joyce's last fragment   1933

30
September
1933

Carolus Verhulst to **Paul Léon**
They have not yet had a reply to their request to Miss Joyce to make new illustrations for Mr Joyce's last fragments as it is impossible for them to eliminate colours from the existing ones, nor to their request to Mr Joyce to put more material in this volume

3 October
1933

Paul Léon to **Carolus Verhulst**
Mr Joyce says there has never been any question of his adding more material, Verhulst is at liberty to change the colours of the *lettrines*, the matter is urgent as a book on Mr Joyce is about to appear which refers to this edition of the fragment

5 October
1933

Carolus Verhulst to **Paul Léon**
They will bring book out before 31 May next, *with copy*

10 February
1934

Carolus Verhulst to **James Joyce**
Has sent proof of pp 23-48 from *The Mime of Mick Nick and the Maggies*, printers cannot go further, he will send proofs of pp 49-80

[30 June
1934]

Carolus Verhulst to **James Joyce**
Account per 30 June 1934 for *The Mime of Mick, Nick and the Maggies*

12 July 1934

Carolus Verhulst to **Paul Léon**
He cannot make a definite proposal until he has seen the *lettrines* of Miss Joyce

13, 15 August
1934

Carolus Verhulst to **James Joyce**
Copies of *The Mime* for the English and American press, *de luxe* copies sent to various persons at Mr Joyce's request, photograph of Miss Joyce, offers to fetch the *lettrines* of Miss Joyce while in London, congratulations on success in USA, *with copy carbon extract from letter of 13 August*

16 August
1934

James Joyce, Hôtel Brasseur, Luxembourg to **Carolus Verhulst,** *carbon typescript unsigned*
Thanks for letter of 13th, thinks it would be a good idea for Verhulst to call on Burns and Oates to inquire about the *lettrines*

26 October
1934

Carolus Verhulst to **James Joyce**, Elite Hotel, Zurich
Received a telegram from Mrs Jolas asking him to report to

Joyce about the publication of the Chaucer *ABC* with *lettrines* by Miss Joyce, he cannot make a definite proposal until he hears from his English and American agents

Carolus Verhulst to **Paul Léon**   8 July 1935
The requested article by Louis Gillet is not in his possession

Publicity leaflet by The Servire Press for *The Mime of Mick, Nick*   c 1935
and the Maggies, including photographs of James Joyce, Lucia Joyce and Eugene Jolas, *4p, 5 copies*

.23   F.J. SHEED OF SHEED AND WARD TO JAMES JOYCE,   SHEED &
HARRIET WEAVER AND PAUL LÉON   WARD
Declines to publish Miss Joyce's *lettrines, 4 letters*   5, 12
                                                                       September
                                                                       1935

.24   TAUCHNITZ VERLAG, CURTIS BROWN LTD AND DR   TAUCHNITZ
D. BRODY IN CORRESPONDENCE WITH JAMES JOYCE
AND SYLVIA BEACH, 10 letters, 1930-31

Barbara Davy, Curtis Brown Ltd to **James Joyce**   28 February
Proposal from Tauchnitz Verlag to publish *Portrait of the Artist*   1930
as a Young Man, annotated in hand of Sylvia Beach 'ecrire au nom de
M Joyce acceptant'

[Dr D.] Brody, Rhein-Verlag to **Sylvia Beach**   21 March
Thanks to Mr Joyce for giving his consent, he wrote to Dr   1930
Goyert who is undertaking the work, will not abuse Mr Joyce's
generosity in autographing *Ulysses,* advises Mr Joyce to accept
Tauchnitz's proposal for *Portrait of the Artist*

Sylvia Beach in correspondence with **Messrs Curtis Brown**   4-24 April
Mr Joyce accepts offer of Tauchnitz Editions to publish *Portrait*   1930
of the Artist as a Young Man, signing of contract and receipt of
cheque, *5 letters*

N. Keller, Bernard Tauchnitz, Leipzig in correspondence with   4-12 March
Sylvia Beach and **James Joyce**   1931
Permission to include Joyce's poem *On the beach at Fontana* in
Professor L. Schucking's anthology of modern English poetry,
3 letters

VIKING
PRESS

.25   B.W. HUEBSCH, THE VIKING PRESS, 18 EAST 48TH STREET, NEW YORK IN CORRESPONDENCE WITH PAUL LÉON AND JAMES JOYCE, 37 letters, 1936-40 and royalty accounts 1922-30, 1938-39

2 March 1936

B.W. Huebsch to **Paul Léon**
Has had an enquiry from a small press which wished to publish a collection of Joyce's poems similar to that planned by Mrs Caresse Crosby of the Black Sun Press, Viking Press will cede to Mrs Crosby the right to include *Chamber Music* in her volume, *annotated by Léon 'Answered on June the 16th saying agreement with Mrs Crosby off and asking to resume conversation with the other Paul'*

1 July 1936

B.W. Huebsch, c/o Barclays Bank, 1 Pall Mall East, London to **James Joyce**
What he knows of Mrs Crosby's projected edition, he has written to New York warning them not to commit themselves to Mrs Crosby, he will be in Paris next week

10 July 1936

[Paul Léon] to **B.W. Huebsch**, Hôtel Louvois, 3 Square Louvois, Paris
Encloses copy of letter which he hopes is what Huebsch wanted him to stipulate for the Viking Press

7 December 1936

Paul Léon to **B.W. Huebsch**
Encloses negative of Augustus John portrait for *Collected Poems*, heard from Mrs Crosby that edition was to come out in mid-November

16 December 1936, 11, 30 March, 4, 13 May, 22 June, 22 August, 24 December 1937

B.W. Huebsch to **Paul Léon**
Mrs Crosby's edition is ready, he had not heard she married again, he learnt from Jolas that he has received a considerable instalment of *Work in Progress* and that copy has been sent to Faber, suggests that the book might be produced in the U.S., Mr Joyce should have received three copies of Mrs Crosby's edition of his poems, if Mr Joyce wants *Work in Progress* published in 1937 it is important to know when the manuscript will be ready, he has ordered Gogarty's memoirs to be sent to Mr Joyce, *Wild Apples* would be easier to get in London, encloses statement of Mr Joyce's earnings in 1934 and of money paid, will *Work in Progress* be ready for publication in Autumn 1938, arrangements for the limited edition, *10 letters, letter dated 11 March endorsed with pencilled notes in hand of Paul Léon*

Paul Léon to **B.W. Huebsch**   4 January
1938

Mr Joyce is very concerned about the date of publication which he wishes to be the 4th of July, the date of his father's birthday, progress in correcting proofs

B.W. Huebsch to **Paul Léon**   26 January
1938

He will discuss the matter with Mr Morley of Faber and Faber, July 4th would be an unsuitable date of publication

B.W. Huebsch to **James Joyce**   1 March 1938

Neither he nor Faber know when Mr Joyce's final copy may be expected, both firms hope to publish in October, time necessary to prepare for publication, impracticable to withold title, would like to increase the number of copies in the limited edition

B.W. Huebsch to **Paul Léon,** *telegram*   7 December
1938

ABSENCE REPLY LETTER SEPTEMBER 20 IMPEDES PUB-LICATION BECAUSE PAPER LIMITED EDITION CANNOT BE ORDERED UNTIL WE TELL FABRE QUANTITY REQUIR-ED STOP SIMULTANEOUS ESSENTIAL TO COPYRIGHT THEREFORE DELAY INTERFERES BOTH EDITIONS STOP PLEASE ANSWER EXPLICITLY IMMEDIATELY

Paul Léon to **B.W. Huebsch**   22 December
1938

Confirms cable by which he agrees to modification of contract for *Work in Progress* as suggested in Huebsch's letter of 20 September, *Work in Progress* is now finished, Mr Joyce is in the throws [*sic*] of proof correction

Paul Léon to **B.W. Huebsch,** *carbon copy of telegram*   7 February
1939

YOUR PERSISTENT INACTION IMPEDING IMMEDIATE ENGLISH APPEARANCE BOOK BESIDES BEING PRE-JUDICIAL VITAL INTEREST SAME IN AMERICA AUTHOR PROPOSES YOU RETIRE FROM PUBLICATION TRANS-FERRING EXISTING CONTRACT RIGHTS INTACT RANDOM HOUSE IF LATTER ACCEPTS AGAINST CABLED REFUND FROM HIM OF ROYALTIES ADVANCE WITH SUITABLE COMPENSATORY INTEREST, *annotated in hand of Paul Léon 'NLT Cerf Following cabled Huebsch today', with manuscript draft*

7 February 1939

Paul Léon to **B.W. Huebsch**
Mr Joyce thinks Huebsch should abandon the idea of publishing his book as Huebsch seems to lack interest in it judging from the delay in publication and the fact that he has not told Faber how many copies of the limited edition they should print for the American market, Léon himself understood that Huebsch would make a special effort to achieve prompt publication, Mr Joyce instructed him to send a cable asking Huebsch to withdraw, Mr Joyce's complaints, *2p with copy and ms draft, 5p*

[11 February 1939]

B.W. Huebsch to **Paul Léon**
YOUR CABLE IMPLIES UNFAMILIARITY WITH SITU-ATION STOP WE ARE EAGER TO PUBLISH BUT THUS FAR RECEIVED ONLY 128 PAGES TEXT REMAINDER REPORTED IN TRANSIT STOP FABERS WILL CONFIRM OUR FULL COOPERATION

11 February 1939

Paul Léon to **Padraic Colum**
Encloses cable reply from Mr Huebsch and letter Léon has written him

11 February 1939

Paul Léon to **B.W. Huebsch**
Huebsch's cable contained no information concerning his decision or date of publication, Faber have ordered paper for limited edition, will Huebsch let him know when the book is to be published, there have been numerous telephone calls inquiring about it, Mr Joyce wishes Léon to stress that no time should be wasted looking for his approbation for the title page or jacket, Faber have already consulted him and carried out his wishes, *with copy*

8 March 1939

B.W. Huebsch to **Paul Léon**
Protests at the content and terms of Léon's letters and cablegrams, *2p*

11 March 1939

Paul Léon to **The Viking Press**
He has received no reply to his letter to Mr Huebsch of nearly six weeks ago, the Paris booksellers have received Viking's catalogue which mentions only the limited edition, queries whether Viking intend to bring out an ordinary edition or to fulfil financial clauses of contract, will they cede their rights to Random House, failing a prompt reply Léon will not be able to

advise Mr Joyce to sign the sheets of the limited edition, *with manuscript draft which also includes 'Thanks kind birthday message and congratulations you both on happy event James and Nora Joyce'*

Paul Léon to **B.W. Huebsch**
17 March 1939
Mr Joyce does not consider Huebsch's letter of the 8th calls for further reply

B.W. Huebsch to **Paul Léon**
22 March 1939
FINNEGAN BINDING TRADE EDITION 6000 COPIES NEXT WEEK STOP PUBLISHING BOTH EDITIONS ABOUT THREE WEEKS AFTER CUSTOMS CLEARANCE OF LIMITED STOP THIRD QUESTION DISINGENUOUS AND INSULTING

B.W. Huebsch to **Monro Saw & Co**
3 April 1939
Acknowledges letter of 24 March saying that Mr Joyce wishes Viking to discontinue payments to Pinker, form of letters of authority from Mr Joyce and from Pinker, Mr Joyce need not 'insist' on payments which will be made by agreement as in the past

B.W. Huebsch to **Paul Léon**
10 April 1939
Sheets of limited edition arrived in New York on 6 April but are still in the customs, Huebsch is telling Léon and Mr Joyce this so they may know he was not dreaming when he declined to name a publication date other than one based on actual possession of the sheets, *endorsed with draft reply in hand of Paul Léon*

James Joyce to **The Viking Press**, *carbon typescript unsigned*
15 April 1939
Letter authorising them to make payments for him to Monro Saw & Co

B.W. Huebsch to **James Joyce**
19 April 1939
Sends six copies of regular edition of *Finnegans Wake*, hopes appearance pleases Joyce though Léon implied Joyce was indifferent to the American edition, sheets of the limited edition have cleared customs after delay caused by non-arrival of consular invoice

Paul Léon to **Viking Press**
9 May 1939
They should have made payment direct to Monro Saw, delay does not surprise Léon

7 July, 12
August, 16
November
1939

B.W. Huebsch, New York and Paris to **Paul Léon**
Huebsch's summer address; thanks Léon for letting him see an essay, does 'Earwicker' correspond to German 'ewiger'; received a letter from Pinker's New York representative saying that Léon agreed to proposal made in Huebsch's letter of 8 September to Pinker

1 February
1940

Paul Léon to **B.W. Huebsch**
Confirms letter from Mr Joyce asking that during the period of hostilities royalties should be paid direct to Mr Joyce because of difficulty of getting money out of England, *annotated in hand of Paul Léon 'The same mutatis mutandis to Cerf'*

1922-30

Royalty accounts of B.W. Huebsch, Inc, Publisher and of The Viking Press for *A Portrait of the Artist as a Young Man*, *Chamber Music*, *Dubliners* and *Exiles*, 7p

1938-39

Royalty accounts of Viking Press for *Collected Poems*, *A Portrait of the Artist* and *Dubliners*, 4p

7.
MISCELLANEOUS BUSINESS CORRESPONDENCE:
FILM PROPOSALS, TRANSLATION RIGHTS, PERMISSION TO REPRODUCE JOYCE'S WORK, REQUESTS FOR CONTRIBUTIONS

FILM
RIGHTS

.1 WARNER BROTHERS, LOUIS ZUKOFSKY AND OTHERS IN CORRESPONDENCE WITH JAMES JOYCE, SYLVIA BEACH AND PAUL LÉON ABOUT THE FILM RIGHTS OF *ULYSSES*, 12 letters, 1932-36

30 August
1932

Paul Léon to **R. Schless, Warner Bros.**, 25 rue de Courcelles, Paris
He has communicated their conversation about the filming of *Ulysses* to Mr Joyce, Mr Joyce's health does not permit him to deal with the matter at the moment

TRANSLATIONS

Virginia Stover, New York to **Sylvia Beach,** *telegram*
Her husband wants to make a proposal for the screen rights of
Ulysses

29 January 1934

Paul Léon to **Virginia Stover**, *typescript of telegram*
He needs more details before submitting an offer to Mr Joyce

[c.30 January 1934]

Paul Léon to **Lou Smith**, Paramount, New York
Mr Joyce's son is going to the U.S.A. and will see him about his
proposal

7 May 1934

[Toni ?] to **Sylvia Beach**
Advice on the sale of the film rights of *Ulysses*, *8p*

7 May 1934

Maxim Lieber to **George Joyce**
Encloses copies of contract for the dramatization of *Ulysses*

5 April 1935

Paul Léon to **Louis Zukofsky**, c/o Mr George Joyce, Beach and
Westwood Avenues, Long Branch, N.J.
Delay in replying to their screen version of *Ulysses* due to
discussions taking place with another firm, Mr Joyce has taken
only a fragmentary cognizance of their work but other critics
while recognising its value have found lapses and errors, Léon
would like to hear from Zukofsky about terms of agreeement
for production

10 July 1935

Louis Zukofsky to **James Joyce**
He and Mr J. Reisman would be glad to receive suggestions as
to any changes Mr Joyce would like in their script, Mr Joyce
should arrange to have their scenario sold with the rights to his
book as the authorized screen version, sale should bring in fifty
to seventy five thousand dollars

18 July 1935

Paul Léon to **Louis Zukofsky**
Mr Joyce has read their scenario and finds it commendable, his
comments, other proposals for the film rights, Léon suggests
Flaherty as film producer

30 July 1935

Louis Zukofsky to **Paul Léon**
They will make every effort to revise the scenario to accord with
the wishes of Mr Joyce, they have read Gilbert's and Budgen's
commentaries, explains their treatment of *Ulysses*; reminder to
Léon to send list of corrections, *2 letters*

12 August, 28 September 'Armistice Day' 1935

221

'Armistice
Day' 1935

Louis Zukofsky to **James Joyce**
They have not yet received Mr Joyce's suggestions for revision
of *Ulysses* scenario which Paul Léon said he would send

20 November
1935, 11
February
1936

Paul Léon to **Louis Zukofsky**
Has not yet replied to letter of 12 August because the person
Mr Joyce wanted to cooperate in the bringing out of *Ulysses* has
been ill, Mr Joyce thinks a review of the script extremely
important and insists on reading the script with this person,
awaits Zukofsky's permission to read his text, *2 letters, original
letters signed by Léon with carbon of letter of 20 November and wrongly
addressed envelope marked 'inconnu'*

TRANSLA-
TIONS

**.2 CORRESPONDENCE OF PUBLISHERS, TRANSLATORS
AND AGENTS WITH PAUL LÉON RE TRANSLATIONS AND
TRANSLATION RIGHTS OF WORKS BY JAMES JOYCE, 37
letters, 1932-39**

11 May 1932-
2 February
1933

Paul Léon in correspondence with **Signora Amalia Risolo**,
Trieste
Italian translation rights of *Dubliners*, *3 letters*

22 August-2
September
1932

Paul Winkler, Agence Internationale Littéraire, 14 rue Auber,
Paris in correspondence with **Paul Léon**
Hungarian translation rights of *Portrait of the Artist as a Young
Man*, *3 letters*

15-17
November
1932

E. Reaves, European Literary Bureau, Paris in correspondence
with **Paul Léon**
Countries which do not yet have a translation of *Portrait of the
Artist as a Young Man*, *2 letters*

2 December
1932

Ernst Wolf, Bonn to **James Joyce**
Asks permission to publish his translation into German of *I
Hear an Army, with translation, 4p*

11-20 January
1933

Paul Léon in correspondence with **Olga Bauer**, Madrid
Advice re Spanish translation rights of *Ulysses*, *2 letters*

23 January
1933

Paul Léon to **Signor Augusto Foa**, Milan
Sends copy of *Ulysses* in connection with Italian translation

TRANSLATIONS

V. Nabokov-Sirin, Berlin to **James Joyce** and **Paul Léon**, *Russian and English*
Translation of *Ulysses* into Russian, negotiations for terms, *3 letters*

9 November 1933-
6 January 1934

Nova, Budapest to **James Joyce**
Hungarian translation rights of *Ulysses*

2 July 1934

Jules Corréard, Villa Sidi Brahim, Mont St Georges, El Biar, Alger to **Paul Léon** and **James Joyce**
Permission to publish a translation into French of *Pomes Pennyeach* by Miss Onslow, *1 letter and 2 calling cards*

9 July, 29 December 1934

A.K. Mukerji, Calcutta to **James Joyce**
Was introduced to Mr Joyce by Mr Joyce's cousin Mrs E. Vanderwert in August 1929, asks permission to translate *A Portrait of the Artist as a Young Man* into Bengali with a foreword and introduction by Joyce, *2p, with leaflet advertising 'The Biblioteca, The Circulating Library', Calcutta*

10 January 1935

R. Fréalle, Saint-Brieuc to **Paul Léon**
Are French translation rights of *Dubliners* still free

9 March 1936

Carlos Maria Reyles, *Sur,* Buenos Aires in correspondence with **Paul Léon**
Spanish translation rights of *Exiles, 5 letters*

22 June-12 August 1936

Alvano Salema, Lisbon to **James Joyce**
Permission to translate *Ulysses* into Portugese

4 April 1938

J. Stork, Storkama, Agence Littéraire, Paris in correspondence with **Paul Léon**
Negotiations for Spanish translation rights of *Ulysses, 8 letters*

19 May-20 October 1938

Klaus Lambrecht, Paris to **James Joyce**
Bermann-Fischer-Verlag, Stockholm wish to acquire Mr Joyce's new work

25 February 1939

Willem Jaspert to **[Faber & Faber]**
German translation rights of *Finnegans Wake*

26 April 1939

.3   CORRESPONDENCE RE JAPANESE TRANSLATION OF
ULYSSES, 22 letters with enclosures, 1932-34

21 May 1932

Yoshisaburo Okakura, Naka-Arai, Outside Tokyo to **Sylvia Beach**
Two Japanese translations of *Ulysses* available in Tokyo, *8p*

[?May 1932]

[James Joyce/Sylvia Beach] to **Professor Y. Okakura**, Naka-Arai, Outside Tokyo, *unsigned typescript annotated 'draft drawn up by JJ'*
Legal position of Japanese translation of *Ulysses*

[?June 1932]

T. Suzuki to **James Joyce**
He was happy to meet Mr Joyce the other day, Japan adhered to the Berne Convention, address of Japanese lawyers, Japanese agencies who could inform Mr Joyce of criticism of his work, *2p*

5 August
1932

Sadamu Nagamatsu, Hitoshi Ito, Idisanori Tsujino to **Sylvia Beach**
Letter from Japanese translators of *Ulysses* offering 200 yen for the rights to *Ulysses*, *2p*

30 August
1932

Sylvia Beach to **Paul Léon**
Encloses letter from Japanese pirates of *Ulysses*

2 October
1932

Yoshisaburo Okakura, 2230/3 chome, Naka-Arai-Machi, Itabash-Ku, Tokyo
His dealings with Japanese publishers of *Ulysses*, *2p*

25 October
1932

Paul Léon to **Monsieur Susuki** [sic], 2 Avenue St Philibert, Paris XVI
Mr Joyce asks Suzuki to go over the enclosed volumes and brochures before his interview with him which is fixed for Sunday

25 October
1932

Paul Léon to **H.B.M. Consul General**, British Consulate General, Tokyo
Encloses memorandum and copies of letters re unauthorised translation and publication of *Ulysses* in Japan for the advice of a Japanese lawyer, *3p, with draft letter and memorandum*

5 February
1933

Sadamu Nagamatsu, Hisanori Tsujino, Hitoshi Ito to **Sylvia Beach**
Will Mr James Joyce accept the 200 yen and permit them to continue with the translation of *Ulysses* into Japanese

JAPANESE *ULYSSES*

Sylvia Beach to **James Joyce**
She still has the 200 yen cheque

[? February 1933]

John Gadsby, Building No. 13, No. 12, Marunouchi 2-chome, Kojimachi-Ku, Tokyo to **Paul Léon**
Legal advice re how Mr Joyce should proceed under Japanese law, *3p, with carbon copy*

24 February 1933

Paul Léon to **John Gadsby**
Returns cheque for 200 yen, thinks 2000 yen would be a suitable fee, what would be the expenses of legal action, *2 letters*

27 March, 26 September 1933

Paul Léon to **H.B.M. Consul General**, Tokyo
He has no reply to his letters to Mr Gadsby

5 December 1933

John Gadsby to **Paul Léon**
The legal situation in Japan, does not think that any good purpose can be served by further legal pressure, *2p, with carbon copy*

30 December 1933

P.D. Butler, H.M.Consul, Tokyo to **Paul Léon**
Mr Gadsby was in England for several months, he has written to Léon, *with carbon copy*

8 January 1934

James Joyce to **John Gadsby**, *carbon copy unsigned*
Letter of authorisation to deal with the matter of the Japanese translation of *Ulysses*

22 January 1934

Paul Léon and **James Joyce** to **John Gadsby**
Has advised Mr Joyce to accept small sum offered, asks Gadsby to act for Mr Joyce and encloses letter of authorisation, *2 letters*

22 January 1934

John Gadsby to **Paul Léon**
Encloses bank draft and copy of receipt given to Daiichi Shobo, *with uncashed bank draft, receipt in Japanese with 2 copy translations and carbon copy of letter*

26 March 1934

Paul Léon and **James Joyce** to **John Gadsby**
Acknowledges letter of 26 March, encloses Mr Joyce's receipt for cheque, *2 letters*

24 April 1934

DANISH
ULYSSES

.4 CORRESPONDENCE RE DANISH TRANSLATION OF *ULYSSES*, 14 letters, August - December 1936.

25 August
1936

Johanne Kastor Hansen, Martins Forlag, Vestervolgade 109, Copenhagen to **Paul Léon**
Mr Joyce who is in Copenhagen asked them to write to ask Léon to send a copy of *Ulysses* to see whether it would be feasible to translate it

3 September
1936

Paul Léon to **Messrs Martins Forlag**
He despatched a copy of *Ulysses* to Mr Joyce

18
September
1936

E. Winther to **Paul Léon**
They have discussed with Mr Joyce what Mr Joyce called the moral aspect of publishing *Ulysses* in Danish, prohibition not likely in Denmark, economic aspect, many people in Denmark read books but few buy them, asks Léon to make a proposal, *2p*

7 October
1936

Johanne Kastor Hansen to **Paul Léon**
They have not yet received an answer to their letter of the 18 September, requests extension of term for deciding on purchase of *Ulysses*, Mrs Hansen received the issue of the *Times* containing John Lane's advertisement for his issue of *Ulysses*

27 October
1936

Paul Léon to **Johanne Kastor Hansen**
He has been too busy with the British edition of *Ulysses* to answer sooner, Mr Joyce asked him to forward the text of *Exiles* which would translate well into Danish, what translator would translate *Ulysses*, Mr Joyce thinks it very important the translation should be well done as Danish is a favourite language of his which he has studied for many years and speaks fluently, Léon must inquire about the amount obtained for *Ulysses* in other countries before he can arrive at a specific figure

11 November
1936

Johanne Kastor Hansen to **Paul Léon**
Mr Winther says they are interested in translating and publishing only *Ulysses*

18 November
1936

Paul Léon to **Johanne Kastor Hansen**
Sorry to note that Mr Winther disposes so lightly of all literary

considerations, asks £200 for rights of Mr Joyce for translation of *Ulysses*

E. Winther to **Paul Léon**
Cannot justify paying £200 for *Ulysses* given the nature of the Danish market, possible translators, will Mr Joyce reconsider, *2p*

30 November 1936

Johanne Kastor Hansen, Fiolstrade 3, III Copenhagen to **Paul Léon**
Writes in her private capacity, she would like to get some director interested in producing *Exiles*

30 November 1936

Paul Léon to **Martins Forlag**
Offers *Ulysses* for $150

10 December 1936

Paul Léon to **Johanne Kastor Hansen**
Has received Hansen's private letter, he would like to get the Danish translation of *Ulysses* settled before taking up the matter of *Exiles*

10 December 1936

E. Winther to **Paul Léon**
Thanks for letter with revised offer of 150 Dollars, they are taking steps to make arrangements with translators

23 December 1936

Paul Léon to **Martins Forlag**
The offer was not 150 dollars but 150 pounds

26 December 1936

E. Winther to **Paul Léon**
150 still too much, regret they must give up the idea of publishing *Ulysses*

31 December 1936

.5 REQUESTS FOR PERMISSION TO REPRODUCE PUBLISHED WORK BY JAMES JOYCE IN ANTHOLOGIES, SET POEMS TO MUSIC, USE QUOTATIONS, PRODUCE *EXILES*, 18 letters, 1932-38

MISCELL-ANEOUS

Peter Lindsay
Permission to set *Strings in the Earth and Air* to music

nd.

1932, 1934-35	**John J. Munson** Permission to reprint several poems from *Chamber Music*, points relating to his forthcoming book, *3 letters*
16 September 1932	**Charles Flato**, Director, Barn Theatre, Boston, Massachusetts to **James Joyce** Permission to perform *Exiles* and to reduce royalty charge
31 October 1932	**Paul Léon** to **Charles Flato** Mr Joyce gives authorisation for six performances with royalty of \$125
October 1932	**E.O. Daughtry** Permission to use verses from *Strings in the earth, with reply giving permission, 2 letters*
November 1932	**Muriel Herbert** Permission to reproduce *She Weeps over Rahoon* and *I Hear an Army Weeping, annotated with reply*
May 1933	**Camille McCole** Permission to quote from *Ulysses* and *Portrait of the Artist as a Young Man*
May 1934	**Robert Gross** Permission to use *Ulysses* as the libretto of an opera
September 1934	**Vernon Duckworth Barker** Permission to reproduce *Araby* in the Budapest review *Nyugat*
September 1934	**Frank Swinnerton** Permission to quote extract from *Ulysses, 2 letters*
July 1935	**Eric Blom** Permission to reproduce a passage from *Ulysses, annotated with reply*
September 1935	**R.J. Wilkinson** Permission to include *All Day I Hear the Noise of Waters* and *I Hear an Army charging upon the Land* in an anthology for Ceylon

PERMISSIONS – REQUESTS FOR CONTRIBUTIONS

Georges Roger
Permission to include *On the Beach at Fontana* in *England Calling*, *2 letters and circular*

May-June 1936

B.A. Young
Permission to use quotations from *Work in Progress*

October 1936

W.G. Healy, Secretary, Irish Stage Society, 18 Upr. Fitzwilliam Street, Dublin to **James Joyce**
The Irish Stage Society wants to produce *Exiles* at the Peacock, they would like information on royalties and Joyce's approval for the production, *annotated in Léon's hand '2nd letter answered and sent on March the 21st 1932 PL'*

4 February 1937

Paul Léon to **W.G. Healy**
Mr Joyce will leave the matter of royalties to the Society's discretion as it is a new venture, should the production be successful they should apply again

9 March 1937

W.G. Healy, The Stage Society, 39 Harcourt Street, Dublin to **Paul Léon**
Unwilling to enter into the arrangement Léon suggests for royalties, would prefer to allot 5% of gross takings, would like Mr Joyce to write a short note of the play for inclusion in the programmme

11 March 1937

Eltham Literary Evening Institute
Permission to set *Lean out of the Window*, *Goldestair* to music

March 1938

.6 REQUESTS FROM PERIODICALS AND EDITORS FOR CONTRIBUTIONS FROM JAMES JOYCE, 30 letters, 1930-39

REQUESTS FOR CONTRIB- UTIONS

Kerker Quinn, *Direction*

n.d.

Gordon Fraser, *Minority Press in Cambridge*

1930

René Meurant, Group d'Études Poétiques, Paris

December 1932

Terence A. St John

August 1932

March 1933	**Elizabeth Parben,** *re lectureship in memory of Professor Herford*
March 1933	**Simpkin Marshall Ltd,** *Books of the Month*
September 1933	**Albert Skira**, *Minotaure*
October 1933	*American Quarterly of Verse*
May 1934	*Literaturnaya Gazeta*, Moscow
June 1934	**Fellowship of Australian Writers**
August 1934	**Writers' International**, *The Left Review*
December 1934	**St. Anthony's Boys' High School, Burma**, *A Garland of Goodwill*
September 1935-March 1936	**Theodore V. Brown**, New York Request for contribution to Frank Harris Memorial Exhibit, *3 letters*
September 1935	**Churyo Fuchida**, *King*, Tokyo Questionnaire
March 1936	*The American [Mercury]*
August 1936	**Dorothy Kissling**, Editor, *Muse*
September 1936	**Allied News Agency**
May 1937	**Les Amis de Mil-Neuf-Cent-Quatorze**
January 1938	**Dorothy Norman**, *Twice a Year*
September 1938	**Alfred O. Mendel**, editor of *The Living Thoughts Library*
March 1939	**Jacques Vallette**, *Le Point*
April 1939	**Paul G. Guillumette, Black Star**
October 1939	**Georg Noble**, *Youth Review*
October 1939	**Frederick C. Packard,** Harvard University Request to redo Joyce's recording of pp 136-37 of *Ulysses*

8.

MANUSCRIPT AND TYPESCRIPT DRAFTS OF POEMS AND OF PAGES FROM *WORK IN PROGRESS*, MISCELLANEOUS PROOFS

.1 *Ecce Puer,* typescript and manuscript drafts in various hands, *6 items, typescript draft of first three lines of Ecce Puer endorsed with 'P.S.' in hand of Paul Léon referring to £1000 at signature of contract and Mr Joyce's opposition to 1,000 signed copies being placed on the American market*

.2 *Stephen's Green* by James Stephens. With Latin translation entitled *Jacobi Jucundi Viridiversificatio* and Italian translation entitled *I Verdsi di Giacomo* both by James Joyce, *typescript, 2p*

.3 *A Portrait of the Artist as an Ancient Mariner,* signed 'J.J', *typescript*

.4 *Pennipomes Two Guineaseach, carbon typescript*

.5 *Work in Progress,* passage beginning 'While, one word burrowing on another, Standfest, the towelturbaned', *carbon typescript with manuscript annotations, 3p*

.6 *Work in Progress,* passage beginning 'Glug; (Mr Seumas Quillad), the bad black boy of the storybooks, who has been sent into disgrace by The Floras...', *typescript with manuscript annotations, 4p*

.7 *Work in Progress,* proof pages marked 'Specimen Q, Maclehose, 488 pages, September 21, 1931', *2p*

.8 *Work in Progress,* proof pages beginning 'As we there are.../unde et ubi' [Faber p. 260] n.d.   .9   *Chamber Music*, I, II, III, XV, XVI, proof pages, 5p

n.d.   .10   *Chamber Music*, translations into German of poems Nos. I, III, IV, IX, XV, XXV, XXX, XXXIII, XXXV, marked 'Alastair', typescript, 3p

9.

NEWSCLIPPINGS ARRANGED IN CHRONOLOGICAL ORDER

including, *inter alia*

November 1932- November 1934	reviews of *Two Tales of Shem and Shaun*,
	news items about Mr Joyce's eyesight,
March- September 1935	reports of the United States court case about *Ulysses*,
	reviews of books about Joyce,
February- April 1936	article from *New York Journal* on Cobina Wright *annotated in hand of James Joyce 'This is the fool woman on whose programme G. is to sing'*, 5 March 1935
January 1938 February 1939- February 1940	reviews of *The Mime of Mick, Nick and the Maggies*,
	reviews of the exhibition at the Leicester Galleries, London of Matisse's illustrations for *Ulysses*,
	reports of jail sentence of Eric Pinker in New York for theft
1877	article about Dr John Henry Newman from *The World*, 17 January 1877

108 items

10.

MISCELLANEOUS PRINTED MATERIAL INCLUDING ISSUES OF PERIODICALS, PAMPHLETS AND ITEMS RELATING TO *ULYSSES* CENSORSHIP AND COPYRIGHT

.1 'Extract from a Private Letter from a Relative in Dublin' Re comments of librarians at Trinity College Dublin and the National Library of Ireland on *Ulysses, carbon typescript, 8 copies*
29 March 1922

.2 Protest against the piracy of *Ulysses* in the United States by Samuel Roth signed by 167 authors, Paris
2 February 1927

.3 James Joyce: *Work in Progress*, Part 11 and 12 [cover title]: continuation of *A Work in Progress, 35p*, n.d., *footnote on page 1 reads 'Since Mr Joyce's health has made it impracticable for him to undertake the complete revision of Part III, the nine installments of which are to appear in transition beginning with the March issue, No. 12, the author has consented to detach the following pages from Part II'; footnote on page 13 reads 'This commences Book III of Mr. Joyce's new work. Book I appeared consecutively in transition nos 1 to 8 and a fragment of Book II was published last month in transition number 11. Book III will continue to appear consecutively with each number of transition'*
[1928]

.4 *The New English Weekly*, Vol. II, No. 12, 5 January 1933 (containing review of *Tales of Shem and Shaun* by D.G. Bridson)
5 January 1933

The New English Weekly, Vol.III, No. 24, 28 September 1933 (containing 'Canto Thirty-Eight' by Ezra Pound which includes a reference to James Joyce)
28 September 1933

.5 *Contempo*: James Joyce issue (Edited by Stuart Gilbert), Volume III, Number 13, 8p., Chapel Hill, N.C. 15 February 1934 *Special First Edition printed on rag paper, Copy No. 1, with covering letter from Milton Abernethy, Editor.*
15 February 1934

1934

.6 *The Modern Library*: a complete list of titles...Spring and Summer [New York] 1934, *including The Portrait of the Artist as a Young Man and Dubliners*

1934

.7 Register of Prohibited Publications (As on the 31st March 1934), Dublin, Stationery Office, 1934, *2 copies*

3 August 1934

.8 United States Circuit Court of Appeals: United States of America, Libellant-Appellant, -against- One book entitled *Ulysses* by James Joyce, Random House Inc.: decree of Augustus N. Hand, Circuit Judge and dissenting opinion of Manton, Circuit Judge, *8 + 8p, copy*

1936

.9 Docteur Geo. Gibier-Rambaud: Rôle de l'infection focale dans les psychoses. Paris, 1936

April 1937

.10 Società Nazionale Dante Alighieri: Comitato di Parigi: [invitation to a conference led by Louis Gillet on the theme 'J. Joyce et l'Italie']

June 1937

.11 'Note read at the XV Session of The P.E.N. Club at Paris (June '37)'
Re *Ulysses* and the copyright law of the United States, *1p, typescript, incomplete*

August 1937

.12 Dublin Tenders Limited: 3 Hour Coastal Cruise on board Pleasure Steamer "John Joyce" sailing from Victoria Wharf, Dun Laoghaire...August 1937

1938

.13 Catalogue of a Sava Botzaris exhibition of sculpture, drawings and caricature. With a prefatory note by Harold Nicolson. [Exhibition held at The Leicester Galleries, London, January-February 1938], London, 1938, *exhibition included sculptured head of James Joyce which is reproduced in the catalogue; a drawing is also listed*

.14 Programme for a *soirée* held under the auspices of Romantisme, a society whose *Comité Artistique* included James Joyce

6 April 1938

.15 List of pornographic literature entitled 'Curious books' including *Ulysses* and *Lady Chatterley's Lover*

n.d.

.16 'Ballad of Persse O'Reilley (as sung by Phoblacht)', *page torn from 'transition'*,

n.d.

.17 Joseph F. McKaig: "Nil desperandum": the chemical man as deduced from the biochemistry of the human blood. Washington, n.d.

c.1932-39

.18 Miscellaneous book announcements and catalogues, 5 *items*

c.1932-39

.19 Miscellaneous printed material, *9 items*

.20 Picture postcards, one of portrait of Mme Récamier, three of scenes in Montana

11.

PERSONAL EXPENSES OF JAMES JOYCE AND OF THE JOYCE FAMILY

.1 Miscellaneous personal receipts, *2 items*

1932

.2 Miscellaneous medical bills for treatment of James Joyce from Drs. Etienne Cheurlot, A.W. Collinson, H. Welti, Charles Bove and J.M. Le Mée, *9 items*

1933-39

1933-38

.3 Antonin Establet, Wine Merchant, Châteauneuf-du-Pape: letters, invoices, receipts and publicity material, *20 items including verses by Joyce? beginning 'Dieu-Dèche...'*

December
1934-39

.4 *The Irish Times:* receipts for subscriptions and three letters from Paul Léon renewing subscriptions, *16 items, receipt dated 12 October 1938 endorsed with annotations in hand of Paul Léon*

1934-35

.5 Miscellaneous personal receipts, bills and invoices, *24 items, includes bill for coat from Schiaparelli endorsed in hand of James Joyce 'my wife begs you to pay this or these'*

1934-35

.6 Hotel bills of James Joyce, *4 items*
Les Golf Hotels, Etretat, 19 [?May 1934]
Carlton Elite Hotel, Zurich, *6p*, 8-14 January 1935, *with receipt from Hug & Co, Musikalien- und Instrumenten-Handlung, Zurich for score by Schoeck*
Savoy Hôtel et Restaurant, Fontainebleau, 11-29 September 1935
Savoy Hôtel et Restaurant, Fontainebleau: bill for Paul Léon, 21-29 September 1935

1934-35

.7 Miscellaneous receipts from establishments in Zurich, *29 items*

1934-39

.8 Invoices from The Galignani Library, 224 Rue de Rivoli, Paris to James Joyce for books sold to him, 8 items, *with two postcards saying Ibsen's Little Eyolf and Riemann's Dictionary of Music are unavailable, February, March 1934, invoice dated 31 August 1938 annotated in hand of James Joyce: 'Please bring this down to 500fr. Still I don't see how it keeps so high as I don't order any books and keep paying off. Also £1 to Dublin. I have had no news of Giorgio or Helen since you left. Weather broken all the time. I hope Mrs Léon is well again. Did you ring Delmas on Sat? Salutations cordiales, J.J*

1935-37

.9 Alfred Imhof Ltd, London: letters, invoices and receipts mainly re record made by Joyce, *15 items*

.10   Murdoch, Murdoch & Co., Music Publishers, re supply of vocal scores to Mr Joyce, *4 items*

29 November– 5 December 1935

.11   Miscellaneous letters and invoices, mainly from book-sellers and including receipt for subscription to A.E. Memorial fund, *27 items*

1936-40

.12   Romeike & Curtice 'The Press Clipping Bureau', London: letters and invoices re press clippings, *7 items*

1939

.13   Miscellaneous receipts, bills and invoices, *3 items*

n.d.

.14   Miscellaneous cards of various persons and establish-ments, *8 items*

n.d.

12.

RESIDENCES, REMOVAL AND HOUSEHOLD EXPENSES, INSURANCE

.1   Compagnie D'Assurances Générales: accounts, policy and notices re household insurance of James Joyce, *10 items*

1931, 1935-37

.2   Correspondence of Marsh & Parsons, The Kensington Auction and Estate Offices, London with James Joyce and Paul Léon re lease of flat at 28b Campden Grove to Mr Taillifer, Taillifers wish to quit, length of their stay depends on outcome of American Presidential election, Mr Joyce wishes to relet flat, terms and length of his contract, statement of account, efforts to relet Mr Joyce's flat, bills, new tenant Mrs Green, Mr Joyce wishes to dispose of both the lease and the furniture, Miss Weaver's instructions to let the flat unfurnished, furniture should be removed, bills, *27 letters*

29 April 1-4 May 1932, 13 August 1932-30 May 1933

| 1932-35 | .3 Société Parisienne de Déménagements et de Garde Meubles: receipts for furniture storage, *11 items* |

| 1933-35 | .4 Maple & Company Ltd, Removals and Warehousing: letters, invoices and receipts, *13 items* |

| April-May 1934 | .5 Letting agreement and rent receipts for James Joyce's flat at 42 Rue Galilée, Paris, *7 items* |

| 9 June 1934 | .6 Letter from Paul Léon to Monsieur Verray, Paris saying that Léon has just received a telephone call from Mr Joyce who does not wish to take the apartment at 51 rue Galilée not because of its price but because of its lack of comfort |

| June 1934-35, 1939 | .7 Estimates, invoices, correspondence, bills and receipts for renovation and redecoration work carried out on the flat at 7 Rue Edmond Valentin, *31 items, invoice of J. Vialtelle dated 18 October 1934 endorsed in hand of James Joyce 'Can't read Levy's letter J.J. Find out if Jolas sent those cigars, please. Never got them'* |

| July 1934-39 | .8 Lease of flat at 7 Rue Edmond Valentin by James Joyce. With associated papers and rent receipts, *20 items* |

| 7 July 1934, 1936-38 | .9 Correspondence of Paul Léon with L. Petit, landlord of James Joyce's flat at 7 Rue Edmond Valentin, *7 items* |

| 8 July 1934, 1936-37 | .10 Correspondence of Paul Léon with Joseph Chabrier about the lease and upkeep of James Joyce's flat at 7 Rue Edmond Valentin, *17 items* |

| 21 July 1934-39 | .11 Compagnie Parisienne de Distribution d'Electricité: electricity accounts and contract, *12 items* |

| 24 July 1933-1940 | .12 Telephone accounts, bills and receipts, *73 items* |

RESIDENCES

.13   Compagnie du Gaz de Paris. Societé du Gaz de Paris: gas accounts and advertising material, *7 items*

end July
1934-35

.14   G. Hamm, Facteur de Pianos et Orgues, Paris: letters, invoices, receipt and rental agreement for piano and radiogram, *11 items, letter of 29 August 1934 annotated in hand of James Joyce 'I told these fools by 'phone on the 15.7 to remove the poste. If they didn't, tant pis. They owe me a month's refund on the piano hire'*

1934-37

.15   L'Urbaine & la Seine: accounts, policy and notices re life assurance of James Joyce, *13 items*

1935-39

.16   Correspondence of Paul Léon with Bonduel & Bayot, insurance brokers re insurance policies of James Joyce, *5 letters*

1935, 1937,
1939

.17   Invoices and receipt for furniture supplied to Madame Joyce by *Au Bûcheron, 4 items*

1935

.18   *"A la Place Clichy"*: cleaning bills, *4 items*

1935-37

.19   Papers associated with the Joyce family's change of apartment to 34 Rue des Vignes, Paris, including a survey of the apartment, and correspondence with Gaston Strauss re rent and heating, *12 items*

April 1939-
February
1940

13.

BANK ACCOUNTS, POSTAGE AND MONEY ORDER RECEIPTS, TAXES

1931-39 .1 Lloyds & National Provincial Foreign Bank Limited: statements, cheques, cheque book stubs, *182 items*

1932-36 .2 Banque Franco-Américaine: statements and correspondence, *26 items*

1932-40 .3 Parcel post receipts showing names of addressees, *86 items*

1933-39 .4 French money order and international money order receipts, *52 items*

c.1932-39 .5 Postal order counterfoils some with names of addressees, *41 items*

1934-39 .6 Correspondence of the Treasury Department, Washington with James Joyce and Paul Léon re demands for United States income tax, *17 items*

1935-40 .7 French tax assessments, demands and receipts, *52 items*,

14.

MEDICAL BILLS AND RECEIPTS OF LUCIA JOYCE

August 1933-
September
1940

Medical bills and receipts of Lucia Joyce principally from
'Les Rives de Prangins', Nyon, Switzerland
Dr Th. Brunner, Sanatorium für Nervenleidende,
Küsnacht bei Zürich, Switzerland
Cavendish Nurses, London
St. Andrew's Hospital, Northampton
Maison de Santé Velpeau, Paris
Dr F. Achille Delmas, Maison de Santé d'Ivry, Ivry

164 items

15.

PHOTOGRAPHS

Photographs of James Joyce, Nora Joyce, Paul Léon and Constantine Curran sent in envelope addressed in hand of James Joyce from the Savoy Hotel, Fontainebleau to Paul Léon in Paris, postmark 21 September 1935

.1   Constantine Curran, Paul Léon and James Joyce standing

.2   Constantine Curran, Nora Joyce and James Joyce standing

.3   Paul Léon and Constantine Curran seated (2 copies)

.4   James Joyce seated with hat on knee

.5   Photograph showing the River Liffey and Christ Church [?by Thomas Pugh, 1934]

See also picture postcard showing Joyce standing beside a windmill sent by Joyce to Léon, 2 August 1934, p. 13

16.

MISCELLANEOUS

.1   Miscellaneous receipts, scraps of paper, printed material, coupons, *21 items*   1932-40

.2   Miscellaneous letters and papers relating to Paul Léon and Alexander Ponikowski, *15 items*   1933-40

.3   Miscellaneous envelopes, three addressed to James Joyce, *7 items*

.4   Envelopes and folders in which the collection was contained

INDEX

INDEX

INDEX

INDEX

INDEX

INDEX